A CONCISE HISTORY OF THE CINEMA
Volume Two   £1.25

*Above: Pierre Clémenti and Catherine
Deneuve in Buñuel's BELLE DE JOUR*

in the same
SCREEN SERIES
edited by Peter Cowie
produced by The Tantivy Press

EASTERN EUROPE
by Nina Hibbin

SWEDEN 1 and 2
by Peter Cowie

FRANCE
by Marcel Martin

GERMANY
by Felix Bucher

JAPAN
by Arne Svensson

THE AMERICAN MUSICAL
by Tom Vallance

THE GANGSTER FILM
By John Baxter

Forthcoming

ITALY
by Felix Bucher

THE WESTERN
by Allen Eyles

 **screen SERIES**

A Concise History of
THE CINEMA

Edited by Peter Cowie

A. ZWEMMER LIMITED, LONDON
A. S. BARNES & CO., NEW YORK

Acknowledgements

THE PUBLISHERS would like to thank all the contributors in various countries, who have worked so carefully to make this project possible. They also acknowledge the assistance of the following where stills are concerned: Academy Cinema, Atlas Film, British Lion, Felix Bucher, Ceskoslovensky Filmexport, Cinecenta, Cinemabilia, Columbia, Contemporary Films (London), DEFA, Goswin Doerfler, Jörn Donner, Film Polski, Mirella Georgiadou, Leonhard H. Gmür, Hungarofilm, Jugoslavija Film, M-G-M (London), Miracle Films, Numberone (Rome), Paramount, Barrie Pattison, Sandrews, Shell Co. of Australia, Svensk Filmindustri, 20th Century-Fox (London), Uniphoto, United Artists (London), Warner Brothers (London), Zagreb Film, Zweites Deutsches Fernsehen.

The two Volumes are divided somewhat arbitrarily at 1940, and readers will note that certain films made after 1940 are mentioned in Volume One and certain films made earlier are mentioned in Volume Two.

The dates after titles in the text usually refer to the date of release in a film's country of origin.

COVER STILLS

Front: Anne Bancroft and Dustin Hoffman in THE
GRADUATE (courtesy of United Artists, London)
Back: Monica Vitti in Antonioni's L'AVVENTURA

FIRST PUBLISHED 1971
Copyright © 1971 *by* The Tantivy Press

Library of Congress Catalogue Card No.: 73–118807
SBN 498 07716 0 (U.S.A.)
SBN 302 02064 0 (U.K.)

Printed in the United States of America

Contents

See Volume One for Select Bibliography

KEY TO CONTRIBUTORS

Each contributor is identified by his initials, which appear at the end of his piece, irrespective of its length.

Roy Armes	*ra*	Ulrich Gregor	*ug*
John Baxter	*jb*	Peter Harcourt	*ph*
Felix Bucher	*fb*	Nina Hibbin	*nh*
Suzanne Budgen	*sb*	Dorothea Holloway	*dh*
Ivan Butler	*ib*	Ronald Holloway	*rh*
Russell Campbell	*rc*	Alan Howden	*ah*
Kingsley Canham	*kc*	Claire Johnston	*cj*
Peter Cowie	*pdc*	Paul O'Dell	*po*
Chidananda Das Gupta	*cdg*	Gerald Pratley	*gp*
Langdon Dewey	*ld*	David Rider	*dr*
Goswin Doerfler	*gd*	Anthony Slide	*as*
William Dyckes	*wd*	John M. Smith	*jms*
Allen Eyles	*aje*	Ralph Stephenson	*rs*
Ken Gay	*kg*	Arne Svensson	*asv*
Mirella Georgiadou	*mg*	Robin Wood	*rw*

1. U. S. A.

F *GONE WITH THE WIND* suggested that Hollywood techniques and showmanship could reach no higher, *Citizen Kane* (1941) gave the industry a massive jolt. Here was a film that used every cinematic device to perfection, that presented a personality larger than life, a personality who laughed at his own vulgarity and made a caricature of the American dream of riches and material success. **Orson Welles** (*b* 1915), who with his co-scriptwriter Herman Mankiewicz created this masterpiece, had come from a background of stage and radio. Already celebrated as a child prodigy (reciting speeches from *King Lear* at seven), he had founded the Mercury Theatre in 1937. This company was to produce players of the calibre of Joseph Cotten, Everett Sloane, and Agnes Moorehead, and made Welles keenly aware of the actor's role. He was invited to Hollywood by RKO and began shooting *Citizen Kane* on very favourable terms. He was clearly attracted by the brash effectiveness of the *March of Time* newsreels, and *Citizen Kane* started with a news-reader's voice booming out the salient facts of Kane's career. No format could have been more appropriate for the obituary of a press magnate. To "forty-four million news-readers," Kane was a colossal, larger-than-life tycoon who dominated four decades of American life. To Susan, his mistress and subsequent wife, he appeared as an awesome monster who launched her on her disastrous career as a singer without even asking her permission. To Leland, his college friend, he was cynical and faintly malevolent ("he never gave you anything, he just left you a tip"). To Bernstein, his General Manager, he was perhaps most congenial, "a man who lost nearly everything he had," a man to be pitied and revered. Using the testimonies and recollections of these and many other personalities, Welles described a Kane very much in the round, a man who was all things to all men, and he did so by stretching the capacities of the medium to their limit. His narrative was brusque and fragmented; though it ranged over a lifetime, the film did not attempt to capture a period quality so much as a human personality viewed from many angles. At the centre of it all was Welles himself, playing Kane with a sonorous authority, frivolous, ambitious, gleeful and disgruntled by turns.

Citizen Kane inspired many directors in Hollywood and in Europe. Gregg Toland's camerawork made deep-focus compositions, hitherto the exception rather than the rule, look essential in the ceilinged rooms of Kane's Xanadu castle or the bustling newsrooms of "The Inquirer." Flashbacks, too, came of age with *Citizen Kane*—although later in his

ORSON WELLES

Deep-focus in CITIZEN KANE. Orson Welles (at left) with Joseph Cotten

Citizen Kane

career Welles was to reject them as they outgrew their competence. The sharp black-and-white imagery of *Citizen Kane* induced a whole series of sombrely-lit films (*Double Indemnity, The Heiress* etc.) during the Forties.

But the success of *Citizen Kane* also demonstrated that a talent so mercurial and headstrong as Welles's would find it difficult to survive in Hollywood. The power of the big studios was too great, the conventions of movie-making too deeply implanted. After shooting his second film, *The Magnificent Ambersons* (1942), Welles went to Rio de Janeiro to embark on a triptych of stories called *It's All True*. The Brazilian episode included some remarkable coverage of the Carnival (in colour), but a dispute with RKO brought Welles hurrying back to Hollywood, to find that the editing of *The Magnificent Ambersons* had been completed behind his back and that his contract was broken.

Even so, this second feature was, in its altogether quieter way, just as rewarding as *Citizen Kane*. A nostalgic glance at turn of the century America, it was concerned, superficially, with the displacement of the horse and carriage by the automobile. But, as in *Citizen Kane,* it was the influence people exerted on one another that fascinated Welles, and his skilful dialogue and direction of players brought alive the personalities of Georgie Minafer (Tim Holt), spoilt and querulous, Fanny Minafer (Agnes Moorehead), put upon and resentful, and Isabel (Dolores Costello), serene and quietly suffering. The Amberson

The Magnificent Ambersons

house was a perfect physical symbol of the family's outlook and way of life, each room reflecting the characteristics of its occupant. The huge kitchen was the setting for one of the film's most sophisticated sequences, with Jack and George teasing Fanny about her love for Eugene Morgan, for minutes on end before an unmoving camera.

Although his style is built on the living, vibrant image, Welles knows as much as any director the value of "real" time on the screen. His films leave an impression of hectic speed and sinuous movement, but there is in each of them a number of calm, reflective scenes that permit the dialogue to exert an authoritative hold over the audience. "The secret of my work," Welles has said, "is that everything is based on the word. I do not make silent films. I must begin with what the characters say. I must know what they say before seeing them do what they do." But the fact remains that a Welles film is pre-eminently a visual experience. Indeed the post-synchronisation applied to his European films makes one all too aware of dialogue that seems unrelated to the characters' position on screen. One senses in them the frustration of a director deprived of Hollywood craftsmanship, a director often dubbing several roles himself and relying on curiously angled back-shots in a desperate attempt to disguise the exigencies of the budget and the poverty of the equipment available to him.

Both *The Stranger* (1946), and *The Lady from Shanghai* (1948) were concerned with the cancerous power for evil in American life.

In each film the Welles hero/villain/dupe was a solitary, a wanderer without a home, hovering on the periphery of a society that could not make up its mind whether or not to accept him. However sympathetically one may be disposed to view *The Stranger* as a pot-boiler shot by Welles at a time when the studios were anxious to capitalise on the postwar fear of fifth columnists, the film remains obstinately unconvincing. After a fine opening passage, melodrama was allowed to run riot, with the casual encounters in a Connecticut town being given a grotesque and absurd weight that offset the pleasing brilliance of the technique. *The Lady from Shanghai,* though at first glance an even more shallow affair, was very rewarding, its exotic yacht cruise a perfect metaphor for the bizarre, lazy, and yet lethal pattern of events involving the footloose Irishman, Michael O'Hara (played by Welles). A preposterous murder plot divulged on the heights above Acapulco harbour, Elsa Bannister's urgent pleading with O'Hara in an aquarium as a pair of hideous fish glided behind the glass of their exhibition tank, the couple's hiding from the police in a dingy Chinese theatre while men on stage wheeled and cavorted with hieratic gestures: these were scenes where the imagery richly acknowledged the themes of ambition and treachery, guilt and craving.

The melodrama that lay at the heart of these films stemmed perhaps from the director's keen admiration for Shakespeare, a playwright who, according to Welles, "never wrote a pure tragedy: he couldn't do it. He wrote melodramas which had tragic stature, but which were nonetheless all melodramatic stories." His next two pictures were both adaptations of Shakespeare. *Macbeth* (1948), a coarse-cut fiasco shot in twenty-three days for Republic, looked and sounded appalling. *Othello,* on the other hand, survived quite admirably the trials and tribulations of a protracted shooting schedule in North Africa. Welles swept the film along at a violent pace; the voices of the characters echoed and ricocheted off the castle walls and lingered menacingly in the air; the tolling of bells and the bubbling of Turkish baths accentuated the restless, brooding aspect of the play; all helped to add verisimilitude to Othello's cry of "Arise, black vengeance, from the hollow hell." But poor dubbing and necessarily fragmented montage again limited the impact of a Welles film, and his next work, *Mr. Arkadin/ Confidential Report* (1955), although adapted from a novel he himself had written, was edited by other hands and suffered from an irritating and illogical structure. The central figure of the racketeer Gregory Arkadin (played by Welles), was, however, sufficiently sly and monstrous to form a strong focal point for *Confidential Report*. "Arkadin created himself in a corrupted world," says Welles. "He doesn't try to better that world, he is a pioneer of it," and even more than Charles Foster Kane he embodied the essential nature of the Wellesian hero. A compelling combination of the solitary and the patrician master of ceremonies, unscrupulously despatching those who stood in his way, Gregory Arkadin excited human sympathy as much as moral disgust.

Welles has always maintained that the best technicians are in Hollywood, and *Touch of Evil,* his 1958 production for Universal-International, was his most fluent film of the decade. A more percipient comment on the anomalies of police "justice" than it was given credit for, *Touch of Evil* again presented a leading character, Hank Quinlan, who nursed a secret grudge against society and turned to corrupt methods in order to gain the power and recognition he believed to be his due. As a police chief on the Mexican border, Quinlan was pitted against Mike Vargas (Charlton Heston), a narcotics investigator, and the clash of wills involved the transference of guilt so often found in Welles's world. The virtuosity of the camerawork was also typical of Welles, although he was unquestionably helped by the Hollywood prowess of Russell Metty and his crew.

The landscapes and buildings of *The Trial* (*Le Procès,* 1962), Welles's next film, achieved the same disquieting effect as the eerie environment of Los Robles in *Touch of Evil.* In both films darkness was a vital constituent of the surroundings, providing cover for those creatures (both played by Akim Tamiroff) like Grandi in *Touch of Evil* and Block in *The Trial* who blink in terror at the light. The huge,

Anthony Perkins and William Chappell in Welles's
THE TRIAL (picture courtesy Uniphoto)

glass-lined Gare d'Orsay was an ideal setting for Kafka's story of disorientation, unexplained menace, and incarceration. Joseph K stands for a society that is to blame for the ghastly knots into which it has tied itself. "In my opinion," comments Welles, "for Kafka, Joseph K was guilty. For me also he is guilty because he is part of the human condition." Anthony Perkins, febrile and uncertain, was superbly cast as K (he even bore a strong resemblance to Kafka), and Welles's intelligent blend of fast-moving shots with staccato moments of violence conveyed a visual impression of the weird panic of *The Trial*. Music has not been a major branch of Welles's style, but the noble chords of Albinoni's Adagio lent dignity to this film.

Angelo Francesco Lavagnino's score for *Chimes at Midnight/Falstaff* (*Campanadas a medianoche*, 1966) was less appropriate to its subject, its Latin tinklings failing to conjure up the "Merrie England" so dear to Welles. A tribute to Falstaff, Shakespeare's rumbustious, often melancholy colossus, the film was shot in Spain and had as its centrepiece a masterly re-creation of the Battle of Shrewsbury, as impressive in its inexorable rhythm as the confrontation on the ice in Eisenstein's *Alexander Nevsky* (see Volume One, Chapter Seven). The solemn gatherings in the castle of Henry IV, and the hilarious conversations with Silence, also demonstrated Welles's intimate understanding of Shakespeare.

There was a distinct bond between *Chimes at Midnight* and *The Immortal Story* (*Une histoire immortelle*, 1968), for both films revolved around aged, basically dissatisfied men. The merchant in *The Immortal Story* is unexpectedly passive, relying on the companionship of his humourless clerk rather as Falstaff relies on Shallow. "I don't like pretence, I don't like prophecies—I like facts," Clay says impatiently, and in his bizarre attempt to turn fancy into reality, he provokes his own death. Sixty-eight minutes in length, *The Immortal Story* was a mere *conte,* but the refulgent colours and the relaxed pace of the film gave it a tone of maturity and, ultimately, of tolerance, qualities often lacking in Welles's more aggressive films.

Welles has become an actor of star status over the years, but, with a few exceptions such as *The Third Man* and *Compulsion,* the movies concerned have barely tested his talent. He is best suited to majestic roles, and for many their image of Welles is of a rather grotesque king, politician, diplomat, or tycoon, delivering his lines with a nonchalance and authority that temporarily overwhelms other actors on-screen. Many of these appearances have been prompted by Welles's desire to finance his own films, and at no stage in his career since *Citizen Kane* has he found studio backing without considerable difficulty. His screen version of *Don Quixote,* in modern dress, remains obstinately incomplete, but still during the past thirty years Welles has managed to build a corpus of work that places him indisputably in the top flight of directors. *pdc*

When Hitchcock went to Hollywood in 1940 he was to all appearances a completely formed film-maker; one might well have speculated as to what effect America would have on his work, but there was little reason to expect the remarkable deepening that was to take place. Nor can his first five American films have caused any great surprise. With the exception of the untypical and disappointingly uninteresting comedy, *Mr. and Mrs. Smith* (1941), they were quite in line with his British work: *Rebecca* (1940) and *Suspicion* (1942) were both set largely in England, and studio-bound in Hitchcock's British manner, with predominantly British casts; *Foreign Correspondent* (1940) and *Saboteur* (1942) were episodic adventure films in the tradition of *The Thirty-Nine Steps*. Then came *Shadow of a Doubt* (1943), and with it the revelation that Hitchcock had it in him to be a profounder, more disturbing artist than could previously have been guessed. Its detailed and sympathetic treatment of American small-town society doubtless owed something to Thornton Wilder (the scriptwriter); but the critical and ironic tone that qualified the sympathy was Hitchcock's. The central theme that emerges from this background was essentially that of Hitchcock's masterpiece *Vertigo:* the leading character's dissatisfaction with a limiting "reality" and her consequent yearning after an alluring, but dangerous and equivocal, world of mysterious glamour embodied in a visitor from outside her known environment. In *Vertigo* the sexes are reversed and the central relationship is very different; but the theme (implicit already in some of the more interesting British films, such as *Rich and Strange*) is clearly very important to Hitchcock and out of it grow some of the films in which one senses him most personally involved. Hitchcock had difficulty with the ending of *Shadow of a Doubt,* and the last part slipped into relatively facile melodrama. In its disturbing ambiguities, both moral and emotional, however, it introduced the series of great films that, interspersed with less successful or slighter works, forms the backbone of Hitchcock's mature art: *Notorious* (1946), *Rope* (1948), *Rear Window* (1954), and the trio of films from what has been to date his richest period, *Vertigo* (1958), *North by Northwest,* which at once sums up and transcends the earlier pursuit films, and *Psycho* (1960). Apart from these, Hitchcock's Hollywood output has been strikingly varied both in quality and kind. In *Lifeboat* (1943), in which the survivors of a torpedoed ship take aboard the captain of the U-boat that sank it, Hitchcock transcended John Steinbeck's schematic script to make a film of characteristically complex and disturbing force. *Stage Fright* (1950) revealed a laborious struggle with intractable material and (Marlene Dietrich apart) bad actors. *Dial M for Murder* (1953) was merely an efficient rendering of a clever stage thriller, undertaken as a technical exercise when no more inspiring material presented itself. *To Catch a Thief* (1955) was attractive but lightweight, lacking the disturbing resonances of Hitchcock's

Hitchcock in the Fifties. Cary Grant and Eva Marie Saint in NORTH BY NORTHWEST (left); and Kim Novak in VERTIGO (right)

best work. Extremes can be clearly represented by *Under Capricorn* (1949), an austere and uncompromisingly serious work shot largely in leisurely and elaborate long takes, thematically anticipating *Vertigo* and *Marnie;* and *The Trouble with Harry* (1955), in which Hitchcock's idiosyncratic and mordant humour found its fullest expression.

One of Hitchcock's main strategies in ensuring commercial success has been the development of techniques of audience-identification. This is not a matter of crudely using the subjective camera device: we do not identify with a character simply because the camera imposes his physical viewpoint on us. Hitchcock builds up identification through his choice of representative characters embodying universal urges, and through the detailed construction of the narrative, and uses subjective shots as reinforcement: the first clearly subjective shot in *Psycho,* for example, comes when Marion Crane, stopped by the traffic lights, watches her employer cross in front of the car. But the use of identification techniques is not merely a matter of commercial know-how—it is closely bound up with all that seems most personal in Hitchcock's work. It is a means of expressing and communicating obsessive or compulsive behaviour with the maximum intensity, and it is behaviour of this kind that clearly fascinates Hitchcock. It is when the obsession involved is one of fundamental significance that Hitchcock's work rises above the level of popular entertainment to become fully achieved art. The films one would choose to represent him at his greatest are perhaps

Rear Window, Vertigo, and the first half of *Psycho* (the latter half, from the introduction of the Vera Miles character, is less consistent in creative intensity). *Rear Window* is concerned, not merely with curiosity, but with the desire to dominate and possess; *Vertigo*'s essential theme is the yearning for an escape from reality into what may be a higher and finer reality or a dangerous world of illusion. Both films for most of their length imprison the spectator within a single consciousness (James Stewart, in both cases); the protagonist's obsessions, by a natural process of universal extension, become ours, and we are led with him, through an ever-increasing involvement, towards understanding and purgation. Hence the films become, for character and spectator alike, a therapeutic and cathartic experience. The first half of *Psycho* carries the identification principle to its extremest development. Here there can be no possible distinction between artist and entertainer. Hitchcock's ability to manipulate audience-reaction, the suspense for which he is popularly famous, are essential aspects of the total effect.

The quality of Hitchcock's post-*Psycho* work is still very much disputed, but *The Birds* and *Marnie,* despite incidental clumsiness, are worthy of their predecessors. *The Birds* (1963), which develops naturally out of the complete undermining of all sense of security in *Psycho,* is Hitchcock's most explicit statement of his view of life, the crystallisation of the sense of utter precariousness, of terrible and unpredictable forces ready to erupt and destroy our brittle, complacent civilised *façade,* that is implicit throughout his work. *Marnie* (1964), a rich and complex work, draws together many thematic threads, notably from *Under Capricorn, Vertigo* and *Psycho,* and is right in the mainstream of Hitchcock's development. Disappointing as *Torn Curtain* (1966) and *Topaz* (1970) are, there is no reason to suppose that Hitchcock's art is in decline.

Hitchcock is a great film-maker, but his work presents the critic with many problems. He is very uneven. Within his total output, the films that demand sustained serious attention are in a minority, and of these only a small proportion are completely satisfying.

As is likely to be the case with creative and talented directors working in Hollywood, the problems arise from the artist's relationship with the commercial system he has to work in, but in Hitchcock's case the nature of the relationship has been significantly different from what one has come to expect. The careers of most distinguished Hollywood directors have been characterised by a series of struggles and protests against interference and the imposition of limitations, on commercial grounds, by producers or studio bosses. Hitchcock has encountered difficulties of this kind, notably in the course of the three films made for Selznick—*Rebecca, Spellbound* (1945), *The Paradine Case.* But in general it is true to say that, far from fighting the "system," he has embraced it wholeheartedly. He has consistently shown great personal concern for box-office response. He speaks in interviews of his responsibilities to the companies whose money is invested in his films, placing these, apparently, before any responsibilities he may feel to any concept of art or towards himself as an artist. *Torn Curtain,* for example, is fatally flawed because Hitchcock gave in to pressure to turn the Paul Newman character into a conventional hero (the resulting artistic confusion, ironically enough, probably accounted for the film's indifferent commercial success). Factors largely extraneous (happily) to Hitchcock's artistic achievement are also relevant here: the public image he has been at pains to create; his readiness to lend his name to long series of television thrillers, and to published collections of short stories, of (to put it politely) only intermittent distinction; the frequent vulgarity and sensationalism of the publicity he allows or encourages, including the "trailers" he makes himself (*Psycho, The Birds*). In such areas as these, Hitchcock has shown no scruples about pandering to the tastes of a culturally degraded and disintegrated society. In his attitude to the public he has set himself to serve, cynicism and contempt play an important role.

Assessment

To the critic who wishes to make serious claims for Hitchcock as an artist such aspects of his career cannot be anything but an embarrassment. They neither invalidate nor harm his few masterpieces, but they bear a significant relationship to his work as a whole and they indicate the causes of its unevenness. Hitchcock has never taken himself really seriously as an artist: only as a craftsman, a technician, a popular entertainer. It seems unlikely that he himself really understands why *Rear Window* and *Vertigo,* for example, are great films. Yet one hesitates to suggest that his art would have benefited from his having a more conscious view of himself as an artist. On the one hand, certain works he *does* seem to have been consciously serious about (*Under Capricorn, I Confess, The Wrong Man*) are, although substantial and respectable, not in the first rank of his films, lacking as they do essential components that go to make up the rich and complex effect of his best work. On the other hand, a number of Hitchcock's most assured artistic successes (*Notorious, Rear Window, Psycho*) have also been among his greatest and most audience-conscious commercial successes. There is a clear enough relationship between certain aspects of *Psycho*—the vein of macabre, sardonic humour that runs through it and makes an important contribution to its tone, the way in which the whole film is constructed and shot to evoke and manipulate audience-reaction—and the Hitchcock of the public image. So that, although the critic is compelled to distinguish drastically between different aspects of Hitchcock's work, he remains continually aware of interconnections between those aspects.

The role Hitchcock has accepted of popular entertainer whose first responsibilities are to his audiences (to keep them amused) and his

16

backers (to ensure safe box-office returns) at once plays a part in determining the peculiar nature of his best work and helps to explain much that is unsatisfactory. It explains why the interest of a number of his films (*Foreign Correspondent, Saboteur*) is only intermittent, the films offering a collection of set-pieces strung together with little regard for overall meaning, their *raison d'être* being the isolated moments rather than any organic movement. It also explains why certain potentially great Hitchcock films are flawed. I have mentioned *Torn Curtain,* where the interest dwindles in the last third as the narrative crumbles in a series of rather tired set-pieces (in the theatre, on the boat) that hark right back to the British period. There is also *Strangers on a Train* (1951). To say that the film deteriorates at precisely the moment when it departs radically from the plot-line of Patricia Highsmith's novel (in which the hero actually performs his "exchanged" murder) is not to suggest that the first two-thirds are slavishly dependent on their original: on the contrary, if one wanted to demonstrate the essential tone, the richness of effect, the sureness of touch, of Hitchcock working at full creative pressure, one could hardly do better than point to the opening train encounter, the fairground murder, the party scene. But, as later in *Torn Curtain,* Hitchcock appears to have drawn back from the full implications of his material out of doubts as to what a popular audience will accept in the nature and behaviour of the hero; and, although the deterioration is never as marked as in the later film, the last part of *Strangers,* for all its brilliance, operates less complexly and disturbingly than what has gone before: a work of art lapses into a work of entertainment. *rw*

Hawks's *His Girl Friday* (1940) was a re-make of *The Front Page,* Lewis Milestone's film, which in turn was based on a play by Hecht. A story of journalism, it was marked by a subtle and very extensive use of over-lapping dialogue, several changes of tone, and a startling pace. Then for the last time Hawks returned for his inspiration to the First World War. *Sergeant York* (1941), the exploits of Alvin C. York, concentrated on its hero's early life in Tennessee and Kentucky, including his religious conversion. The rural setting was made to bear a weight of symbolic and patriotic meaning that is unusual in Hawks; family life was depicted with great sensitivity. This remains one of Hawks's simplest films in construction and the final example in his career of a conflict of ideas (in this case between religious duty and patriotic duty) which is *felt* as such. John Huston was among the scriptwriters.

Ball of Fire (1942), written by Billy Wilder and Charles Brackett, was a comedy quieter than those preceding it. It concerned a scholar's research into slang, his initiation into experiences quite new to him, and the reconciliation of tendencies at first thought to be incompatible. America's war-time preoccupation with unity emerged with Hawks's

Howard Hawks own concept of group endeavour in *Air Force* (1943), written by Dudley Nichols, with a significant contribution from William Faulkner: individualism is here subsumed into the corporate unity of a bomber crew. *To Have and Have Not* (1945) was only distantly related to Hemingway's novel. Jules Furthman and Faulkner produced the script, and the cast was headed by Humphrey Bogart and Lauren Bacall (her *début* in the cinema). Set in Martinique, the film dealt with the long-delayed and outraged intervention of an American in the struggle of the Free French against Vichy.

Hawks's first postwar film was *The Big Sleep* (1946), an adaptation, written by Faulkner, Leigh Brackett, and Jules Furthman, of Raymond Chandler's novel. The film emerged as a parody of the *film noir,* deliberately confused and bizarre. Like the previous film, it gave Bogart and Bacall the chance to give deeply characteristic performances which accorded perfectly with Hawks's own conception. Both the playing and the dialogue were witty; the atmosphere of claustrophobia and duplicity was subtly achieved.

By contrast, *A Song Is Born* (1948) was an uneasy and inferior re-make of *Ball of Fire,* but Hawks's last film of the Forties represented a return to form. *I Was a Male War Bride* (*You Can't Sleep Here* in G.B., 1949) was a comedy taking place in Europe immediately after the war, in which a French Captain, played by Cary Grant, is humiliated first by a woman, then by American bureaucracy. Finally he has to resort to woman's dress and the status of "war bride" in order to reach his beloved America. *jms*

Humphrey Bogart and Lauren Bacall in THE BIG SLEEP

William Wyler (*b* 1902) was not prolific in the Forties. The most outstanding characteristic of his work during the decade was the highly-developed efficiency and precision with which he used the technique of composition-in-depth, with individuals, groups, and objects, to re-inforce dramatic continuity and frequent theatricality of his subject matter. The austerity with which he used this method contrasted with the more flamboyant exploitation of similar techniques by Orson Welles. The collaboration of Wyler with Gregg Toland, who perfected deep-focus photography, was therefore of great importance, since it was Wyler who made the most extensive and ambitious use of Toland himself (Welles did not work with Toland after *Citizen Kane,* while Ford and Hawks made no great technical demands upon him). He produced and directed *The Letter* in 1940. This was adapted by Howard Koch from W. Somerset Maugham's short story. Tight, constricted, and exotic, it was set in Singapore and a nearby plantation, with Bette Davis as the planter's wife who murders her lover. The tension was sustained by the web of deceit that the woman creates in order to hide her guilt. Wyler's continuing interest in deep-focus photography (even without Toland, the film being shot by Tony Gaudio) was always to the fore.

Wyler's next two features reunited him with Toland. *The Westerner* marked one of his very few returns (the first, in fact, since sound) to the *genre* in which he had begun his career so prolifically—the Western. The combination of Wyler, Toland, and dramatist Lillian Hellman (which had earlier produced *Dead End*) was now re-constituted for *The Little Foxes* (1941), based on Hellman's play. It studied a group of corrupt people, in a story of the deep South at the turn of the century, and concerned the setting up of a cotton mill to be run on cheap labour. Wyler did not attempt to disguise the theatrical nature of the piece, but used careful composition and a slow, deliberate pace. The acting of Bette Davis, Herbert Marshall, and Dan Duryea was excellent.

During the Second World War, Wyler made one feature and two documentaries. *Mrs. Miniver* (1942) was set in wartime England and concentrated on one English family. Heroic, propagandist, and un-abashedly sentimental, it included a sequence dealing with the small boats of the Dunkirk rescue; Wyler received his first Academy Award for this film. Then came the two documentaries. *Memphis Belle* (1944), which Wyler conceived, directed, partially photographed, and edited, was in 16mm Technicolor. It was made for the U.S. Air Force, and—with a spontaneity very unusual in Wyler—sensitively conveyed the tension of both the waiting for and the execution of the raid that is the film's climax. *Thunderbolt* (not released until 1947 and never released in Britain) was co-directed with John Sturges, and concerned the activities of fighter bombers in Italy.

Returning to the feature field, with Gregg Toland as his lighting cameraman once more, Wyler shot *The Best Years of Our Lives* (1946), which was noticeably more naturalistic than his prewar work, sober and avoiding the intense conflicts that had earlier seemed so characteristic of him. It dealt with the problems of ex-servicemen returning to civilian life, and their difficulties in readjusting to their homes and coming to terms with the postwar world. Three characters represented different problems: they were played by Fredric March, Dana Andrews and Harold Russell, the latter a real-life veteran without previous acting experience. But the all-too-neat solutions to each man's predicament were found by many to be facile and arbitrary.

With *The Heiress* (1949), Wyler turned again to literary adaptation. Henry James's *Washington Square* was adapted by Ruth and Augustus Goetz from their Broadway play. It focused on a girl's relationship with her father, and her revenge on a suitor who deceived her. The casting and direction, however, removed the film some considerable distance from James's conception, simplifying the characters, blunting the conflict, and altering the tensions. Nevertheless the stiff, enclosed world of the Victorian house and the emotional repression of its inhabitants were portrayed with Wyler's customary clarity, discipline, and careful *mise en scène.* Ralph Richardson was sternly impressive as the *pater familias,* and Olivia de Havilland revealed a surprising range of expressions as the daughter. *jms*

JOHN HUSTON

The scriptwriting career of **John Huston** (*b* 1906) continued into the Forties. His script work on his own films was to be extensive. His remarkable *début* as director was on *The Maltese Falcon* (1942), a brutal and sordid, yet witty description of a corrupt society. This thriller, dark and enclosed, became almost an archetype for the American *film noir* of the Forties, and powerfully influenced the developing career of Humphrey Bogart; it was important in fixing his image as the man who, in spite of everything, remained free and sardonically humorous. The immense success of the film led to Huston's undertaking a much more expensive production—*In This Our Life* (1942), an anti-racist study of a rich and patriarchal Southern family, featuring Bette Davis and Olivia de Havilland.

Across the Pacific (1943) reunited the leading actors of Huston's first film in a spy drama, heavy in atmosphere. The imposed ending was not shot by Huston. He then made three remarkable documentaries. The first of these was *Report from the Aleutians* (1943), a picture of an American base in a hostile natural environment. *The Battle of San Pietro* (1945) was filmed under fire in the Liri valley on the road to Rome in 1944. Huston's stress on the heavy casualties sustained by the Americans was removed before the film's release. The third of these documentaries, *Let There Be Light* (1945) was suppressed by the Pentagon and never released. It dealt with the treatment by hypnosis of battle neuroses. Though optimistic, it made clear the depth of the patients' suffering.

Huston's already high reputation was further increased by *The Treasure of Sierra Madre* (1948), set in Mexico in the Twenties. Its story of three penniless prospectors battling with nature in search of a fortune in gold was enlivened by the impressive performances of Bogart and Walter Huston (the director's father). The struggle itself was more significant than the derisive outcome.

Richard Brooks collaborated with Huston on the scenario of *Key Largo* (1948), in which Bogart played a war veteran face to face with a gangster, a remnant of the prewar world. The concept of courage was examined here by Huston with skill and irony. His next film, *We Were Strangers* (1949), was not well received. Set in Havana in 1933, it was concerned with a revolutionary anti-Fascist plot, which brings together five strangers whose conspiracy is finally abortive.

Billy Wilder (*b* 1906), an Austrian expatriate, had come to America in 1934; by 1940 he had to his name several major scriptwriting credits, which continued into 1941. His first film as a director was *The Major and the Minor* (1942), which like all his work in the Forties, with the exception of *Double Indemnity,* he co-authored with

BILLY WILDER

Humphrey Bogart with Lee Patrick in THE MALTESE FALCON

Charles Brackett. The latter also produced Wilder's Forties films (but not *The Major and the Minor* or *Double Indemnity*). Wilder's first picture was a comedy, taking place in wartime, in which Ginger Rogers played a disillusioned career-woman whose misadventures resulted from her adopting the disguise of a twelve-year-old in order to travel home at half fare. He followed this successful effort with *Five Graves to Cairo* (1943), a topical spy thriller set in the Libyan desert with Erich von Stroheim supremely authoritative as Rommel. Wilder then collaborated with Raymond Chandler on the script of *Double Indemnity* (1944), a suspense drama told in flashback, with an attempted "perfect" crime and doomed lovers in a seedy Los Angeles. This *film noir* broke new ground in Hollywood by depicting its stars (Barbara Stanwyck and Fred MacMurray) as unsympathetic murderers. But the bitter pessimism of the story was relieved by continual flashes of repartee and world-weary wit in the dialogue.

The Lost Weekend (1945) was even more daring. It told of a single weekend in an alcoholic's life—his craving for drink, his stealing, his desire for suicide, his spell in a hospital alcoholic ward (shot on location), and his descent into *delirium tremens*. Wilder's next film was in complete contrast to this study of degradation. *The Emperor Waltz* (1948), in which Bing Crosby played a phonograph salesman at the court of the Emperor Franz Josef of Austria, was a comedy musical. In *A Foreign Affair* (1948), the setting was Occupied Berlin, including footage of the shattered city, but this was nevertheless a satirical comedy in which G.I.s fraternised with their recent enemies, and Marlene Dietrich and Jean Arthur represented the womanhood of their respective countries.

ROBERT SIODMAK

Trained like Wilder at Ufa, **Robert Siodmak** (*b* 1900) already had directorial work of distinction to his name when he left Germany for France in 1933; in 1940, escaping from Paris the day before the Germans arrived, he went straight to Hollywood. He endured the direction of seven films unworthy of his talent, culminating in *Cobra Woman* (1943), a Maria Montez vehicle, and *Son of Dracula* the same year. His subsequent American work, however, was outstanding—a series of films characterised mainly by extreme studio realism, menacing atmosphere, and pathological characters. *Phantom Lady* (1944) was a murder mystery in downtown New York during a heat wave, dealing with the search for a woman who can provide an alibi for a man accused of murdering his wife. It had an intricate soundtrack and claustrophobic sets, and like much of Siodmak's work it investigated the nightmarish world concealed by respectable exteriors in a huge city.

In *Christmas Holiday* (1944), Siodmak concentrated on a happy young couple—but the man was a dissipated murderer and after his trial and conviction his wife was reduced to poverty. *The Suspect* (1945) unfolded in the London of 1902 and was based on the Crippen murder case. Charles Laughton played the gentle, sympathetic man who murdered his hateful wife and married a young girl before being discovered. The murder sequence made skilful use of subjective camera-work.

New England gentility concealed hatred and incest in *The Strange Affair of Uncle Harry* (1945). An imposed ending revealed, without conviction, that it was "only" a dream. Also set in New England, *The Spiral Staircase* (1945) concerned a psychopathic family that included a homicidal sex-maniac: the camera movements were exceptionally flexible, the soundtrack (as often in Siodmak's work) was meticulously constructed; and the sets were a triumph of art direction. *The Killers* (1946), produced by Mark Hellinger, was an uneven and awkward expansion of a terse Hemingway story. Burt Lancaster made his *début* in this film. Grotesquerie and pathology were the characteristics of *The Dark Mirror* (1946) and *Time Out of Mind* (1947), both of which fell below the standard Siodmak had set himself. Urban night life was evoked with considerable care and authenticity in *Cry of the City* (1948), which contained much location work. The performances of the cast, headed by Richard Conte and Victor Mature, were finely observed; the film remains powerful, detailed, and absorbing. *Criss Cross* (1949) was more ponderous and superficial than its predecessor, but *The Great Sinner,* also released in 1949, was an expensive production adapted by Ladislas Fodor and Christopher Isherwood from Dostoievsky's *The Gambler,* and Siodmak's direction was suitably polished.

JULES DASSIN

Jules Dassin (*b* 1911) was busily making shorts in 1940–41. The last of these, *The Tell-Tale Heart* (1941), was responsible for his being given the opportunity to direct his first feature, *Nazi Agent* (1942), which dealt with the breaking up of a Nazi espionage ring in America. *The Affairs of Martha* (1942) took place in a small town whose inhabitants were upset when a housemaid writes a book about her experiences. Dassin's next film, *Reunion in France* (1942), used Occupied Paris as its setting, where a *couturière* helped an American airman to avoid capture. This modest and pleasing film indicated the increasing assurance of Dassin's style.

After two minor films, *Time Fortune* (1942) and *Young Ideas* (1943), he was given the chance to direct Charles Laughton in a comedy, *The Canterville Ghost* (1944), in which the family ghost was unable to rest until a descendant performed an act of heroism. Two lightweight films followed: *A Letter for Evie* (1946), a match-making comedy, and *Two Smart People* (1946), a comedy thriller. Dassin's last three Hollywood films were very superior. In *Brute Force* (1947), written by Richard Brooks and produced by Mark Hellinger, Dassin showed a side of his personality that could hardly have been suspected from his earlier work. It dealt with prison conditions, but not in a documentary fashion. The corruption and viciousness of the authorities, and the violent revolt of the prisoners were depicted with an almost operatic flourish; there was a direct line from the social protest melodramas of the Thirties to *Brute Force,* but the impact of the war was also unmistakably felt. Hellinger produced Dassin's next movie, *The Naked City* (1948), which focused on crime in the New York streets, with a great deal of location work in a manner typical of the period, and created sympathy for a murderer. His final Hollywood film was *Thieves Highway* (1949), in which a warehouse owner who cheated poor workers was killed by one of them. Dassin's social conscience was now much in evidence in his work; he was soon to leave the U.S.A. of McCarthy for Europe.

MICHAEL CURTIZ

The career of **Michael Curtiz** (*b* 1888) continued to be extraordinarily prolific into the Forties, though as the decade wore on his output lessened compared with the halcyon days of the Thirties. His virtuosity, vigour, and directness, allied to his forthright dramatisation of American political moods, had already often swayed his work towards propaganda; the early Forties saw the best use possible made of his pamphleteering talents. *Virginia City* (1940), set in the Civil War and the years immediately following, was concerned with the healing of divisions in the nation. *The Sea Hawk,* also released in 1940, ended Curtiz's series of films with Errol Flynn. The story of the Spanish Armada threatening England held an obvious parallel for viewers at the time. The break with Flynn signalled a widening in Curtiz's range of subject matter. *The Sea Wolf* (1941) was a faithful and powerful adaptation of Jack London's novel. In the superb *Casablanca* (1942), Rick's café was a haven for European refugees; Bogart's role here personified the sentimental involvement with Europe and the breakdown of American isolationism. *Casablanca* can now be seen as the entertainment film of the Forties *par excellence,* and the masterpiece of Curtiz's career.

Yankee Doodle Dandy (1942), a musical biography of George M. Cohan, featured one of James Cagney's most energetic performances, and was a sentimental celebration of traditional American values and patriotism. One of the film colony's most direct gestures towards the war effort was *This Is the Army* (1943), a large-scale musical dedicated by Curtiz to Irving Berlin. *Mission to Moscow* (also 1943) was an adroit and impressive piece of pro-Stalin propaganda.

In the later Forties Curtiz seemed most at home in bitter melodramas, set in carefully observed milieus, such as *Mildred Pierce* (1945), which detailed the social and financial rise of a housewife, played with brilliant *hauteur* by Joan Crawford, or the sinister murder story, *The Unsuspected* (1947), with its accomplished and characteristically smooth performance by Claude Rains. *Night and Day* (1946) was a musical biography of Cole Porter; *Life with Father* (1947), a period comedy. Throughout the Forties, Curtiz's work was tending to grow more lavish, softer, and more sentimental than in the previous decade. *jms*

In 1939 Busby Berkeley made a social drama, *They Made Me a Criminal,* and at this point in his career, he left Warners and joined M-G-M, beginning a new cycle of musicals with *Babes in Arms* (1939), which was followed by *Forty Little Mothers* (1940), *Strike up the Band* (1940), *Blonde Inspiration* (1941), *Babes on Broadway* (1941), *For Me and My Gal* (1942), *The Gang's All Here* (1943), *Cinderella Jones* (1946) and *Take Me Out to the Ball Game* (1949).

Busby Berkeley

In the films he directed, Berkeley paid little attention to the story line; the narrative existed merely as a means to explore his fantasies. His choreography did not depend on the dance steps themselves, but on the movement of great masses of dancers, and in this sense it was architectural rather than anything else. This grandiose conception of the musical was highly abstract in its effect, the constantly shifting patterns of interlocked bodies often achieving an almost surrealist effect. Berkeley's kind of escapism was particularly popular in the Depression days, and his series of Gold Digger films is perhaps his most magic and memorable achievement. What is particularly striking about his early films is the eroticism of much of the choreography; *Roman Scandals* in particular, achieves a kind of abstracted sensuality that is quite unique.

While Berkeley retained many of his famous effects in his musicals in the Forties, and most notably in the famous "Polka-Dot Ballet" in *The Gang's All Here,* which featured masses of girls twirling glowing metal hoops together with huge multi-coloured polka-dots, his musicals in general became more intimate in conception, and *Take Me Out to the Ball Game* based on Kelly and Donen's scenario marked a distinct move in the direction of the intimate modern musical, which they later perfected.

Since 1949 Berkeley has not directed another musical, his large-scale conceptions having been proved to be far too expensive. However, he has worked on a few musicals as a dance director, among them *Two Weeks with Love* (1950), *Call Me Mister* (1951), *Easy To Love* (1953), *Small Town Girl* (1953), *Rose Marie* (1954) and *Billy Rose's Jumbo* (1962). cj

After the remarkable impact which Mamoulian made in Hollywood in the Thirties, his career suffered a sharp decline, and he began to turn more and more to the stage. In 1940 he moved to Twentieth-Century Fox, where he made his first swashbuckler, *The Mark of Zorro,* which was a fairly routine re-make of Fred Niblo's silent version. Next followed *Blood and Sand* (1941) the story of a matador, in which Mamoulian again experimented with the use of colour, the result being rather mannered and self-conscious, in what was a grossly sentimental view of bull-fighting. In *Rings on Her Fingers* (1942) Mamoulian again turned to comedy before leaving Fox and working for the stage for the next five years. In 1944 he was assigned to direct the thriller

Rouben Mamoulian

Laura and prepared the script and cast but was replaced by Otto Preminger after a few days' shooting. However, he returned in 1947 to direct a musical, *Summer Holiday,* based on O'Neill's play *Ah, Wilderness* about young people growing up in an American small town. Despite its inventiveness in the use of song and dance numbers to aid the narrative, the film was not a success, and Mamoulian returned to the theatre once more. However, his final return to the cinema could not have been more spectacular; *Silk Stockings* (1957) proved to be one of the most outstanding musicals ever made. The story of a Russian commissar who falls in love with a capitalist in Paris, with music by Cole Porter, and starring Fred Astaire and Cyd Charisse, *Silk Stockings* combines aspects of the more intimate musical with modern numbers to trace the growing love affair between Fred Astaire and Cyd Charisse. Curiously Mamoulian succeeds in capturing with far greater depth than he has ever achieved since *Applause* a psychological reality which informs the whole texture of the film.

Mamoulian was involved with two more projects: the film of *Porgy and Bess* which he began working on until he was taken off the project, and *Cleopatra* which he began shooting and then abandoned. Clearly, Mamoulian is one of the casualties of the Hollywood system, but unlike so many directors who have fallen foul of the system, his approach to the cinema is neither political nor intellectual. In fact, most of his films are extremely reactionary in their world view.

His difficulties seem to have been personal rather than anything else. However, his theatrical experience came at a crucial time for the cinema, and his interest in absorbing new techniques was particularly important. Mamoulian is best seen as a showman, as an interpretive rather than a creative artist whose formalistic preoccupations were particularly important in the development of the musical as a *genre. cj*

Donen and Kelly

The partnership of **Stanley Donen** (*b* 1924) and **Gene Kelly** (*b* 1912) marked a major step in the development of the American musical. Both men began their careers as dancers on the stage, meeting in 1940 in the stage version of *Pal Joey* in which Kelly starred. This was Donen's first job as a dancer, and Kelly gave him a job as his assistant in *Best Foot Forward,* his next stage assignment. Both of them then moved into films, Donen as a dance director and Kelly as a performer, arranging his own choreography. Their first picture together was Charles Vidor's *Cover Girl* (1944), the first of the modern musicals in which they experimented with choreography which develops naturally out of character and plot. In *Anchors Aweigh* (1945) Donen worked as Kelly's dance assistant and together they developed the famous dance routine using a cartoon mouse. In Busby Berkeley's *Take Me Out to the Ball Game* (1949), they collaborated on the script in addition to arranging some of the dance routines, and the time seemed ripe for their first directorial assignment, which came the same year

Vera-Ellen and Gene Kelly in a number from ON THE TOWN

with M-G-M. *On the Town* (1949), the story of three sailors on leave in New York marked the culmination of their partnership. *Singin' in the Rain* (1952) was a story of back-stage life, and their last film together; *It's Always Fair Weather* (1955) was again set in New York and was concerned with the pre-arranged meeting of three ex-G.I.'s. The spontaneous sense of gaiety, incorporating elements of crazy comedy, that pervades the world they create is always tinged with a sense of melancholy. The streets of New York are transformed into a poetic evocation of this same ambiguity. Kelly's dancing style, which he has described as "a sythesis of old forms and new rhythms" is a mixture of athleticism, tap and classical forms. This combined with Donen's interest in stylistic experimentation and his aesthetic sense of satire, brought about the entirely unique quality of their work together.

Since 1955 both men have directed on their own, Donen making a number of musicals, the earliest ones for M-G-M, notably *Royal Wedding* (1950) and *Seven Brides for Seven Brothers* (1954), and the later ones for Warners: *The Pajama Game* (1957) and *Damn Yankees* (1959), both made in collaboration with George Abbott. As well as dancing in a number of musicals, most notably those directed by Minnelli including *An American in Paris* (1951) and *Brigadoon* (1954), Kelly has directed a number of films including *Invitation to the Dance* (1956), *Gigot* (1962) and *Hello Dolly!* (1969). However, since the dissolution of their partnership neither of them has produced work of the same quality. *cj*

Vincente Minnelli (*b* 1910) was really responsible for the re-birth of the musical during the modern period. With a brilliant reputation on Broadway, he was brought to Hollywood by Arthur Freed and made his *début* as a director with *Cabin in the Sky* (1943). Minnelli's verve and sincerity came to the fore with *Meet Me in St. Louis* (1945), which starred his future wife, Judy Garland. *Yolanda and the Thief* (1945) and *The Pirate* (1948) were, for many, further demonstrations of Minnelli's dazzling use of *décor,* colour, and elaborate, infectiously joyful dance sequences. "The Trolley Song" in *Meet Me in St. Louis,* the South American rhythms of *Yolanda and the Thief,* and the climactic encounter of Gene Kelly and Judy Garland in the Caribbean whirl of *The Pirate*: these were among the most inspired achievements of Forties cinema, celebrating a very special American *genre. pdc*

EDWARD DMYTRYK

Edward Dmytryk (*b* 1908) directed his first film privately in 1935; between 1939 and 1943 he made a large number of pictures, mainly thrillers. A considerable talent for propagandist cinema revealed itself in his *Hitler's Children* (1943), an early depiction of life in Nazi Germany, dealing with divided loyalties and the Hitler Youth movement; in *Behind the Rising Sun* (also 1943), where an American-educated Japanese was killed in action, and his father realised his country's mistakes; and in *Tender Comrade* (1944), concerning the wives' wait for their husbands' return.

Based on a Raymond Chandler novel, Dmytryk's *Murder My Sweet* (1945) was a technically-accomplished thriller. *Back to Bataan* (released the same year) dealt with the organisation of guerrillas in the Philippines, while the personal and emotional aftermath of war was the subject of both *Cornered* (1945) and *'Til the End of Time* (1946). *So Well Remembered* was shot by Dmytryk in England during 1947, although its release was delayed. The film recounted the story of a North Country newspaper editor's marriage. *Crossfire* (also 1947), with an excellent performance by Robert Ryan, daringly attacked American anti-Semitism, and used its city-by-night settings with documentary flair. Refusing to deny his Communist sympathies, Dmytryk could no longer work in America. *Obsession* (1949), a comedy-thriller, and *Give Us This Day,* both shot in England, were his last films of the decade. *Give Us This Day* had its background in the New York slums and described the unfortunate fate of an Italian bricklayer and his family. *jms*

The dominating name in Forties comedy is that of **Preston Sturges** (1898–1959). His films have such an individual flavour, an easily recognisable reflection of his own quirky temperament, that it is true to say that had he been an on-screen performer rather than the unseen writer-director his work would have the same universally popular standing as that of the great screen comedians among film enthusiasts. Sturges never worked in collaboration on his major scripts, and he expresses through them a personal vision of a world in which chance determines success and insecurity is an enforced way of life for his leading characters. He peopled the backgrounds of his pictures with a contingent of battered faces belonging to the character actors who made up his stock company (most notably William Demarest, Georgia Caine, Esther Howard, Frank Moran) who by way of contrast are seen clinging to their way of life.

Sturges had been a screenwriter during the Thirties, his best work being *Easy Living* (1937), a script fully characteristic of his later work and directed with unobtrusive efficiency by Mitchell Leisen. After *Remember the Night* (1940), another excellent comedy also handled by Leisen, Sturges won the opportunity to direct his own script of *The Great McGinty* (1940) by agreeing to the minimum possible fee. This almost unprecedented step opened the way for a great many other writers to direct their own work, and *McGinty,* although made cheaply and with an inexpensive cast, picked up an Oscar for its script and was a popular success. Over the next four years, Sturges turned out seven more films in an amazing display of stamina, and only one of these, *The Great Moment* (1944) could be considered as anything less than completely successful (and this film. the biography of the dentist who first killed pain, is in fact underrated for its admittedly odd but extremely effective approach, extracting typical Sturges humour from the basic situations).

Sturges's films brilliantly exploited two standard elements of comedy. One was visual incongruity in which characters of some dignity are involved in slapstick situations. Examples of this are the governor (Brian Donlevy) and the political boss (Akim Tamiroff) battling away in the governor's mansion in *The Great McGinty;* a millionaire's son so dazed and outwitted by the machinations of a female (Barbara Stanwyck) that he falls over things, including her extended foot (*The Lady Eve,* 1941); dental patients going berserk on a dose of experimental anaesthetic in *The Great Moment* (1944); a small town boy (Eddie Bracken) forced to masquerade as a war hero in *Hail the Conquering Hero* (1944); a town cop (William Demarest) trying to coax a prisoner (Eddie Bracken) to escape from his jail in *The Miracle of Morgan's Creek* (1944).

Linked to these situations was the second point of humiliation, involving embarrassment and despair, as in the hoax played on the white-collar worker (Dick Powell) of *Christmas in July* (1940) or the chain-gang experience of a Hollywood director (Joel McCrea) stripped of his identity in *Sullivan's Travels* (1942), Sturges's defence of his own and Hollywood's general practice of entertaining rather than deliberately provoking audiences with a message.

Sturges's films are very American in their concern with material success, yet owe much to his upbringing in Paris and the style of the French boulevard farce. They are very masculine in their appreciation of (and respect for) the wiles and sex appeal of a woman. They are very insistent on the dangers of pride and ambition. But most of all they are richly funny in their inimitably fast paced, contradictory, confused and very alive manner; and if they come up with happy endings, this doesn't dispel the atmosphere of disquiet about the risks involved in taking an adventurous approach to life. From 1945 Sturges's career went into a decline, and only the untypically polished and well-structured *Unfaithfully Yours* (1948) approached the standard Sturges had set earlier. Somehow he lost the good judgement and depth of inspiration that had served him so well earlier.

Billy Wilder (*b* 1906) was another screenwriter of the Thirties (usually collaborating with Charles Brackett, as on such memorable films as *Midnight* and *Ninotchka,* both 1939) who gained control of his scripts as a director (with Brackett producing). His *début* in this dual role was *The Major and the Minor* (1942), an ingenious comedy with an audacious plot that involved Ginger Rogers masquerading as a twelve-year-old. *A Foreign Affair* (1948) was Wilder's other major comedy of the decade, showing its director's celebrated "bad taste" in exploring the disreputable goings-on between the occupiers and the occupied in postwar Berlin.

George Cukor directed *The Philadelphia Story* (1940), a witty, glossy picture adapted by Donald Ogden Stewart from the Philip Barry play. Seemingly light and forgettable, it is—like the earlier *Holiday*—made into much more by the central performance of Katharine Hepburn. Based on a staple Thirties situation with Cary Grant reclaiming his ex-wife from an unfortunate re-marriage in the brink of time (very much as in *His Girl Friday* and *The Awful Truth*), it allowed Miss Hepburn to convey the inner distress of a society woman trying to find herself, and happiness of mind. Hepburn later partnered Spencer Tracy in other comedies for M-G-M: *Woman of the Year* (George Stevens, 1942), *Without Love* (1945, Harold S. Bucquet) and *Adam's Rib* (1949) (as well as *Pat and Mike* in 1952). Stevens's handling of *Woman of the Year* was as polished (if slightly awkward technically) as in his *The More the Merrier* (1943), and both comedies had slapstick highlights, no doubt inspired by his early days of photographing

Laurel and Hardy, and warm performances by the stars (the latter film with Jean Arthur, Joel McCrea—a most underrated comedy performer, and Charles Coburn). Stevens also made during the Forties a wordy and intelligent comedy, *The Talk of the Town* (1942), which dealt with the clash between the law and the individual, and a sentimental and nostalgic piece of reminiscence for a vanished age, *I Remember Mama* (1948) which had a gentle edge of humour.

Frank Capra made a film version of *Arsenic and Old Lace* (1944) with none of his usual preoccupations and concomitant depth of feeling, but his *It's a Wonderful Life* (1946) was a bold return to form, a small town fantasy with James Stewart as the figure rescued from suicide by an angel's demonstration of what his life has meant to others; and, though it did not appeal in the cynical postwar climate, it can now be seen as a splendid piece of filmcraft which sweeps one along on the strength of its director's convictions. Capra used the Tracy-Hepburn team for his *State of the Union/The World and His Wife* (1948), an absorbing study of politics and one man's attempt to throw over the system that cannot really be classified as a comedy any more than *Mr. Smith Goes to Washington* could earlier.

At the end of the decade, the former writer and producer Joseph L. Mankiewicz directed and wrote two brilliant studies of feminine psychology, *A Letter to Three Wives* (1948) and *All about Eve* (1950), but his civilised handling of *The Late George Apley* (1946), satirising Boston manners with a beautiful central performance by Ronald Colman, and of *The Ghost and Mrs. Muir* (1947), a light piece of whimsy engagingly played by Rex Harrison, had previously indicated a man with a genuine talent for delicate humour.

Lubitsch (*To Be or Not To Be*) and Chaplin (*Monsieur Verdoux*) made worthwhile contributions to Forties comedy, but otherwise the further important comedies were dominated by the star comedians, even if their importance is now more a matter of their popular success than great artistic worth.

Olsen and Johnson starred in two comedies, *Hellzapoppin'* (1941) and *Crazy House* (1943), which frenziedly defied all logic, even that of confining the film to the screen as at one point the audience were involved by the shadows of "departing patrons" on the screen. They carried Groucho Marx's Thirties technique of chatting to the audience a stage further; but their complete disregard for any form of conventional structure or depth of characterisation meant that their success rested somewhat precariously on the degree of imagination of each of their gags as it came up.

Bob Hope (*b* 1903) came into his own in the Forties, appearing as the star of nearly twenty features, the best-remembered of which are the *Road* series with Bing Crosby and Dorothy Lamour. *The Road to*

Bob Hope (leering) in one of the many "Road" comedies: THE ROAD TO MOROCCO

Singapore was the first (1940), followed by *Zanzibar* (1941), *Morocco* (1942), *Utopia* (1945) and *Rio* (1948). Hope portrayed the cowardly, smart-aleck type forever being duped into tight corners but responding instinctively rather than heroically with a wisecrack. The success of Bud Abbott and Lou Costello in the same period is a yet-to-be-explained phenomenon of the time, for the squealing tubby Lou and obliging straight man Bud neither had the precision and style nor the warmth and subtlety to make them as obviously appealing as all previously successful comedians. Danny Kaye had more obvious talent and his films were far more lavish in conception and execution, yet there was something too impersonal and superficial about his work which relied over-heavily on mannerisms and a fast tongue to make him a major figure of comedy. *aje*

The impact of television brought about an overwhelming change in Hollywood during the Fifties. Under its influence the American film industry faced its first consistent fall in cinema attendances since the depression, but television was no temporary setback—it was a permanent fact of life. If the "talkies" had saved the industry during the depression, perhaps technical innovation could again save the day? Cinerama and 3-D photography proved too inflexible to be generally acceptable, but the success of Cinerama showed that there was a ready audience for the sort of spectacular entertainment that television could not rival and in 1953 Twentieth Century-Fox introduced CinemaScope. Rather earlier, in the late Forties, there had however been a different and, so it seemed to some, an alternative approach to winning back dwindling audiences by moving away from the more predictable, escapist plots towards stories which reflected attitudes and problems of the postwar society. This social realist trend was developed during the Fifties, often by independent producers rather than the major studios and it later came to encompass a wider spectrum of controversial subject matter, such as drug-taking, which tended to bring film-makers into direct conflict with their own self-censorship organisation—the Hays Office. By the end of the decade, however, the two apparent alternatives of wide-screen spectaculars on the one hand and modestly budgeted "adult" subjects on the other had, to a large extent, been mutually assimilated.

Developments during the decade brought about a relatively stimulating, if somewhat uncertain creative climate but in retrospect an aura of melancholy hangs over the memory of Hollywood at the beginning of the Fifties. Under the dark cloud of McCarthyism a number of distinguished film-makers were blacklisted and unable to work. Even the greatest names were not spared. In 1952 Chaplin delivered his valedictory film—*Limelight,* a sad but moving testament, and shortly afterwards quit America for good. Other great directors continued their exiles for different reasons. Stroheim, since the Twenties regarded as unemployably extravagant, made a poignant acting appearance as Norma Desmond's butler in Billy Wilder's *Sunset Boulevard* (1950)— a role that reflected his association with Gloria Swanson in *Queen Kelly* over twenty years earlier. Von Sternberg, a notoriously intractable talent, returned briefly to direct *Macao* (1952) and *Jet Pilot,* begun in the early Fifties by producer Howard Hughes as a sort of gargantuan successor to *Hell's Angels.* Not released until 1957 when RKO-Radio was in its death throes, *Jet Pilot,* with its embarrassing cold-war propaganda, was almost a total disaster and Von Sternberg returned to exile. Even the *enfant terrible* of the Forties, Orson Welles, made only one film in Hollywood during the succeeding ten years—*Touch of Evil* (1958), a quirky though characteristic thriller with Charlton Heston and Janet Leigh.

Of the active and established directors of the early Fifties, John Ford, William Wyler, George Stevens, Billy Wilder and John Huston were perhaps the five held in the greatest contemporary esteem. Hitchcock was regarded with mild indulgence as a potentially great talent who chose to dissipate his ability on trivial thrillers. Howard Hawks, though his comedies might be praised, remained unrecognised as a distinctive, let alone distinguished director. He was more usually placed alongside Michael Curtiz, Mervyn LeRoy and Raoul Walsh as a skilful craftsman. George Cukor was however recognised as a civilised if light-weight director of agreeable comedies.

The work of many of the older directors remained relatively unchanged by the upheavals of the Fifties. Hitchcock abandoned the stylistic experiments of *Rope* and *Under Capricorn* and renewed his identification with the thriller. Ford continued to mix commercial assignments like *When Willie Comes Marching Home* (1950) with personal projects such as *The Sun Shines Bright* (1954). However, with the shift towards more intellectual Westerns presaged by *The Gunfighter* (1950) and *High Noon* (1952), Ford almost withdrew after 1950 from this, his most personal area of activity. There was only *The Searchers* (1956) until *The Horse Soldiers* (1959) marked his return to the *genre* in earnest in the Sixties. Howard Hawks, though less prolific, continued to make comedies and adventure films of which *Rio Bravo* (1959) was the supreme example. Only *Land of the Pharaohs* (1955), in aiming to exploit the spectacular potential of CinemaScope, resulted in failure.

Henry King and Henry Hathaway, both of whom had worked consistently at Twentieth Century-Fox since the Thirties, were directors who seemed content to accept studio assignments. It would be almost as difficult to find one of their later films that clearly expressed the personal style and outlook of its director as it would be difficult to find a Ford film which did not. King's handling of such lively material as *In Old Chicago* (1938) and *Alexander's Ragtime Band* (1938) was assuredly professional but his lethargic treatment of more pretentious themes extended from the false sentimentality of *Seventh Heaven* (1936) to the bathos of *Carousel* (1956). *Twelve O'Clock High* (1949) was therefore the more remarkable for its bleak, almost ascetic approach to its theme of leadership and courage in war. Apart from *The Gunfighter* (1950), an intelligent Western which followed *Twelve O'Clock High,* King's work in the Fifties was mainly on cumbersome, quasi-literary adaptations such as *The Snows of Kilimanjaro* (1952) and *The Sun Also Rises* (1957). Along with the dull biblical romance of *David and Bathsheba* (1951) and *Love is a Many Splendoured Thing* (1955) they survive essentially as anonymous studio products.

Some of Henry Hathaway's films of the period, like *White Witch*

Doctor (1953) and *Garden of Evil* (1954), tend to be cloaked in the same studio anonymity, though they are at least livelier and less pretentious. Since the Thirties he had shown a confident if impersonal approach to adventure films like *Lives of a Bengal Lancer* (1935), but he was also a pioneer in the application of semi-documentary technique to thrillers such as *The House on 92nd Street* (1945) and *13 Rue Madeleine* (1946). Either a lack of taste or failure of resilience in the face of studio pressure is suggested by *Fourteen Hours* (1951), an intelligent and, in many ways, admirable story of a lonely young man's threat to commit suicide by jumping from the ledge of a New York building. The film is almost fatally compromised by a mawkishly contrived sub-plot involving two young people in the watching crowd. Hathaway again came into his own with the more uninhibited type of adventures like *North to Alaska* (1960) that became popular later in the decade.

The work of Stevens, Wyler and Huston seemed, by contrast, more self-aware and consciously intelligent. Each, in the early Fifties, embarked on an adaptation of a serious literary work: Stevens's *A Place in the Sun* (1951) from Theodore Dreiser's *An American Tragedy*, previously filmed by von Sternberg, Wyler's *Carrie* (1952) from Dreiser's *Sister Carrie* and Huston's *Red Badge of Courage* (1951) from the novel by Stephen Crane. *Red Badge of Courage* was flawed by serious studio interference, wittily chronicled by Lillian Ross in her book *Picture,* resulting in the release of a truncated version. It seemed to confirm the popular conception of the artist sacrificed on the altar of commercial expediency, though the difficulties also hinted at Huston's impending transition from the distinguished craftsman of the Forties to the self-conscious artiness of his European period and the indifference of his later Hollywood films. The flaws in *A Place in the Sun* and *Carrie* arose more from a deliberate attempt to romanticise the material.

George Stevens (*b* 1904) had already shown a predilection for sentimental subjects in *Penny Serenade* (1940) and *I Remember Mama* (1947). Although von Sternberg's earlier film had also discarded much of Dreiser's social criticism it did not anticipate Stevens's use of lingering dissolves to make the aspirations of Dreiser's central character seem sympathetic. The clever but overtly sensitive performance of Montgomery Clift and the casting of Elizabeth Taylor as the spoilt society girl, though persuasively romantic, added to the falseness. In the Forties Stevens had been more successful as a maker of agreeable comedies such as *Woman of the Year* (1941), *Talk of the Town* (1942) and *The More the Merrier* (1943). In the Fifties each new film seemed to be striving for more serious recognition. In *Shane* (1953) Stevens largely succeeded. Despite Alan Ladd's weak performance as the reticent gunfighter, *Shane,* along with *High Noon,* became a primary influence in the regeneration of the Western idiom.

Giant (1956), an exceptionally long adaptation from the novel by Edna Ferber, gave the first hint of the elephantiasis which was to overwhelm the later work of many directors in their struggle to buy success with large budgets. Stevens brought his personal qualities to bear on many of the intimate domestic scenes, well played by Rock Hudson and Elizabeth Taylor, but the treatment of more dramatic sequences was somewhat naïve. James Dean, in his last and most demanding role, was only partially successful in portraying the middle-aged oil baron of the later scenes, though as a young man he was, as ever, compelling. *The Diary of Anne Frank* (1959)—only Stevens's fourth film of the decade—is a sober, long and unpopular adaptation of the true story of a Jewish family's incarceration in an Amsterdam attic during the Nazi occupation. Flawed again by false romanticism in the portrayal of Anne herself, the film remains a sincere but tedious account of human endurance. Despite the decline of his more ambitious projects, however, Stevens never lost the gentle humanity which illuminated his earlier films. It was a sad but honourable defeat.

William Wyler seemed equally unable to recapture his earlier success. Neither his handling of two fashionably violent subjects—*Detective Story* (1951) and *The Desperate Hours* (1955)—nor of two films partly concerned with man's attitude to violence—*Friendly Persuasion* (1956) and *The Big Country* (1958)—displayed the stylistic felicity of his earlier masterpieces. *Ben-Hur* (1959), like Stevens's *The Greatest Story Ever Told* (1965) suggested that no one could rival Cecil B. DeMille in the treatment of quasi-biblical stories. With *Ben-Hur*, Wyler seemed to be lost in the machinery.

For Billy Wilder the Fifties was a period of growing independence, and he avoided the pitfalls of ambitious prestige projects with the possible exception of *Spirit of St. Louis* (1957), a sober but dull account of Lindbergh's historic Atlantic flight: significantly it was one of Wilder's few commercial failures. Following *Sunset Boulevard* (1950), Wilder parted company with Charles Brackett and became his own producer. A raucous cynicism pervaded his first solo film, *Ace in the Hole* (*The Big Carnival*, 1951) and persisted in *Stalag 17* (1952), which was criticised for some of its more light-hearted insights into life in a German P.o.W. camp, though it was not until *Some Like It Hot* (1959) that Wilder displayed his consummate ability to walk a tightrope across an abyss of bad taste, with his brilliant handling of this tranvestite comedy. Though Wilder's most memorable females—Barbara Stanwyck in *Double Indemnity* (1944) and Gloria Swanson in *Sunset Boulevard*—are not among the most likeable personifications of their sex, he can also be credited with giving Marilyn Monroe two of her best comedy roles in *Some Like It Hot* and *The Seven Year Itch* (1955).

Hollywood in the Fifties. Wyler's re-make of BEN-HUR (left); and Alan Ladd, Jean Arthur, and Van Heflin in Stevens's SHANE

Influenced by the social realism of the postwar European cinema, Hollywood began, in the late Forties, to assimilate a measure of liberal involvement with contemporary issues into its own productions. This tradition also influenced the crime film, and Twentieth Century-Fox in particular made several, incorporating a semi-documentary treatment of FBI methods such as *Call Northside 777* (1948). Richard Widmark as the archetypal smiling killer took over where Cagney left off ten years earlier. And, benefiting from the techniques evolved for war-time documentaries, location photography became commonplace with films like *The Naked City* (1948, *dir* Jules Dassin).

Elia Kazan (*b* 1909) was one of the foremost directors to emerge from the new school of social realism. His first film, *A Tree Grows in Brooklyn* (1945) based on Betty Smith's novel about an unhappy adolescent girl's upbringing, attracted immediate attention for Kazan's sensitive direction. *Boomerang* (1947) is, however, a key film in the use of on-the-spot technique to tell what is, in essence, a detective story about the apparently unmotivated killing of a New England Priest while also investigating local corruption and political expediency which threatens to lead to the execution of an innocent man. *Gentleman's Agreement* (1947) and *Pinky* (1949) exemplify Kazan's liberal treatment of two aspects of racial prejudice—by then a fashionable and potent theme for several films. Kazan's last film in the social

Elia Kazan

realist manner was *Panic in the Streets* (1950), about the tracking down of a criminal believed to be a carrier of bubonic plague. In 1951 Kazan went to Warner Bros. to make *A Streetcar Named Desire,* one of the first films to be adapted from the work of playwright Tennessee Williams. Kazan, with his Group Theatre background, found it an ideal subject: Marlon Brando was cast in his first major role following his *début* in *The Men* (1950), and Vivien Leigh returned to Hollywood after an absence of ten years to play Blanche DuBois. The success of *Streetcar* revealed that the public would now accept a more cerebral treatment of character and motivation than hitherto, as well as the divorce of sex from glamour—at least within the hot-house environment of a Tennessee Williams story.

Kazan made two further films with Brando. In *Viva Zapata!* (1952), drawn on a broad canvas, Brando gives a carefully studied performance as the Mexican peasant leader while Kazan makes passing acknowledgement to Eisenstein in some of the formal groupings and the editing of at least one siege. *On the Waterfront* (1954) was a return to social realism, but with the drama centred on the dawning moral responsibility of an inarticulate longshoreman—Brando—played against a background of dockland violence and Union corruption. The closing sequence, in which a bruised and beaten Brando wins the allegiance of the other longshoremen by staggering heroically to work in defiance of the corrupt Union bosses, signified to some contemporary critics a betrayal of values which the film was seeking to affirm. It had, however, a powerful dramatic impact; so much so that Brando has, almost

Marlon Brando in Kazan's ON THE WATER- FRONT

38

habitually, been submitted to beatings in several subsequent films— perhaps most bloodily in *The Chase* (1966, *dir* Arthur Penn).

Baby Doll (1956), *A Face in the Crowd* (1957) and *Wild River* (1960) suggested a growing disregard for his audience and a tendency toward hysterical overstatement on Kazan's part. *East of Eden* (1956) adapted from Steinbeck, was a considerable success however, particularly because of James Dean's performance. Dean, who died in a motoring accident in 1955, before the release of his last film, *Giant,* combined some of the mannerisms of Brando with an embodiment of those 'teenage attitudes which found an accurate reflection in the increasingly youthful audiences of the period. His death gave rise to a cult of morbid obsession amongst his admirers on a scale perhaps unrivalled since Valentino.

Social realism provided a springboard for several directors whose later work moved into quite different areas. **Robert Rossen** (1908–1966), hitherto a writer of several excellent screenplays, directed *Body and Soul* (1947) which was a vigorous boxing story with John Garfield, and *All the King's Men* (1949), adapted from Robert Penn Warren's novel about the rise of a Southern state governor as a people's champion, his corruption in the exercise of power and eventual moral decline—a story reputedly based on Huey Long. More impressive in intention than execution, *All the King's Men* has a rather disorganised narrative carried along by several powerful individual scenes and the Academy Award performance of Broderick Crawford. Rossen's later work took the shape of several diverse and unrelated projects: *The Brave Bulls* (1950) was a somewhat diffuse though ambitious attempt to penetrate the mythology of bullfighting while *Alexander The Great* (1955), though more literate than the historical epics of its day, also demonstrated the perils of international casting and Rossen's unmodulated narrative technique. *Island in the Sun* (1957), made in England, and *They Came to Cordura* (1959) used increasingly overheated plot material but it was not until *The Hustler* (1961) that Rossen found a subject which, in returning to the more enclosed *milieu* of pool-room gambling, vindicated the promise of *Body and Soul.*

The career of **Richard Brooks** (*b* 1912), though more prolific, is similar to that of Rossen. After some unlikely early work as a writer of Maria Montez adventures at Universal, Brooks scripted *Brute Force* (1947, *dir* Jules Dassin). *Crossfire* (1947, *dir* Edward Dmytryk), the first Hollywood racialist drama, about the murder of a Jew, was adapted from a novel by Brooks (though in the novel the victim was a homosexual). *Crisis* (1950), a thriller with Cary Grant, was Brooks's first

Social Realism

film as a director and was made for M-G-M where he remained as a contract director throughout the succeeding decade. During that time he made only one film, *Deadline* (*Deadline U.S.A.,* 1952) away from the studio: made for Fox, with Bogart as the editor of a dying daily newspaper, *Deadline* is, in many ways, the most personal of his early films, revealing an empirical rather than utopian idealism. During his early years at M-G-M Brooks was apparently unhappy with the pictorial style imposed by the studio, and in *Deadline* he used a darker, more textured photography closer to the brooding style of his later independent production *Elmer Gantry* (1960). It was a wise decision, because the brightly lit backgrounds that accompany the M-G-M gloss dangerously compromised *The Blackboard Jungle* (1955), threatening to topple the treatment of an already sensational novel by Evan Hunter about classroom violence into glib sensationalism. Brooks apparently sees the writing of the screenplay as the central creative process, and his films from the scripts of others are mainly undistinguished. Of his later films *Something of Value* (1957), set in Kenya during the Mau Mau outrages, and his two adaptations from Tennessee Williams, *Cat on a Hot Tin Roof* (1958) and *Sweet Bird of Youth* (1961), are effective, personal works; and *Elmer Gantry* (1960), scripted by Brooks from the novel by Sinclair Lewis, remains his most consistent and fully realised work to date. *The Brothers Karamazov* (1958), on the other hand, with its over-emphatic colour effects anticipated the worst excesses of *Lord Jim* (1965).

Yet another director whose career took shape in the late Forties was **Fred Zinnemann** (*b* 1907), who, after a varied career directing shorts and second features of little distinction, went to Europe to make *The Search* (1948), a touching story of a war orphan befriended by an American G.I. With its topical humanitarianism *The Search* won widespread admiration, and Zinnemann followed it with two further films about the ravages of war, *The Men* (1950) for Stanley Kramer about the rehabilitation problems of a paraplegic ex-serviceman, played by Marlon Brando, and *Teresa* (1951), a love story in war-torn Europe and the later problems of a G.I. married to an Italian bride. *Act of Violence* (1949), a thriller in the *Crossfire* tradition, also had its drama rooted in an act of war-time cowardice. In *High Noon* (1952) Zinnemann effectively transferred his humanitarian concern to a Western which, despite its somewhat over-simplified and calculated plot, was a critical and commercial success of some magnitude. A certain measure of opportunism grew apparent in Zinnemann's treatment of the more ambitious projects which now came his way. His handling of *From Here to Eternity* (1952), while undeniably faithful to the raw quality of James Jones's novel with its cynical, brutalised view of humanity, seemed lacking in his earlier idealism though the skilful transcription won him an Academy Award. *Oklahoma!* (1955) was a conscientious but unoriginal transcription of the Rodgers and Hammerstein stage success, the first to be filmed in Todd-AO, for which Zinnemann disappointingly retained much of the outmoded theatrical idiom. He was more at home with *A Hatful of Rain* (1957), an adaptation of a Broadway play about an ex-serviceman's struggle to keep knowledge of his addiction to drugs from his possessive father while being harassed for money by a sadistic peddler. However, in being faithful to the original, the film became overloaded with fashionable psychological trappings. *The Nun's Story* (1959) and *The Sundowners* (1960), on the other hand, showed an increasing determination to extract the greatest possible emotional effects by falsifying and emphasising every dramatic moment.

Joseph L. Mankiewicz (*b* 1909), often classified as a literary and, therefore, un-cinematic director made the relatively unusual transition from producer. Working for Fox, his first film as a director was *Dragonwyck* (1946), a stylish, doom-laden period drama from a novel by

Gary Cooper in the climactic gun-fight of HIGH NOON

Anya Seton. *A Letter to Three Wives* (1949), with its Cukor-like story of suburban marital tensions, brought Mankiewicz critical recognition for his witty and civilised treatment and led naturally to *All about Eve* (1950) after a brief excursion into social melodrama with *No Way Out* (1950). Bette Davis's career was at a crossroads and *All about Eve* gave her the best role for some years, with dialogue studded with jewelled epigrams. *The Barefoot Contessa* (1954), with its exotic echoes of Lewin's *Pandora and the Flying Dutchman* (1951) in the use of colour and casting of Ava Gardner, tended to reveal the weakness of Mankiewicz's self-effacing pictorial style, but he remained a brilliant director of actors—most notably in *House of Strangers* (1950) and *Julius Caesar* (1953)—as well as actresses. *Guys and Dolls* (1955), which showed Mankiewicz's discreet intelligence somewhat at odds with the brashness of Runyon, also suggested a commendable ability to withstand the pressures of "block-buster" production without abandoning every vestige of personal taste—a highly relevant factor in the rescue operation Mankiewicz was later called upon to perform on *Cleopatra* (1963) when it threatened to become the cinema's biggest financial disaster. *The Quiet American* (1958) was a strangely off-beat successor to *Guys and Dolls*. Mankiewicz made it for his own company in Italy and on location in Vietnam but audiences were indifferent to the political situation in South-East Asia and the film failed, despite a good performance by Michael Redgrave as Graham Greene's tortured anti-hero. *Suddenly Last Summer* (1959), also made in Europe, was a commercial success: the casting of Elizabeth Taylor and the challengingly controversial story adapted from Tennessee Williams with its references to revenge consummated by cannibalism ensured that, but the sensibilities of Mankiewicz were hardly matched to such traumatic material. The success of the film was however a minor landmark in staking out the broadening bounds of dramatic propriety.

The Fifties were a testing period for the Hays Office as film-makers attempted a more adult approach to sexual matters and the treatment of hitherto forbidden subjects. **Otto Preminger** (*b* 1906) became a prominent tactician in skirmishes with the censor. When approval was withheld from *The Moon Is Blue* (1953) because the heroine—played by Maggie MacNamara—referred to herself as a virgin, the hypocrisy of the existing censorship was underlined. Preminger openly challenged the Hays Office with *The Man with the Golden Arm* (1955), which dealt with the forbidden theme of drug addiction. The film was released without approval and met with widespread success. Such moves effectively undercut the censor's position, forcing a retrenchment to a more liberal attitude. By 1959 Preminger was able to introduce the word "contraceptive" into *Anatomy of a Murder* without objection.

Such details are, of course, peripheral to Preminger's quality as a

film-maker. Sometimes criticised for the icy detachment of his films, which are distinctly objective in their treatment of character, Preminger may also be admired for his clarity of expression and the freedom he allows to the spectator in forming his own attitudes. The conventions of the Hollywood star system have however created a dilemma, making it difficult for audience and critics to see his films with the same objectivity. Dana Andrews, the corrupt police officer of *Where the Sidewalk Ends* (1950) is iconographically inseparable from Dana Andrews, the handsome, virile *likeable* star. Fritz Lang exploited precisely this effect, using the same actor in *Beyond a Reasonable Doubt* (1956), relying on audience sympathy for the actor as an innocent man wrongly convicted of murder before revealing he is the real killer.

A surprising weakness in a director who is also an actor is the uneven quality of the performances Preminger elicits, though Clifton Webb in *Laura* (1944) and Charles Laughton in *Advise and Consent* (1962) are memorable exceptions. It may however account, in part, for the problem of *Where the Sidewalk Ends*. But there are many compensating strengths: during the Fifties Preminger tackled an unusually wide range of subjects, ranging from the brittle sex comedy of *The Moon Is Blue* to the despair of *Bonjour Tristesse* (1958), from the Western adventure of *River of No Return* (1954) to the thoughtful if disastrously unsuccessful adaptation of Shaw's *Saint Joan* (1957), from the Negro musical of *Carmen Jones* (1954) to the "problem picture" of *The Man with the Golden Arm* (1955). The alterations Preminger made to *Saint Joan* suggest a particularly careful attempt

43

to balance Joan's motivation between her reason and her "voices," thereby frustrating judgement of the character. This is the keynote of Preminger's work. Expressed also through an uncommitted and fluid camera style it points to a unifying factor for the disparate nature of his films. *ah*

Independents   Many of the successful films of the late Forties were, by Hollywood standards, relatively inexpensive. Location photography in contemporary settings saved costly studio sets and this, in turn, made it possible for independent producers to operate competitively without an affiliation to a major studio. **Stanley Kramer** (*b* 1913) was particularly successful and influential. In 1949 he made *Champion* (*dir* Mark Robson), a boxing film somewhat in the style of Rossen's *Body and Soul*. Produced on a highly condensed shooting schedule the film is reputed to have earned its modest cost four times over in the American market alone. Kramer continued to produce low-budget features dealing with important subjects: racial prejudice in *Home of the Brave* (1949, *dir* Mark Robson), rehabilitation of ex-servicemen in *The Men*. The success of *High Noon,* made like all his previous films for United Artists, took Kramer to Columbia under a unique deal which provided studio, finance and distribution while leaving Kramer almost complete independence. Kramer broadened his choice of subjects to include adaptations of a number of off-beat (by Hollywood standards) books and plays. The first was *Death of a Salesman* (1952) with Fredric March as Arthur Miller's tragic figure of Willy Loman. **Laslo Benedek** (*b* 1907) directed the film with uncompromising integrity, even managing the flashbacks without recourse to optical effects: unfortunately the film's commercial failure tended to vindicate the traditional view that stage plays require extensive re-working for the screen.

The Columbia contract called for thirty films in five years and though Kramer embarked on new projects at a prodigious rate it soon became apparent that he had not brought with him a Midas touch. Adaptations like *The Four Poster* (1952, *dir* Irving Reis) and *The Member of the Wedding* (1953, *dir* Fred Zinnemann) fared little better, while even more vigorous subjects like *The Sniper* (1952, *dir* Edward Dmytryk) and *My Six Convicts* (1952, *dir* Hugo Fregonese) achieved only modest box-office success. Perhaps the most original of the Columbia films was *The 5,000 Fingers of Dr. T* (1953), a musical fantasy in Technicolor from a script by Dr. Seuss, the children's writer, about a small boy's daydreams concerning his piano teacher. Even this excursion into Disney territory failed commercially and by 1954 Kramer turned to more obviously successful subjects. *The Wild One* (1954, *dir* Laslo Benedek) had Marlon Brando as leader of a motor-cycle gang who terrorised a small town; it was banned by the British censor who saw it as a blueprint for imitative social disorder. Kramer's last film for Columbia was an uncharacteristically star-studded adaptation of Herman Wouk's novel *The Caine Mutiny* (1954, *dir* Edward Dmytryk) with Humphrey Bogart giving a conscientious performance as the paranoiac Captain Queeg.

It seems likely that the unfulfilled promise of Kramer's Columbia films may have been due to the departure of Carl Foreman, until 1952 Kramer's closest associate. Foreman, who scripted all the early films, fell victim to the McCarthy witch-hunt and went into anonymous exile in Britain where he has continued to reside. In 1955 Kramer returned to United Artists, abandoning the attempt to produce large quantities of films: instead he embarked on more ambitious individual films which he directed himself. The first, *Not as a Stranger* (1955) was a somewhat overblown hospital drama, adapted from a contemporary best-seller; his later work reverted in type to his original choice of subjects—racial tolerance in *The Defiant Ones* (1958), atomic disaster in *On the Beach* (1959), religious bigotry in *Inherit the Wind* (1960). All show him to be a director with a facile but undistinguished style and a tendency to contrive his dramatic situations as exercises in didactic liberalism.

Another important independent company was Hecht-Lancaster, formed in 1947 by producer Harold Hecht and the actor Burt Lancaster. The participation of stars in production had certain advantages and though in some cases the companies created had only paper substance, others—like Hecht-Lancaster and Kirk Douglas's Byrna Productions—achieved notable results. Hecht-Lancaster's first films were colourful action pictures like *The Crimson Pirate* (1952, *dir* Robert Siodmak), but in 1954 under a deal with United Artists they became more ambitious. Lancaster had an unusually demanding role as an Indian in *Apache* (1954, *dir* Robert Aldrich) which was a further significant step in Hollywood's sympathetic treatment of the Indians pioneered by *Broken Arrow* (1950, *dir* Delmer Daves), while *Vera Cruz* (1954, *dir* Robert Aldrich) brought an unusual measure of wit and maturity to an adventure yarn, creating a style discernible in many subsequent films from *Bandido* (1956, *dir* Richard Fleischer) through to Richard Brooks's *The Professionals* (1967) and Aldrich's own *The Dirty Dozen* (1967).

Marty (1955, *dir* Delbert Mann) was influential in quite a different way. It was adapted from a television play by Paddy Chayevsky, filmed in black-and-white with little expansion of the original action. Lancaster did not appear: Marty, the shy and unattractive New York butcher, was played by Ernest Borgnine, hitherto a supporting actor, who won an Academy Award for his performance. *Marty,* in rejecting the doctrine of CinemaScope, colour and spectacle in favour of material originally written for the domestic screen, polarised Hollywood attitudes to television. The commercial success of *Marty* encouraged other television adaptations: Hecht-Lancaster filmed *Bachelor Party* (1957, *dir* Delbert Mann) from another Chayevsky play, while other independent units made *Twelve Angry Men* (1957, *dir* Sidney Lumet) and *Patterns of Power* (*Patterns*, 1956, *dir* Fielder Cook) from plays by Reginald Rose and Rod Serling. The vogue spread to major studios, particularly M-G-M who made *Wedding Breakfast* (*The Catered Affair*, 1956, *dir* Richard Brooks) from Chayevsky, *The Rack* (1956) from Serling and *Ransom!* (1955). By 1958, however, it became apparent that this was a transitional phase: live drama on television was by that time almost extinct, replaced by filmed series commanding predictable weekly audiences and produced in Hollywood on the stages vacated by the demise of the second feature. The television influence persisted, however, through the dramatic transfusion of talent and ideas that had taken place. Prominent among the young directors recruited from television were **Delbert Mann** (*b* 1920), **Sidney Lumet** (*b* 1924) and **John Frankenheimer** (*b* 1930). **Paddy Chayevsky** (*b* 1923), **Rod Serling** (*b* 1924) and **Reginald Rose** (*b* 1921) have all subsequently written original screenplays, while the style they evolved—with Chayevsky's ear for colloquial idiom, Serling's facile but acutely observed dialogue phrasing and Rose's literate perceptions of social attitudes—has been assimilated in countless other scripts.

No discussion of independent production in the Fifties would be complete without mention of four unique and unrelated films: *Kiss Me Deadly* (1955, *dir* Robert Aldrich), a dazzling if brutal exercise in style adapted from an incomprehensible story by Mickey Spillane; *Night of the Hunter* (1955), Charles Laughton's only film as a director, from a script by James Agee, which combined outstanding performances by Shelley Winters and Evelyn Varden and brilliant "barnstorming" by Robert Mitchum as a deranged phoney preacher, with an eclectic but beautiful pictorial quality; *Sweet Smell of Success* (1957), a Hecht-Hill-Lancaster production directed with astonishing incisiveness by Alexander Mackendrick from a play by Clifford Odets; and *Paths of Glory* (1957, *dir* Stanley Kubrick), a black, uncompromising condemnation of military cynicism and injustice.

Studio Influence
Though the Fifties saw the beginning of the end for the film factory system established by the major studios in the Twenties, some distinctive groups of films continued to roll off the conveyor belts. Richard Brooks's work for M-G-M has already been noted, but Metro was also the home of Vincente Minnelli, whose reputation in 1950 rested on his series of elegant musicals. By 1954 the musical was, however, in decline: *The Bandwagon* (1953), which splendidly united Fred Astaire and Jack Buchanan, as well as giving Astaire his best dancing partner for many years in Cyd Charisse, was also the last of Minnelli's musicals conceived as a film original. The theatrical origins

*George Peppard
and Audrey
Hepburn in
BREAKFAST
AT TIFFANY'S*

of *Brigadoon* (1954), *Kismet* (1955) and *Gigi* (1958) were more apparent but they remained decoratively distinguished despite a diminished emphasis on dancing as a principal element. Comedies such as *The Long Long Trailer* (1954) and *The Reluctant Debutante* (1958) show Minnelli's style to be quintessentially that of M-G-M for whom he has worked throughout his career, while his two films about the people who make films—*The Bad and the Beautiful* (1953) and *Two Weeks in Another Town* (1962)—crystallise between them an image of Hollywood in transition.

During the Fifties perhaps the most impressive stylist was **Douglas Sirk** (*b* 1900) whose body of work for Universal-International comes close to rivalling that of von Sternberg in the Thirties. All except three of the seventeen films made by Sirk for Universal between 1952 and 1959 were in colour and, as with Minnelli, Sirk's pictorial style tended to define the studio's "house style." Though he had worked in Europe and Australia since 1929 Sirk did not arrive in Hollywood until 1943; his formal camera style and mastery of lighting, colour and effects were not fully revealed, however, until *Magnificent Obsession* (1954), *All That Heaven Allows* (1956) and *Written on the Wind* (1957)—the last, arguably, being his most complete achievement in transmutation of meretricious plot material.

At Columbia the spirit of social comedy was re-kindled by *Born Yesterday* (1950, *dir* George Cukor), a story of innocence, in the "dumb blonde" personality of Judy Holliday, triumphant over corruption. This and Cukor's two subsequent films with Judy Holliday provided patterns for *The Solid Gold Cadillac* (1956) and *Full of Life* (1957), made by the same actress for **Richard Quine** (*b* 1920), Columbia's most promising young contract director. Though Quine attracted notice with several lively musicals like *All Ashore* (1953) and the thriller *Drive a Crooked Road* (1954) at the beginning of his career his later work failed to live up to this promise and he was overtaken by **Blake Edwards** (*b* 1922), a frequent script collaborator on Quine's early films. Edwards's comedies were generally brighter and more consistent than Quine's although his best work did not come till he left Columbia to make *Operation Petticoat* (1959). The delicately balanced moods of *Breakfast at Tiffany's* (1961), handled with grace and precision by Edwards, confirmed his ascendancy.

A more robust comic tradition was developed in the films of **Frank Tashlin** (*b* 1913), whose earlier experience as a newspaper cartoonist can be discerned in his use of broad caricature and simple gag construction. His two films with Jayne Mansfield, *The Girl Can't Help It* (1956) and *Oh! For a Man* (*Will Success Spoil Rock Hunter?*, 1957), parodying the mythology of success in "Rock and Roll" and the Madison Avenue rat race, were acutely observed and highly inventive while his frequent work with Jerry Lewis seemed to be pointing toward the creation of a new and original comedy style.

M-G-M, under its young executive producer **Dore Schary** (*b* 1905) embarked on a series of original second features, of which *Mystery Street* (1950, *dir* John Sturges) and *Stars in My Crown* (1950, *dir* Jacques Tourneur) were particularly interesting. **John Sturges** (*b* 1911) later produced several well-constructed Westerns—*Bad Day at Black Rock* (1955), *Gunfight at the O.K. Corral* (1957) and *Last Train from Gun Hill* (1959) were the best—but failed to develop a distinct personal style.

Of the directors who first worked for Dore Schary, **Nicholas Ray** (*b* 1911) is perhaps the most important. Ray's first film was *They Live by Night* (1949), one of a group produced under Schary at RKO-Radio before his move to M-G-M: other notable companion pieces were *Crossfire, The Set-Up* (1949, *dir* Robert Wise) and *The Window* (1949, *dir* Ted Tetzlaff). *They Lived by Night* and Ray's next film *Knock on Any Door* (1949) seemed to belong to the school of social realism, though they were realised with an unusual density of perceptive detail. The merit of much of Ray's later work lies more in the manner of its execution, but even stylistic felicities could not save assignments like *Flying Leathernecks* (1951). *Johnny Guitar* (1954), a Republic western with Joan Crawford, had, however, such a bizarre quality with unconscious references to Kraft-Ebbing and Pirandello, that it commanded considerable critical attention and is considered by some to be Ray's best film. This honour may more properly belong to *Rebel without a Cause* (1955) which, along with *The Young Stranger*

(1956, *dir* John Frankenheimer), first defined the "generation gap" and the incoherent disenchantment of the younger generation with the values and aspirations of their parents—an attitude brilliantly embodied in James Dean's performance. It has been suggested that *Rebel without a Cause* demonstrates Ray's central theme—the idea that each human relationship forms its own morality, but many of his films like *Party Girl* (1958) may quite simply be enjoyed for their stylistic qualities. Unfortunately Ray's style was unable to transcend the front-office interference on *Bitter Victory* (1958), potentially one of his more personal works, nor the gargantuan vulgarity of *King of Kings* (1961).

Ray intermittently displayed a social conscience, which earned him regular critical attention: the films of **Samuel Fuller** (see separate article below) on the other hand were treated derisorily or ignored because of the crudity and violence of their political perceptions. After an early career in journalism and several years as a film writer Fuller showed an immediate and confident grasp of technique in his first feature, *I Shot Jesse James* (1949) which was constructed mainly in close-up to disguise low-budget shortcomings in the sets. With its central character an assassin the film is typical of Fuller's use of violent, even brutal heroes—like Widmark's squalid pick-pocket in *Pick-Up on South Street* (1952). Fuller's self-declared interest is in the emotional potential of film: violence is not so much condoned as used for the physical expression of emotion in a visual medium. Perhaps one of the cinema's genuine "Primitives," Fuller has apparently remained faithful to his own unfashionable view of the world until now, in hindsight, his work has not only integrity but an unsuspected relevance.

Fuller was, of course, not alone in his dramatic use of violence: **Robert Aldrich** (*b* 1918) in *Kiss Me Deadly* created a world with violence as its anarchic ethic though the emotional brutality of *The Big Knife* (1955) and *What Ever Happened to Baby Jane?* (1962) seems to be his predominant characteristic. In *The Prowler* (1950), **Joseph Losey** (*b* 1909), with Aldrich as his assistant, handled a story of squalid ambition pursued with cold calculation which established the tone of their later work. **Phil Karlson** (*b* 1908) and **Don Siegel** (*b* 1912) both increased their stature in the mid-Fifties with a series of crime thrillers to which they brought style and integrity. The most effective were Karlson's *The Phenix City Story* (1955) and *The Brothers Rico* (1957) and Siegel's *Baby Face Nelson* (1957) and *The Line-Up* (1958). Siegel, however, had already made *Riot in Cell Block 11* (1954) a violent subject, but belonging to the social realist school, executed in a vivid and remarkably unsentimental manner, and *Invasion of the Bodysnatchers* (1956), a catchpenny title concealing an honest and thoughtful treatment of the seminal theme—the destruction of human identity. Karlson's career later declined but Siegel successfully extended his work into the Sixties.

Though the work of Fuller, Aldrich, Losey and Siegel reveals a logical continuity into the Sixties it has little bearing on the apparently divergent trends of wide-screen colour spectaculars on the one hand and low or medium-budget films of intelligence and concern with human issues on the other. In many ways, however, the divergence was resolved in 1957, but not in Hollywood. Britain had become the centre for a great deal of Hollywood-financed production. *The Bridge on the River Kwai* (1957, *dir* David Lean) provides a forceful example of what happened. Firstly it was an independent production (Sam Spiegel), but financed and distributed by a major Hollywood company (Columbia). Secondly it was a spectacular story (photographed in CinemaScope and colour) but with a serious, liberally-minded theme (about courage, loyalty and integrity in war). By 1958 the influence was felt in Hollywood. *The Bridge on the River Kwai* was a great commercial triumph; the success of Hollywood's own productions was less certain. Television adaptations met with diminishing returns and the source was drying up. The novelty of CinemaScope had worn off in the five years since its introduction. The vast traditional audience of lower-paid middle-aged people were lost almost permanently, held captive by their television sets. The remaining audience was younger, better paid, perhaps more intelligent. By 1958 it was they whom Hollywood had to please to survive. *ah*

William Holden on the warpath in THE BRIDGE ON THE RIVER KWAI

By the early Sixties a new pattern of film production could be seen to be emerging in Hollywood. The unease brought about by the McCarthy era and the invasion of Hollywood by television had now been overcome. Although audiences continued to dwindle, they did so at a greatly reduced rate. The huge Hollywood companies were gradually taken over by larger industrial complexes, and the old-style studio producer began to die out, being replaced by the new independent producer, increasingly a director in his own right. Many of these producers were based in New York rather than Hollywood itself, so that increasingly, New York became an important centre for the industry. The beginning of the Sixties witnessed a considerable movement of young directors into films from television, among them Franklin Schaffner, Arthur Penn, John Frankenheimer, Sidney Lumet and Martin Ritt. Several of their films—indeed, a large number of so-called "American" films of the Sixties—were in fact produced in England, using English technicians and facilities.

Franklin Schaffner (*b* 1920), having worked both in the theatre and for television, made his first film, *Woman of Summer* (*The Stripper*) in 1963, a poignant story of back-stage life realised with documentary authenticity. *The Best Man,* made the following year, was also documentary in its approach, and was a bitingly witty comedy about American political life. However, it was with the epic that Schaffner came into his own as a film-maker. *The War Lord* (1965), a historical epic set in early Medieval Europe, was a fatalistic and haunting evocation of an era, rich with its doom-laden imagery of mists and forests. Schaffner's next film, a spy thriller, *The Double Man* (1967) showed little of his former flair, suggesting the thriller to be a *genre* largely unsuited to his talents. *Planet of the Apes* (1968), a science fiction film about a group of astronauts stranded on an unknown planet governed by apes who have come to regard human beings as wild animals, was undoubtedly Schaffner's finest film to date, ending on a note of extreme pessimism when it was revealed that the planet was, in fact, earth itself, 2,000 years in the future. *Patton: Lust for Glory* (*Patton*) was also conceived on an epic scale, depicting the campaigns of the idiosyncratic figure of General George S. Patton towards the end of the Second World War.

Arthur Penn (*b* 1922) also worked in television, although his reputation was made in the theatre. His first film, *The Left-Handed Gun* in 1957, a Western about Billy the Kid, was one of the most remarkable directorial *débuts* in the history of the cinema; his depiction of Billy as sensitive yet inarticulate, drawn into a life of violence ending his suicide, was a significant contribution to the Western *genre*. The feeling of physical intensity which is always linked with a feeling of inadequacy of expression has dominated Penn's work, and this was explored in greater depth in his next film, *The Miracle Worker* (1962),

the story of the education of a blind, deaf and dumb child, Helen
Keller by Annie Sullivan. The extreme physicality of Penn's world and
the performances he succeeds in drawing from his actors are his most
distinctive contribution to the cinema. Physical violence played an important part in his work, particularly in his next three films, all of which
fell loosely into the gangster *genre. Mickey One* (1964) was the most
abstract and overtly symbolic of all Penn's films, the study of a night
club entertainer over-burdened by a sense of guilt, who attempts to
lose his identity among the down-and-outs. *The Chase,* made a year
later, was a more persuasive film, the story of a Texan town overrun
by prejudice and violence. However, it was *Bonnie and Clyde* in 1967
that marked the culmination of Penn's work in the gangster *genre* and
represented his most explicit statement on the nature of violence in
society. The film is an exploration of the legend of Bonnie and Clyde
rather than their reality; what concerns Penn is the way in which his
characters derive a sense of identity from the legend they create, a theme
that preoccupied him in *The Left-Handed Gun.* With *Alice's Restaurant* (1969) he abandoned these concerns in favour of exploring the
alternative value system of the hippie movement. This was undoubtedly
Penn's least successful film in which he failed to come to terms with
his material. Nevertheless, the folk-singer Arlo Guthrie bears a strong
resemblance to other Penn heroes, and his final rejection of the hippie
dream of brotherhood and peace parallels the rejection of organised
society in Penn's earlier work.

   John Frankenheimer worked primarily in television before turning
to the cinema with *The Young Stranger* in 1956. Frankenheimer's approach to film-making is marked by a search for the striking image,
which can too often degenerate into a striving for visual effects for
their own sake. His early films were documentary in style, displaying
a great feeling for urban landscape. All Frankenheimer's protagonists—
the young Puerto Ricans in *The Young Savages* (1961), the prisoners
in *Birdman of Alcatraz* (1962), the brain-washed soldiers in *The
Manchurian Candidate* (1962)—are alienated from organised society
in some way, but his examination of that society appears simple and
often naïve. In this way his later films never appear to really succeed
in conveying a personal vision, except in the purely formal sense. *The
Train* (1964), *Grand Prix* (1966), *The Fixer* (1968) and *The Gypsy
Moths* (1969) all suggested a growing divergence between form and
content which was not so evident in the earlier (and much the most
successful) phase of his career.

*Opposite: the work of three younger American directors. Top left: Alan Bates in
Frankenheimer's THE FIXER. Top right: George C. Scott in Schaffner's PATTON.
Below: Faye Dunaway and Warren Beatty in Penn's BONNIE AND CLYDE*

Martin Ritt (*b* 1920) began his career in a similar way to Frankenheimer, working in the theatre and television before making his first film *A Man Is Ten Feet Tall* (*Edge of the City*) in 1957. An immensely assured and schematic first film, *A Man Is Ten Feet Tall* traced the relationship between a neurotic adolescent and a Negro docker who initiates him into adult life. Ritt's treatment of the racial theme was particularly interesting, and it is a theme that has recurred throughout his work. His least successful films have been literary adaptations, such as *The Long Hot Summer* (1957) and *The Sound and the Fury* (1958), both based on William Faulkner novels. After *The Black Orchid* (1959), Ritt was gradually to assume a more pessimistic tone with *Five Branded Women* (1960), *Paris Blues* (1961) and *Hemingway's Adventures of a Young Man* (1962) which culminated in *Hud* (1963), a modern Western that dwelt on the uncertainty of personal relationships. This sense of ambiguity was the focal point of *The Outrage* (1964), a re-working of Kurosawa's *Rashomon*. Ritt became increasingly interested in characters with divided allegiances; the double-agent in *The Spy Who Came in from the Cold* (1965), the half-caste Indian in *Hombre* (1966), the gangster torn between his Sicilian roots and the world of big business in modern America in *The Brotherhood* (1968). In *The Molly Maguires* (1970), Ritt's most accomplished film to date, the study of a mining community in Pennsylvania infiltrated by a company spy, Ritt makes a plea for social action, even if it may prove self-destructive. In this film, Ritt's mastery of dialogue, colour and movement proves conclusively that he has long since transcended his theatrical origins.

Sidney Lumet laboured far longer under stage conventions, having worked in the theatre first as an actor and then as a producer, before moving into television in the early Fifties. His first films were theatrical in style and content: *Twelve Angry Men* (1957), *Stage Struck* (1958), *That Kind of Woman* (1959), *The Fugitive Kind* (1960), and *A View from the Bridge* (1961). With *Long Day's Journey into Night* (1962) Lumet did succeed in adapting O'Neill's theatricality for a purely cinematic purpose, and from then on his career was marked by a self-conscious search for stylised forms of expression. His next three films *Fail Safe* (1964), *The Pawnbroker* (1965) and *The Hill* (1965) all explored the effects of authoritarianism. *The Group* (1966), an adaptation from Mary McCarthy's novel about a group of girls in the Thirties and their assault on adult, male-dominated life, was notable for its performances, which mark out all his later films, *The Deadly Affair* (1967) and *The Sea Gull* (1969).

Stanley Kubrick (*b* 1928) has had a fairly imaginative career in the film industry, shooting, scripting and editing his early independent films such as *Fear and Desire* (1953), *Killer's Kiss* (1955) and *The Killing* (1956), all of which were expressionistic thrillers, making use

Manic expressions in Kubrick's DR. STRANGELOVE. George C. Scott (left) and Sterling Hayden (right)

of striking and meaningful visual effects. From then on Kubrick's projects became more ambitious with *Paths of Glory* (1957), a memorable film about the dreadful reality of war, and *Spartacus* (1960), an epic on which he was unfortunately not allowed the freedom he required. His next two films led him further into the realms of fantasy, revealing a talent for the absurd that had not been evident previously: *Lolita* (1961), a surrealist tragi-comedy about a middle-aged man's infatuation with a pre-pubescent girl, and *Dr. Strangelove, or How I Learned To Stop Worrying and Love the Bomb* (1963), a burlesque anticipation of the Third World War. Kubrick then embarked on his most ambitious project, *2001: A Space Odyssey,* which must be counted as the greatest science fiction film ever made, dwarfing all other films in the *genre* in its breadth of vision in which the idea of time itself is shown to have no meaning, and in its technical bravura.

Irving Lerner (*b* 1909) began his career in a similar way to Kubrick, making low-budget, independent thrillers such as *Edge of Fury* (1958), *Murder by Contract* (1958) and *City of Fear* (1959), but his transition into big-budget film-making was much less successful, and productions like *Royal Hunt of the Sun* (1969) displayed little of Lerner's original talent. **Frank Perry** (*b* 1930) is another independent director, based in New York, who has made a significant contribution to the American cinema of the Sixties with a series of studies of American life, all of which are scripted by his wife Eleanor Perry. *David and Lisa* (1962), a moving account of the relationship between a pair of adolescent schizophrenics, gained him an immediate reputation as a director. In all his other films Perry's characters have been vainly searching for the tenderness and ability to communicate with one another that David and Lisa achieved through madness. His later films, *Ladybug, Ladybug* (1963), *Trilogy* (1968), *The Swimmer* (1968), *Last Summer* (1969), and *Diary of a Mad Housewife* (1970) were extremely intimate in style and modest in intention. **John Cassavetes** (*b* 1929), the actor, is perhaps the independent director to have had most influence in the Sixties. *Shadows* (1960) which was shot on 16mm and depended heavily on improvisation for its effect was a major breakthrough in technique. Cassavetes's move into commercial film-making was not an entirely happy one, though *Too Late Blues* (1961), the story of an idealistic jazz musician who sells his talents to commercialism, still remains impressive. *A Child Is Waiting* (1963), a film about a school for retarded children, was much less persuasive as a whole, which may be due to the fact that it was re-edited by the studio. With *Faces* (1968), Cassavetes returned to working independently on 16mm with a study of the crack-up of a marriage in middle-age, which depended less on pure improvisation than *Shadows,* and for this reason is less formless and more forceful.

The Sixties also saw the growth of independent film-making on the fringes of Hollywood, much of it encouraged and financed by the entrepreneurial genius of director and producer Roger Corman. **Irvin Kershner** (*b* 1923) made his first film, *Stake-Out on Dope Street,* in 1958 which was produced by Corman, and went on to shoot two more thrillers, *The Young Captives* (1959) and *Hoodlum Priest* (1961). Originally a cameraman, Kershner's early films all convey a strong visual sense and a feeling for locations. In 1964 Kershner left Hollywood to make an independent film in Canada, *The Luck of Ginger Coffey,* a bleak but humorous study of unemployment set in snow-clad Montreal. He returned to America in 1966 to film the crazy comedy *A Fine Madness* and *One Born Every Minute* (*The Flim Flam Man*), the story of a professional confidence trickster. Another director to be financed by Corman is **Monte Hellman** (*b* 1930) who made his first film *Beast from Haunted Cave* in 1959. Originally an editor, Hellman's visual style is highly schematic, placing great emphasis on montage to achieve a sense of spatial dislocation, which is evident in his war film *Back Door to Hell* (1965) but developed and refined in his two Westerns, *The Shooting* and *Ride the Whirlwind* in 1966. Hellman's work has received little recognition in America, although his Westerns arguably represent the most significant contribution to the *genre* in the Sixties. *cj*

The A features of the war years were keyed largely to escapism, encompassing a subdued W. C. Fields's encounter with the boisterous Mae West in *My Little Chickadee* (1940) and Fritz Lang's *Western Union* (1941) as well as Raoul Walsh's *They Died with Their Boots On* (1942), the most romanticised and stirring of the films of Custer's life. One important exception film that sought to counter the Western myths was William A. Wellman's *The Ox Bow Incident* (1942), which was a harsh indictment of lynching that argued its case too didactically until its moving end scene in a saloon where the letter written by one of the lynch mob's victims is read by two cowpunchers.

In the postwar years there began the abandonment of straightforward narrative and the generally elementary characterisation that had accompanied it. The *genre* henceforth extended itself, either in cycles or under the impetus of particular directors, and many of the most significant pictures were those that used the mythical values of the Western to explore concepts of integrity and self-respect with a clarity that would have been difficult set against the more complex contemporary world.

Niven Busch's screenplay for Raoul Walsh's *Pursued* (1947) introduced the idea of psychological disturbance to the Western: the central character, played by Robert Mitchum, was haunted by memories of an experience in childhood and menaced in adulthood as the still innocent victim of a man's warped scheme of revenge. The film was quite extraordinarily forceful, a production of great artistry and technical expertise. Two years later, Walsh made another dark Western (part of a "tragic ending" cycle) that anticipated *Bonnie and Clyde:* the ruthless pursuit of an outlaw (Joel McCrea) in *Colorado Territory.*

Busch (*b* 1903) also wrote the novel on which producer David O. Selznick based his screenplay for *Duel in the Sun* (1948), a film of massive scale and great dramatic intensity that successfully kept the balance between the foreground figures and the epic setting of a great ranch founded and ruled by a pioneer settler (Lionel Barrymore) in conflict with the relentless march of progress. Directed by King Vidor and (uncredited) William Dieterle, the film's big scenes developed from the characterisation which further involved a half-breed girl (Jennifer Jones) tragically torn between the two sons of the rancher, one the dull, upright representative of good and the forces of law and order, the other the devil-may-care, appealing representative of self-interest and anarchy. At heart, the film was a compelling morality piece told with rare and satisfying bravura that only occasionally toppled over into exaggeration.

That same year Howard Hawks made *Red River,* a further study of a range king forced to mend his self-sufficient ways and move with the times, set against a massive cattle drive from Texas northwards which ends up at a newly arrived railroad link. Borden Chase was

Joseph Cotten and Jennifer Jones in DUEL IN THE SUN

part responsible for the script and went on to write several key Westerns in the Fifties. As in *Duel in the Sun,* Dimitri Tiomkin contributed a notable score that matched the grandeur of the images and the dramatic force of the story.

John Ford John Ford was the least affected by changes in the *genre*: in *She Wore a Yellow Ribbon* (1949), he created a sentimental but affecting account of the close of a cavalry officer's career, and through the use of traditional songs and rich-hued colour photography (by Winton Hoch), gave a poetic, eloquent picture of an old West in which honour and devotion to duty were inspirational ideals. His other two films about the Cavalry, *Fort Apache* (1948) and *Rio Grande* (1950) were not so well organised and an excess of sentimentality overcame *Three Godfathers* (1949) with its self-conscious parallel with the Three Wise Men, though the feeling of the parched, sandy desert was vividly conveyed. *My Darling Clementine* (1946) displayed Ford's genius at elaborating on an indifferent script, while *Wagonmaster* (1950) was Ford's one anti-romantic picture—episodic, idiosyncratic, lacking in star players, and shot through with a powerful visual sense and emotional response towards the hardy pioneers who settled the West.

Other films of the period with points of interest were Hathaway's *Rawhide* (1951) with its details of the operation of a stage line and a well-developed suspense situation of outlaws holding a stage station; *Vengeance Valley* (1951, Richard Thorpe) with its strong story of family conflict and depiction of ranch operations; and William Wellman's *Yellow Sky* (1948), with its excellent use of a ghost town setting and some remarkable, sharp monochrome photography by the late Joe MacDonald.

Broken Arrow and *Devil's Doorway* began a new cycle in 1950 by portraying the Indian in a sympathetic light. They were the first Westerns of two directors, **Delmer Daves** (*b* 1904) and **Anthony Mann** (1907–1967), who were to make a substantial contribution to the *genre* in the Fifties. The former film dealt with the marriage of a Westerner to an Indian squaw and showed Apache chief Cochise as a peace-loving statesman. The latter had a land-owning Shoshone as its leading figure, a man who had fought valiantly for the whites in a war but lost his ranch under discriminating laws. The outcome for the Indian was tragic, as it seemed destined to be for the central character

John Wayne leads the troop in SHE WORE A YELLOW RIBBON

in Robert Aldrich's *Apache* (1954), a lone figure who resisted attempts to move him to a Florida reservation with the rest of his tribe. Burt Lancaster's excellent performance gave considerable strength to the film, and his reprieve at the end has perhaps been unjustly criticised.

Winchester '73 (1950, *dir* Anthony Mann) was the most accomplished of a set of films that dealt with particular weapons (by having a strong theme if episodic plot), with *The Siege at Red River* (1954, *dir* Rudolph Maté), dealing in part with the Gatling Gun, the best of the others.

Henry King's *The Gunfighter* (1950) was perhaps the first fully reflective Western, sombrely presenting the disillusionment of an aging gunfighter (Gregory Peck), continually forced to defend his reputation while making a last grasp at a happy future. Its influence was enormous and it became rare indeed for Western heroes to glory in their prowess with a gun or for gunfighters not to regret their way of life.

High Noon (1952, *dir* Fred Zinnemann) and *Shane* (1953, *dir* George Stevens) enjoyed far greater popularity and brought new prestige to the *genre* by the approval of critics; both were thoughtful in the new manner. *High Noon* in fact mirrored the McCarthy witch-hunt era in Hollywood, and depicted a craven community unwilling to support an upright marshal (Gary Cooper) who wavers in the face of duty, paralleling the Hollywood writing community's weak-kneed support for its politically-victimised members. It applied a contemporary set of values to a situation in which courage and self-reliance were not long before considered automatic in a Western. It was also a film designed to generate suspense (with near unity of time and place) and it started the tradition of title songs (with the voice of Tex Ritter) that persists to this day. *Shane* was a far more subtle, delicately handled picture, improving on a fine novel by Jack Schaefer; based on an already familiar situation (the oppression of small farmers by the big rancher) and set of characters, it distilled the essence of the Western myth, its title figure (Alan Ladd) the angelic but doomed wanderer with a sad but firm awareness of having no place in the civilised scheme of things except to render temporary assistance.

On a more traditional level, the Westerns of George Sherman, such as *The Battle of Apache Pass* (1952) deserve mention for their visual appeal and sincere concern for Indian life and welfare, while *Apache Drums* (1951, *dir* Hugo Fregonese) allowed producer Val Lewton to transfer his notion of the terror of the unseen from the horror field by making the Indians a menace that was felt rather than seen.

In 1953 the first full Western by John Sturges appeared, *Escape from Fort Bravo,* and mixed a certain tenderness in the humanising of an army officer by a woman visitor to a fort with a frighteningly vivid, lucidly staged sequence of an Indian attack on a patrol. The overall balance of Sturges's handling and the opportunities of the script mark this as his finest Western.

The same year saw the appearance of *The Naked Spur,* one of Anthony Mann's most striking Westerns exploring the tensions between a small group in remote highland territory and using the price on a wanted man's head as a compelling illustration of greed and in-humanity—far more effective than the more usual quest for a material object such as gold. Arduous settings were also to be seen in Mann's *Bend of the River/Where the River Bends* and *The Far Country,* both starring James Stewart, and scripted by Borden Chase with a strong emphasis, characteristic of the writer's work, on a man's obligations to others.

Hondo, Johnny Guitar and *Vera Cruz* were memorable Westerns of 1954: the first, directed by John Farrow, was shot for 3-D showing and combined sensitive characterisation and good action scenes with excellent desert scenery (the participation of John Ford in shooting a sequence seems to have inspired the rest); the second has been ac-curately dubbed a "Freudian Western" and behind the novelty of two formidable women in conflict (Joan Crawford and Mercedes McCam-bridge) lay some purposeful and imaginative direction by Nicholas Ray; the third was a tongue-in-cheek adventure yarn, pungently directed by Robert Aldrich, with Gary Cooper and Burt Lancaster as two comrades drawn to an inevitable shoot-out.

The arrival of CinemaScope enhanced the pictorial qualities of the Western and at Columbia Rudolph Maté's *The Violent Men/Rough Company* and Anthony Mann's *The Man from Laramie* (both 1955 re-leases) showed how the wide image could be used to powerful effect. The latter also introduced a scene of violence—the deliberate shooting of hero James Stewart through the hand—that seemingly initiated the trend to emphasise the brutality and violence of the Old West that per-sists to this day in contrast to the painless wounds and deaths of most earlier Westerns.

John Ford returned to the *genre* with *The Searchers* (1956), dealing with a long-drawn-out attempt to rescue a girl abducted and brought up by Indians; and this problem of characters involved in two cultures loomed large in Westerns from the mid-Fifties. It was the pivot of Ford's own later *Two Rode Together* (1961), of Huston's moody *The Unforgiven* (1960), and in Samuel Fuller's *Run of the Arrow* received its fullest analysis: this 1957 film depicted a white Southerner (Rod Steiger) deliberately choosing to join the Sioux rather than admit defeat in the Civil War and being brought to a realisation that a man cannot disown his roots.

With *Seven Men from Now* (1956) Budd Boetticher moved into a mature phase of work in the Western. It was followed by six other Westerns in five years, all starring Randolph Scott. Those scripted by

Burt Kennedy with recurring themes, situations, and lines of dialogue (*Seven Men from Now, The Tall T, Ride Lonesome, Comanche Station*) are excellent examples of unpretentious, richly pleasing work developing a particular ease through the harmonious efforts of cast and crew, encompassing both gritty humour and rough violence, and exploring a curious and powerful interaction of characters.

Delmer Daves was responsible for several fine Westerns: *Drum Beat* (1954, another study of Indian affairs like *Broken Arrow*); *Jubal* (1955, a drama of passion and jealousy within an unusually well realised setting of ordinary ranch life); *The Last Wagon* (1956, one of the most intense and rigorous Westerns ever made, a study in survival); *3.10 to Yuma* (1957, a psychological essay based on the unequal relationship of an outlaw and his captor farmer); *Cowboy* (1958, an absorbing attempt to disentangle legend from reality via a tenderfoot's initiation into the life of a cowboy); and *The Hanging Tree* (1959, a moody and affecting story of a love almost defenceless against the excesses of a wild mining camp).

Howard Hawks, whose earlier Western of the decade, a story of pioneers called *The Big Sky* (1952), was disappointingly sluggish, created in *Rio Bravo* (1959) a finely polished entertainment that successfully incorporated Hawks's recurring ideas about independence and self-respect. The stimulus for the film was a reaction against *High Noon* where the marshal asked for help to get his job done; in *Rio Bravo* John Wayne's marshal rejects the offers of help except from a professional gunfighter but learns to admit his need of others such as Angie Dickinson's delectable character called "Feathers." A keen sense of humour largely overcomes the apparent slack in Hawks's long film, and one can later appreciate that its relaxed quality is part of its charm.

On a more epic scale, William Wyler, who had cut his teeth on a large number of B Westerns in the late silent period and made in *The Westerner* (1939) a "class" Western of some interest, came out with *The Big Country* (1958), where superior production values gave some quality to an awkward, familiar story of a pacifist hero (Gregory Peck) caught up in a feud between two large ranchers. The regrettably short-lived Technirama process produced visuals of stunning beauty and clarity as they had done in the system's introductory picture, the flaccid *Night Passage* (1957).

The late Fifties also produced a gem of comedy, *The Sheepman* (1958, *dir* George Marshall); a film of quiet, glowing beauty, *The Proud Rebel* (1958, *dir* Michael Curtiz); and two Westerns of interest from Anthony Mann: *The Tin Star* (1957), his most openly thoughtful picture, and *Man of the West* (1958), his most intense and savage work (superbly photographed by Ernest Haller).

The early to mid-Sixties saw a sharp reduction in the output of Westerns, particularly of supporting features (the main source being a

Two outstanding Westerns. Joel McCrea and Randolph Scott in GUNS IN THE
AFTERNOON (above), and Marlon Brando and Karl Malden in ONE EYED JACKS

series of feeble, hurried pictures produced by A. C. Lyles and peopled by veteran players down on their luck). The production of Westerns in Europe caught fire and American players were attracted to lend their names to these pictures dubbed for the English-language market. Ones from Germany in the "Winnetou" cycle had high pictorial standards but like those from Italy showed little or no understanding of the subtleties of the *genre*, substituting in place of a reasoned plot and detailed characterisation cipher-like figures and a series of violent high-lights—this exemplified particularly by the "Man with No Name" series starring a newcomer, Clint Eastwood, and beginning with *A Fistful of Dollars* (1964). These films had a certain "camp" appeal and Clint Eastwood was able to star in real Hollywood films. Hollywood itself went to Spain to make Westerns on the cheap (others were largely made in Mexico with very few able to afford to shoot within the U.S.A.).

Good Westerns continued to appear from Hollywood: entertainments like *The Comancheros* (1961, Curtiz's final film) and Hathaway's boisterous "North-Western" *North to Alaska* (1960); the ambitious and powerful *One Eyed Jacks* (saturated with Marlon Brando's moody genius in his sole film to date as a director as well as star); and John Ford's moving *The Man Who Shot Liberty Valance* (1962) which in personal terms placed a tragic price on the march of progress in the West as the law of the gun gives way to that of the courtroom and simple cowboy John Wayne finds himself out in the cold.

The Western seemed to be dying for lack of new development and new talent. The appearance of *Ride the High Country/Guns in the Afternoon* (1962) brought out a new talent—director Sam Peckinpah—but was otherwise in a brilliant fashion a form of summation of Westerns past, with Joel McCrea and Randolph Scott, two semi-retired Western stars, portraying figures trying to adjust to increasing age, lack of usefulness, and vanishing glory. The film is one of the indisputable masterpieces of the *genre*—every shot falling into place and working as part of the whole—and it has a deeply moving finale with the heroic demise of the McCrea character.

Many Westerns since then have shown its influence, most notably Tom Gries's remarkable *Will Penny* (1967) with Charlton Heston in the title role as the ordinary cowboy with great powers of endurance but a sad knowledge that his time is past for a happy, settled life with an attractive woman he encounters and helps. Despite excesses in the characterisation of some menacing outlaws, Gries's film had dialogue of a vivid naturalism and a real sense of the hard life of the times, helped particularly by the careful work of cameraman Lucien Ballard (who had earlier achieved wonders on Peckinpah's film).

Another worthwhile film about the onset of old age was *The Good Guys and the Bad Guys* (1969) with Robert Mitchum and George

Kennedy as the two men reluctantly entering the new style Twentieth century. It was directed by Burt Kennedy who had earlier made in *Mail Order Bride/West of Montana* (1964) and a modern Western *The Rounders* (1965), two ultimately slight but wholly charming films, as a writer-director (the latter based on an excellent Max Evans novel). Kennedy also directed the only worthwhile all-out satirical Western of the Sixties, *Support Your Local Sheriff* (1969), written by William Bowers (who had co-scripted the equally successful *The Sheepman*), although the humorous side of two films by a new writer, William Norton—*The Scalphunters* (1968) and *Sam Whiskey* (1969)—came off very well.

Although John Wayne, in his sixties, continues successfully as a leading man, he too has appeared in films that reflect on declining powers and lost opportunities such as Howard Hawks's *El Dorado* (1967), a loose re-make of his earlier *Rio Bravo* with an increased sense of frailty in its characters and uncertainty about the outcome of situations, and *True Grit* (1969), a straightforward but assured treatment of an excellent novel by Charles Portis, full of shrewd humour and convincing period trappings.

Sam Peckinpah's *The Wild Bunch* (1969) stirred up considerable controversy for its explicit and extended treatment of raw violence and, apart from the questionable validity of this, displayed a lack of tautness and drive in its construction plus weaknesses of characterisation that had been sadly evident in his earlier *Major Dundee* (1965), which had however been ruthlessly cut by the studio. Tom Gries's *100 Rifles* (1969) was another disappointment, lacking the personal qualities that had distinguished *Will Penny*. George Roy Hill's *Butch Cassidy and the Sundance Kid* (1969), based on an original screenplay by William Goldman, mingled elements of comedy and fantasy quite adroitly and displayed again that the Western is in the throes of sorting out a new approach unbound by the conventions of the past. *aje*

Samuel Fuller (*b* 1911) began as a newspaper copy boy at the age of fourteen; by seventeen he was the youngest crime reporter in the business. He has carried this experience into his eighteen films, which reflect it in their impact and concentration. He creates the story, writes the script, directs and often produces his own pictures, with the result that he has been restricted to working for small independent companies or on lower budget films for major studios, notably Fox and Columbia.

An extremely didactic film-maker, Fuller works within a simple framework of basic ideas that are interwoven throughout all his cinema with a differing emphasis. He is not deliberately subtle, his dialogue can be banal and unsophisticated, and his political views are sometimes forced on to a film with unhappy results. His didacticism is only partial in that he does not offer solutions to the problems he raises or describes.

Richard Widmark and Jean Peters in Samuel Fuller's PICK-UP ON SOUTH STREET

He presents them in terms of the emotions of his characters, so that prostitutes, criminals, and professional soldiers are the leading figures. The code of ethics in their profession is violated by the hero, who has been led to a new awareness by his contact with the heroine (as in *Pick-Up on South Street,* 1952; *Run of the Arrow,* 1957; *Verboten,* 1958; *The Crimson Kimono,* 1959; and *Underworld USA,* 1960). Some are fortunate enough to survive, as does Rod Steiger in *Run of the Arrow,* playing an embittered Southerner who cannot accept the Civil War defeat, and deserts to the new Yankee/American enemy—the Indians, until a squaw proves to him that his place is with the whites, facing up to his problem. James Shigeta as a Los Angeles detective who quarrels with his white partner over a female witness with whom they both fall in love, ends by marrying the girl and preparing to face the problems of a mixed marriage. Others, like Cliff Robertson in *Underworld USA,* playing a delinquent who grows up with the sole purpose of avenging his father's murder, achieves his end and does the job that an indifferent and uncaring society should have done, but loses his life in the process.

Fuller's films are accommodated within the three main action *genres* of American cinema, namely war, crime, and Westerns. Significantly, they take place in times of political and social crisis and change, with the result that the films are violent, contradictory, and unconventional. They are not bound to treat "contemporary" or "real-life" subjects, and are not limited by a set of structural, dehumanised *clichés* in making their points valid.

The main themes of Fuller's cinema comprise Southern bigotry (*Run* of the Arrow, Forty Guns, 1957; *Shock Corridor* and *The Naked Kiss*, both 1963); racialism and pleas for integration (*The Steel Helmet*, 1950; *House of Bamboo*, 1955; *China Gate*, 1957; *The Crimson Kimono* and *Shock Corridor*); a strong distaste for war and the professional soldier (*The Steel Helmet, Fixed Bayonets*, 1951; *Merrill's Marauders*, 1961) allied to a powerful sense of patriotism, national duty, and suspicion of Communists and Germans (*Pick-Up on South Street, Verboten, Run of the Arrow, Shock Corridor*). Fuller's world is one in which people perform the right actions for the wrong reasons (*Hell and High Water*, 1953; *Pick-Up on South Street, Underworld USA*). But minor recurrent themes such as criminal organisations being run on para-military lines, and lesser characters who act as a conscience for the unfeeling/unaware central figures, are always very much in evidence. These are presented with a high degree of technical competence that sometimes exceeds the end result in quality. *kc*

With the coming of the Second World War, the fashion for horror films dwindled. Schoedsack directed an effective "mad scientist" story, *Dr. Cyclops,* in 1940, wherein the Doctor reduces a group of people to six inch miniatures. The 1940 remake of *The Phantom of the Opera* by **Arthur Lubin** (*b* 1901) was a poor effort, and that of *Dr. Jekyll and Mr. Hyde* by **Victor Fleming** (1883–1949) the following year was interesting on account of Spencer Tracy's psychological approach, but weak in shock-impact. 1943 was notable partly for a small-scale yet genuinely chilling ghost story, *The Uninvited,* directed by **Lewis Allen** (*b* 1905), but mainly for *The Cat People,* directed by **Jacques Tourneur** (*b* 1904) and produced by **Val Lewton** (1904–1951). Its totally unexpected success started a fantasy-horror cycle which lasted until two or three years after the war, dwindled briefly, re-emerged in horror-science-fiction, and has lasted more or less until the present day. Val Lewton left his mark as producer on a brief but memorable series of horror films. A great believer in "the greater menace of the *un*seen," his productions were written, edited, and in particular photographed with a rare restraint and subtlety. Notable among them were *The Leopard Man* (1943), *I Walked with a Zombie* (1943), *The Body Snatcher* (1945), and *Bedlam* (1946).

Great Britain made a late but very effective entry into the field with *Dead of Night* (1945), a compilation film directed by several hands and telling a series of macabre episodes with a linking story that rose to a fine climax and a subtle double-trick ending.

The mid-Forties upsurge ended with Robert Florey's *Beast with Five Fingers* (1947). **Florey** (*b* 1900) had originally been engaged to make a version of Frankenstein before Whale's film appeared and had worked on the script. In 1932 he directed Poe's *Murders in the*

THE HORROR FILM

Rue Morgue, with dialogue by John Huston. He was later co-director on Chaplin's *Monsieur Verdoux* (1947).

The division between horror and science fiction in the cinema has always been a hazy one. The growing tendency to dwell on the horrific aspects of scientific activities really dates from the early Fifties, when an increasing number of Things, Blobs, Martians and Nuclear Monsters began to arrive. Notable early examples were *The War of the Worlds* (1953) directed by Byron Haskin from the novel by H. G. Wells, and *Them!* (1953, Gordon Douglas), with its outsize ants. The Japanese monster *Godzilla* appeared in 1955 and, inevitably, encountered King Kong a few years later. One of the most intelligent and disquieting of all these films was *The Invasion of the Body Snatchers* (1956) directed by Don Siegel. Though saddled with a prologue and epilogue, against the director's wishes, which weakened the impact, this cautionary tale of substituted personalities remains a minor masterpiece of the macabre. Jack Arnold's *The Incredible Shrinking Man* (1957) was another example of a fantastic thriller raised to near-epic quality by imaginative treatment.

A high point in non-fantastic horror was reached in 1955 with the French *Les Diaboliques,* directed by Henri-Georges Clouzot. The drab story of plot and counterplot in a seedy provincial boys' school leads to a murder of uncompromising nastiness, and works up thereafter to a truly terrifying climax.

Hammer Films, practically synonymous with horror, started on their spectacular career in 1957 with the appearance of *The Curse of Franken-stein,* directed by **Terence Fisher** (*b* 1904), with Christopher Lee as the monster. The resounding success of this film was repeated in the following year by *The Horror of Dracula,* also under the direction of Fisher. Lee played the vampire, a part he has undertaken in several sequels. The Hammer output, and that of Fisher, their most prolific director, has been very uneven: the chief faults being poor scripts and a determination to shock at all costs, the chief virtues a fairly constant high quality of technical production, an often infectious sense of enthusiasm, and every now and then a notably good example of the *genre.* Among these are *The Damned* (1961) directed by Joseph Losey; *Taste of Fear* (1961) and *The Nanny* (1965), both from **Seth Holt** (*b* 1923); *Fanatic* (1965) from **Silvio Narizzano** (*b* 1927), with a great piece of Grand Guignol from Tallulah Bankhead; and, despite a rather obviously *papier-mâché* snake-woman, *The Reptile* (1966), directed by **John Gilling** (*b* 1912).

An above average production in 1958 was Jacques Tourneur's *Night of the Demon,* which treated the occult with some intelligence. It contained a magnificently effective storm-conjuration, but lost grip when the devil appeared—unseen demons are best.

Two films from France during this period may be noted. Outstanding in its combination of horror and beauty is *Eyes without a Face (Les Yeux sans Visage)*, directed by Georges Franju. Interpretable on several levels, this subtle and disturbing film is illuminated by a beautiful performance from Edith Scob, masked almost throughout and left with only her eyes through which to convey her emotions. The second film, *Blood and Roses (Et Mourir de Plaisir)*, directed by Roger Vadim, is a version of Sheridan le Fanu's story *Carmilla,* somewhat pretentious and overblown, but with several effective scenes and some attractive camera-work.

The boundary between the horror film and the suspense thriller is often difficult to define, but Alfred Hitchcock may be said to have crossed it in *Psycho* (1960), which contains possibly the most famous and terrifying murder in the cinema—the stabbing of the girl under the bathroom shower. Despite his own deprecation of the film, its general atmosphere of menace beneath the apparently normal, its slow tightening of tension during long build-ups to shattering climaxes, its subtle clues and hints are representative of the director at his very best.

The same year also saw the first of a series of Edgar Allan Poe adaptations directed by **Roger Corman** (*b* 1926)— *The Fall of the House of Usher.* Corman had previously directed or produced a large number of films of all kinds, often at high pressure, including several horror or science fiction subjects—e.g. *The Day the World Ended* (1956), *The Attack of the Crab Monsters* (1957), *War of the Satellites* (1959), *A Bucket of Blood* (1960). It was with Poe, however, that he really achieved recognition, though the adaptations were often very free. *The Pit and the Pendulum* appeared in 1961, *The Premature Burial* and *Tales of Terror* in 1962 and *The Haunted Palace* in 1963. His two best were both made in 1964, in England and on a less restricted budget: *The Masque of the Red Death* and *The Tomb of Ligeia.* All Corman's later horror films are notable for a flair and a feeling for atmospheric settings which frequently overcome limitations of budget. He works very often with Vincent Price, a gentle-voiced actor who has lightened more than one turgid script with his panache and his welcome lurking humour.

A noteworthy non-Hammer British production of 1964 was *Witchcraft,* directed by **Don Sharp** (*b* 1922), who conjured up an unusually convincing sense of brooding evil, aided by some excellently menacing photography by Arthur Lavis.

Throughout the Fifties and early Sixties a flood of small-scale horror films arrived from Italy. The most successful were those of **Mario Bava** (*b* 1914). His *Black Sunday,* or alternatively *Revenge of the Vampire* (*La Maschera del Dèmonio,* 1960), is a fine Gothic story of witchcraft, starring the indispensable Barbara Steele. This was followed by *Black Sabbath* (*I tre volti della paura,* 1963), *Blood and Black Lace* (*Sei donne per l'assassino,* 1964) and *Danger—Diabolik* (*Diabolik,* 1967),

Jack MacGowran and Roman Polanski in silhouette in
Polanski's DANCE OF THE VAMPIRES

among others. Unfortunately, all these Italian films were ruined in English-speaking countries by execrable dubbing.

Robert Wise (*b* 1914), who earlier directed two Val Lewton productions, was responsible for an excellent ghost story in *The Haunting* (1963). With no visible horrors, he contrived most successfully to convey the animosity of an old building towards interlopers, aided by a splendidly menacing soundtrack.

From Great Britain came a macabre masterpiece from Jack Clayton, *The Innocents* (1961), adapted from William Archibald's stage version of Henry James's classic, *The Turn of the Screw*. Retaining a subtly ambiguous attitude towards the actuality or otherwise of the ghosts, Clayton created a film of authentic beauty and terror, also using sound with great imagination to convey horror as much through the ear as the eye.

One of the finest examples of non-fantastic horror was *Repulsion* (1965) directed by Roman Polanski. This study-from-within of a neurotic girl's disintegration into madness and mania, set almost wholly in a dingy Earls Court flat, unnerves the spectator to a far deeper degree than the most fearsome story of the supernatural. It is a film of the utmost complexity, with a brilliant, if occasionally over-emphasised, use of symbolism. The soundtrack, often of very subtly distorted everyday noises, adds greatly to the general effect. Polanski followed this with *Cul-de-Sac* (1966), a black comedy with macabre undertones; *Dance of the Vampires* (1968) a delightful, underrated horror pastiche of great photographic beauty (by Douglas Slocombe) and sardonic humour; and, in 1969, *Rosemary's Baby,* a very successful story of modern-day witch-craft which courageously followed through its implications. Keeping closely to Ira Levin's original novel, and boldly declaring the impossible to be all too possible, it also demonstrated again Polanski's skill in bringing out the latent menace of a setting—in this case an old New York apartment house.

Two highly accomplished Japanese productions of the Sixties were *Kwaidan* (1964), directed by Masaki Kobayashi and *Onibaba* (*The Hole,* 1965), by Kaneto Shindo. The latter tells an exceedingly grue-some story of legendary Japan, set entirely in fields of man-high grass. *Kwaidan* is a volume of three contrasted ghost stories, exquisitely photographed. A fourth episode, *The Woman of the Snow* (*Yuki-Onna*), was released separately.

Early in 1969 Boris Karloff died at the age of eighty-one. An Englishman whose real name was William Henry Pratt, he was without question the doyen of horror film actors. Known chiefly for his portrayal of the monster in the early *Frankenstein* pictures, he numbered among the best of his numerous parts those in *The Mummy* (1932), *The Old Dark House* (1932), *The Black Cat* (1934), *The Body Snatchers* (1945), *Bedlam* (1946) and *The Sorcerers* (1967). Though he appeared in many films unworthy of his abilities, with his imposing presence and beautifully modulated voice he brought a dignity and integrity to any role he undertook, however inane the script. *ib*

UNDERGROUND CINEMA

The origins of underground cinema can be traced to the "agony and experience" experimental school of films by **Maya Deren** (1923–1961), **Kenneth Anger** (*b* 1932), and **Curtis Harrington** (*b* 1924), during and immediately after the Second World War. The films were personal statements concerned entirely with feelings. Anger's *Fireworks* (1947) and Harrington's *Fragments of Seeking* (1946) now rank as underground films. Many of the film-makers concerned with the underground reject all narrative; their films have technical faults, often deliberately included to create an amateurish texture; some use no movement, others nothing but movement or multiple impositions; running times vary from seconds to hours, while there is more total nudity than in commercial cinema. This, combined with obscene language and strong themes, resulted in frequent police raids during the pioneer days. Thus screenings were held in comparative secrecy, and hence the label *underground.* Today, a majority of the directors involved have banded themselves together under the title of the Filmmakers Cooperative, a

Origins

non-profit-making organisation that has slowly secured a wider audience for underground and *avant-garde* movies. Similar co-operatives have been established in Europe.

Warhol, Mekas and others

Andy Warhol (*b* 1928), originally a painter, began with static camera experiments such as *Empire* and *Sleep* (both 1964). He achieved the widest reputation of any underground film-maker with *Chelsea Girls* (1966)—two separate images on adjacent screens with only one soundtrack audible at any time; and more recently he has explored male homosexuality with *Flesh* and *Lonesome Cowboys* (both 1969). Other influential Warhol films have been *Harlot* (1965), and *Bike Boy* (1967). **Jonas Mekas** (*b* 1922), a Lithuanian, has been the crusader spreading the gospel of the new cinema since he arrived in America in 1949; his films include *Guns of the Trees* (1961), *The Brig* (1964), and *Hare Krishna* (1966). His brother, Adolfas Mekas, who co-directed *The Brig,* produced probably the funniest of all recent underground films, *Hallelujah the Hills* (1963), which adroitly satirised several *genres* of film-making. **Jack Smith** (*b* 1932) brought the fight

Underground imagery: Anger's THE INAUGURATION OF THE PLEASURE DOME

against official censorship into the open with *Flaming Creatures* (1963), which dealt with male homosexuality and female impersonation ("drag"), and contained frequent genital exposure. Arrests, confiscations, and destruction of prints followed screenings of this film, which could not be publicly shown until March 1969 without some form of legal intervention. It thus brought notoriety to the underground. The success of public exhibitions of *Chelsea Girls* proved, however, to be the real breakthrough to total recognition of the underground.

This recognition is still limited to specialised audiences, for none of the other film-makers grouped under this heading have enjoyed the commercial success of Warhol. Anger is less prolific, obsessively exploring sexual deviation in *Scorpio Rising* (1961) and *The Inauguration of the Pleasure Dome* (1958), while Harrington has moved into the commercial American cinema with *Night Tide* (1961) and *Games* (1967). **Ron Rice** (1935–1964) experimented with sensual and visual effects, created by repeated use of superimpositions in *Senseless* (1962) and *The Queen of Sheba Meets the Atom Man* (1963), mingling exotica and erotica as subject matter. **Harry Smith** (*b* 1923) displayed a similar interest, terming his films "cinematic excretia." His output displays a higher degree of technical competence than most—he won the Seventh Independent Film Award in 1965—and consists of "batiked" abstractions made directly on film from 1939 to 1946; optically printed non-objective studies; semi-realistic animated collages; and superimposed photographed actualities. His best known works are *Early Abstractions* (1951) and *Heavenly and Earthly Magic* (1943–58).

One of the more renowned personalities of the West Coast school is **Bruce Conner** (*b* 1933), who is equally well established as a painter. His films have often consisted of material grafted from works made for different purposes, reassembled into an aggressively hostile montage of fast pace and vicious humour, like *A Movie* (1958) and *Cosmic Ray* (1961) while *Report* (1966) deployed rhythmical and ritual effect (plus some of his own blood smeared on a number of prints), repetition and subjective editing on footage of President Kennedy's assassination.

Bruce Baillie (*b* 1931) also used counterpoint of imagery for maximum impact in *Castro Street* (1966), while in *Tung* (1966) he filmed the reflections of natural phenomena such as Sun and Moon on a revolving disc, double exposing the negative image of an Oriental girl into a mass of colour. **Robert Nelson** (*b* 1930) also favours montage. Like Conner he uses multiple separate images, yet unlike him he frequently incorporates his own footage into existing stock material, adding a dimension of personal irony to the flip hipster doctrine. Thus, in *Oh Dem Watermelons* (1965), race prejudice: Negro—Watermelon—the image he has to carry. Ben Van Meter combines qualities of Baillie, Conner and Nelson in the non-conformist dogma of *Up Tight . . . L.A. Is Burning . . . Shit* (1966). They all share the West Coast thematic preoccupation of the non-conformist reacting against the square, middle-class, mechanical society.

Robert Breer (*b* 1926) and **Stan VanDerBeek** (*b* 1931) both pre-date the New American Cinema Movement in their work with collage. Art is one of Breer's main preoccupations—he is yet another painter—but is probably best known for *Breathing* (1963) in which the animation is so rapid that it has been described as creating visual orgasms. VanDerBeek is one of the most politically minded and socially oriented of all underground film-makers, and his black humour is best seen in *Science Fiction* (1958–65). Others of the New York school include an Austrian, Peter Kubelka, who shoots extremely short, strongly-impacted films; and Gregory Markopoulos (*b* 1928), who has been involved with cinema since the late Forties. His *Swain* (1950), *Galaxie* (1960), *Serenity* (1963), *The Iliac Passion* (1967), and *Himself as Herself* (1968) are all extremely complex in visual and thematic composition, displaying an almost obsessive preoccupation with homo-erotic motives. *Himself as Herself* is based on a mystical novel by Balzac, entitled *Seraphita,* about the androgynous son/daughter of a male and female angel. Markopoulos and Anger are the only examples of underground film-makers who have turned to literary adaptations for their movie material.

The most way-out of all is the work of **Stan Brakhage** (*b* 1933), who carried superimposition to the extreme with *Dog Star Man* (1959–64), which combined images of a woodsman climbing a hill and chopping down a tree, a beating heart, lungs, bloodstream, microscopic cells, telescopic shots of the sun, moon and stars in a staggering mixture of individual and blended images. Other work by Brakhage has included *Unglassed Windows Cast a Terrible Reflection* (1953), *Desistfilm* (1953), *The Way to Shadow Garden* (1955), *Thin Line Lyre Triangular* (1963), and *Window Water Baby Moving* (1963).

Ed Emshwiller (*b* 1925) not only pre-plans, but also edits his films very carefully, and with the success of *Relativity* (1963–66) is now able to execute his ideas with greater control than his contemporaries. **Peter Emanuel Goldman** (*b* 1939) is another who has moved into fully professional, commercial film-making via the successful underground movie, *Echoes of Silence* (1962–65), although the impact of underground cinema on the industry is reflected not only by the entry of underground directors into full-scale studio work. Its influence can be seen more plainly in the type of material now considered suitable for filming. Movies like Schlesinger's *Midnight Cowboy,* Hopper's *Easy Rider,* Franck's *Born Losers,* and Mazursky's *Bob and Carol and Ted and Alice* all concern themes and situations that could not have reached the screen in past years as legitimate commercial film material. Similarly, the technical experiments of the underground have been mirrored by the industry, though for admittedly opposing reasons. Underground cinema is also partially responsible for the increase in the sex-exploitation cycle, since this has been a natural offshoot from the very risqué path that the underground trod where sex was concerned.

Audience participation in or involvement with underground films depends solely on individual taste and inclination. They can be seen as mere entertainment, but because of their construction and intention, this could be wearing both physically and emotionally. They serve a definite purpose in that they provoke discussion, while the determination of their directors to make their own films in their own way, refusing to knuckle under to the commercialism of the studios, and the monetary domination of the banking interests running American and British cinema, is to be admired. *kc*

Some talented directors, although not strictly members of the underground movement, have had to be content with similarly slender budgets and modest production methods in order to achieve freedom of expression. **John Korty** (*b* 1933) is director of photography on his own films and has revealed a turn of mind both lyrical and whimsical in *The Crazy Quilt* (1965), *Funnyman* (1967), and *Riverrun* (1969). **Shirley Clarke** (*b* 1925) co-directed a documentary, *Skyscraper* (1958) with Willard van Dyke before achieving an international name with *The Connection*, a Brechtian study of the world of drug addicts, released in 1960. Her *Portrait of Jason* (1967) veered more towards *cinéma-vérité*, as a Negro male prostitute talked about his life, almost liberating himself in the eyes of a dispassionate camera. Jim McBride's two features, *David Holzman's Diary* (1966), and *My Girlfriend's Wedding* (1968) also adopt a semi-documentary approach involving the actual film-maker with his characters and subject-matter to a marked degree. Finally, a man closely associated with the New York experimental group, **Lionel Rogosin** (*b* 1923), has directed a number of radical films, including *On the Bowery* (1955) and *Come Back Africa* (1958). He runs the Bleeker Street Cinema in Greenwich Village and this has been the showcase for several underground films.

No survey of recent American cinema would be complete without mention of **Mike Nichols** (*b* 1931), whose *The Graduate* (1967) proved to be among the most popular films of all time, and who proceeded ambitiously to satirise war in *Catch 22* (1970), an adaptation of Joseph Heller's complex novel. But on an artistic level Nichols's work is still uneven, while Dennis Hopper, whose *Easy Rider* (1969) exerted tremendous influence both on the studios and on audiences throughout the U.S.A., must also make more films before his position can be assessed. *pdc*

Trevor Howard and Celia Johnson in David Lean's
BRIEF ENCOUNTER, scripted by Noël Coward

2. Britain

THE SECOND WORLD WAR marked a great turning-point in British cinema. With the total involvement of the population, the audience was no longer interested in irrelevancies. The war experience was roughly on two levels. There were the accumulated details of day-to-day living, and there was the intimate experience of danger and anxiety, the bitterness of grief, and the emptiness of loss. Documentary films came to have a great importance; they gave instruction and described processes, and gave information about the various services, civil and military. To people who had friends and family in those services this information was precious, and documentaries were received with a rapt attention which they had never before commanded.

The Crown Film Unit scored an unimagined success with *Target for Tonight* (1941), and in the same year produced **Humphrey Jennings's** *Listen to Britain.* Jennings (1907–1950) stands alone in the cinema. A product of Cambridge, he was liberal, socially involved, and forward-looking, with great intellectual gifts. He became interested in Mass Observation and in the Surrealist movement; this last found expression in painting, and the two came together in film-making. He joined the GPO Film Unit in 1934, as a designer under Cavalcanti, but was soon writing scripts and co-directing, eventually taking his place as a fully-fledged director with a group of short films in 1939. He found the Unit congenial, and, in a country at war, he found an audience that could respond to his patriotism. He was intensely conscious of the continuity of history, and his vision of England embraced all those who had helped to form her. The truth and honesty of his own emotions allowed him to be at home with people of all classes and backgrounds, so that he embodied the feelings of his countrymen everywhere. His were primarily documentaries of feeling and, seen now, evoke the state of mind of England at that time. He made people aware of themselves and one another, and revealed to them their own unity of purpose. In *Fires Were Started* (*I Was a Fireman,* 1943) he described, factually, the process of fire-fighting—but as the expression of a dedicated will and self-forgetting purpose. With *Listen to Britain* and *A Diary for Timothy* (1945), this film contained all that is most characteristic in his work. He was engaged on a project for a complex work on the Industrial Revolution when he was tragically killed in an accident in Greece.

The war had awakened a keen sense of patriotism, and it was perhaps the English quality of Noël Coward that accounted to a large extent for the popularity enjoyed by the films which he wrote for **David**

Humphrey Jennings

David Lean   Lean (*b* 1908). The first of these, which Coward also co-directed, was *In Which We Serve* (1942), a fiction film with a naval background aiming at a factual and emotional authenticity. *This Happy Breed* (1944) followed—a kind of working-class *Cavalcade*—and, after that, *Blithe Spirit* (1945), which repeated the success of the play. *Brief Encounter,* however, made in the same year, was conceived as a film, and exploited the power of the cinema to catch subtleties of feeling beyond the outward performance. The film broke new ground in that it claimed one's minute attention for an affair of the heart between middle-aged people, who finally decided that duty and home ties were more important than their own grief.

In the following year Lean turned to Dickens, and, in *Great Expectations,* made one of the major prestige films of this country. The Dickensian inheritance had for many years manifested itself in a tiresome proliferation of gratuitous character parts, but in this film Lean brought to life true characters and refreshed the whole conception of character acting. Though confirming Lean's ability to re-create, rather than adapt, from literature, *Oliver Twist* (1948) did not repeat the success of the

Darkness and light in Carol Reed's THE THIRD MAN

earlier film. Lean maintained a steady, polished output, giving, in *Summer Madness* (1955), another portrait of middle-aged love, but he scored his next great—indeed overwhelming—success in 1957 with *The Bridge on the River Kwai*. This was visually the most extended film he had yet made, paving the way for the great visual excitement of *Lawrence of Arabia* (1962) and the scale and scope of *Dr. Zhivago* (1966). David Lean entered the field of direction with an enormous general technical experience. With his own qualities of lucid exposition and professional discipline, this has made him a master of the well-made film and an accomplished, at times inspired, interpreter of literary works.

Another greatly respected professional is **Carol Reed** (*b* 1906), who, after considerable theatrical experience, entered films as a dialogue director, working for a time as assistant to Basil Dean, and making his first film, *Midshipman Easy*, in 1934. He has been a good judge of his own talent, so that his films have a poise and lack of strain, and his choice and direction of actors are sensitive and sure. There is a strong masculine style in his work which has made him particularly successful in the direction of actors, Trevor Howard (*The Third Man*, 1949, *Outcast of the Islands*, 1951, and *The Key*, 1958) and James Mason (*Odd Man Out*, 1947) giving performances that have persistently stayed in the mind. *Carol Reed*

Reed in his halcyon days made perceptive and telling use of literary sources, his association with Graham Greene being especially fruitful, as was beautifully exemplified in *The Fallen Idol* (1948). Visually, he has shown a documentary feeling for urban landscape—e.g. *The Third Man* and *Odd Man Out*—and city streets glistening in the rain are almost a hallmark of his style.

He has been successful in a number of different *genres*. *Bank Holiday* (1938) was an early example of entertaining social realism; *The Stars Look Down* (1939) sprang from a serious social conscience; *Night Train to Munich* (1940) was an extremely persuasive thriller; *The Young Mr. Pitt* (1942) was a carefully documented historical film, with a memorable performance by Robert Donat; *The Way Ahead* (1944) was one of that group of war films which marked a renaissance in British cinema; and, with *Oliver* (1968) he achieved the most ambitious musical drama in British films so far.

But war and postwar films were not all rooted in a realistic observation. **Michael Powell** (*b* 1905), who started with Rex Ingram in Nice, brought to British cinema a rich, baroque, sensuousness, and an essentially European imagination. After varied experience, he was soon briskly at work in direction. His great individuality made itself felt in *The Edge of the World* (1937), which was conceived as a silent film, with a minimal, atmospheric soundtrack. His sympathies are wide-ranging and international, and his *49th Parallel* (1941) and *The Life* *Michael Powell* *and Death of Colonel Blimp* (1943) were remarkable, in wartime, for their emotional scope and for a certain supra-national structure of narrative. *A Matter of Life and Death* (1946) showed a preoccupation with the realities of war, translated into impressively imaginative terms, with again an emphasis on the international—indeed intersecular—brotherhood of man. The film was remarkable for its use of colour for atmospheric and emotional, rather than naturalistic, truthfulness. *Black Narcissus* (1947) used colour to ravishing effect, and in 1948 *The Red Shoes* combined a European temper, a visual richness, and a baroque imagination, in a film which epitomises Powell's work and achievement. In the picture it gave of the ballet as a close-knit international family, united in a common dedication, and of the Diaghilev-like central character (Anton Walbrook), the film found a strength which lifted it above occasional weaknesses, and confirmed its overall distinction and style. In 1957 Powell's long association with Emeric Pressburger as producer came to an end with *Ill Met by Moonlight*, a wartime thriller illustrating Powell's discerning eye for landscape. Pressburger, born in Hungary, and having worked in Germany and France before coming to England, contributed to the international, European tone of the films.

The war had broken down social barriers in Britain and had made men and women aware of themselves as a people, while the wartime presence of refugees from all over Europe served to emphasise national characteristics. This preoccupation with national character encouraged a group of films from Ealing, which, under Michael Balcon, was an almost family concern, with a sense of community and genial co-operation reflected in the unfailing good humour of the films themselves. The most important single factor was the scriptwriter, T. E. B. Clarke. His script for *Hue and Cry* (1947), directed by **Charles Crichton** (*b* 1910), originated as an idea for a thriller, with children the dominant interest and adults out of sight. The *Magnet* and kindred papers seemed to offer an appropriate closed world, and the idea then grew of having a gang of international spies use a children's paper for exchanging information. This is the essence of the Ealing comedies. They were not just vaguely British, but precise, local, finding in established institutions the source of their basic situations. They marked a break with tradition in that they were conceived in terms of cinema instead of either plays or the old music hall. *The Lavender Hill Mob* (1951) represented the Ealing style at its purest; an established institution, a form of crime which causes no injury, criminals who wouldn't hurt a fly, and a complete absence of any erotic factor whatever. It has a deft script (T. E. B. Clarke) and the tone throughout is genial and affectionate. Although Crichton has tried his hand successfully at other *genres* (e.g. *The Divided Heart*, 1954, a real-life tragedy), his real bent is comedy, the last successful one being *The Battle of the Sexes* (1959).

Michael Balcon and Ealing Studios

Sandwiched between *Hue and Cry* and *The Lavender Hill Mob* was *Whisky Galore* (1949), one of the best of all the Ealing films, directed by **Alexander Mackendrick** (*b* 1912). Mackendrick, a Scot though born in America, had a long training in documentaries and newsreels, which, coupled with much experience as a scriptwriter, enabled him to make of *Whisky Galore,* his first full-length feature, a portrait of a highly individual community. *The Maggie* (1954), was, like *Whisky,* made mostly on location, and it, too, opposed the genial cunning of the local people to the organisational skill of the worldly outsiders, with the implication that the locals were operating a superior scale of values as well. Mackendrick has been a very successful director of children; *Mandy* (1952) combined a beautiful performance by the child with the documentary interest of the Royal Residential Schools for the Deaf, where much of it was filmed. More recently *A High Wind in Jamaica* (1965) again testified to his skill with children, while his eye for realism supplied the necessary substance to the narrative.

In the same year as *Whisky* there appeared also from Ealing a cheerful film about the eccentricities of England called *Passport to Pimlico,* with a script again by T. E. B. Clarke and directed by **Henry Cornelius** (1913–1958). It was a celebration of the rights which we enjoy under the law, a meditation upon those freedoms which, virtually alone in Europe, this country retained. Cornelius came from South Africa, worked in the theatre in Berlin, having been a pupil of Reinhardt, and entered films as an editor; this included editing *The Ghost Goes West* for René Clair. Perhaps his most famous film was *Genevieve* (1953), which in its story about the veteran car rally from London to Brighton conveyed graphically the nature of an enthusiasm which relegates women to a wholly peripheral role. It was notable for a splendidly original performance by Kenneth More.

The most distinguished individual talent to be nurtured by Ealing was perhaps Robert Hamer (1911–1963). He was trained as a mathematician but was attracted to films during his time at Cambridge. After various jobs in the studios, he became an editor, first for Mayflower—he edited *Vessel of Wrath*—then for Ealing (1940). He wrote scripts and was soon given a chance to direct, his first full-length feature, *Pink String and Sealing-Wax* (1945) already marked by an elegant sense of period and style. *It Always Rains on Sunday* (1947), which he wrote as well as directed, showed his skill with social realism, but it was in 1949, with *Kind Hearts and Coronets,* that he created something quite new in British cinema. It was a comedy conceived outside the normal conventions of morality and inviting one's sympathies for a multiple murderer. Hamer wrote for it a civilised and elegant script, witty both in language and situation, and directed it with a control, a relish, and a moral elegance that made it one of the most distinguished films ever to appear in England. *His Excellency* (1952) was a mixture of upper-

Dennis Price and Alec Guinness in KIND HEARTS AND CORONETS, one of the finest Ealing comedies

and lower-class comedy and drama, but in *Father Brown* (1954) Hamer again found his true style, and it is, after *Kind Hearts,* his most successful film. *The Scapegoat* (1959) lacked conviction, and *School for Scoundrels* (1960), though stylish and amusing, did not have the substance of his best work. His early death was a tragic loss to British cinema. *sb*

Asquith's Wartime Films

Like most of his contemporary directors in England, Asquith was obliged to turn his hand to a series of films designed, in one way or another, to help the war effort. In a sense it was a cruel barrier to his progress, and yet much of Asquith's work in the five years 1940 to 1945 has endured remarkably well, and both *The Demi Paradise* (1943, *Adventure for Two* in the U.S.A.) and *The Way to the Stars* (1945, *Johnny in the Clouds* in the U.S.A.) deserve a high place in any assessment of British cinema.

Asquith had planned to make two films with Leslie Howard, but these projects were frustrated by the war, and so in 1940 he made *Freedom Radio* (*Voice in the Night* in the U.S.A., released 1941), a drama about the German underground movement starring Diana Wynyard. His short films for the Ministry of Information included *Channel Incident* (1940), about the Dunkirk rescue operation, *Rush Hour* (1942), a comic impression of the hectic dash to and from work, and *Welcome to Britain* (1943), which let American troops know what to expect when they arrived in the country, with guest work by Burgess Meredith, Bob Hope, and Beatrice Lillie.

Following two moderate pot-boilers, *Cottage to Let* (1941) and *Uncensored* (1942), Asquith directed one of the war's tautest and least sentimental pictures, *We Dive at Dawn* (1943), about a British submarine's limping home after a successful mission in the Baltic. *The Way to the Stars* was even more persuasive, "a war film without any fighting; a flying film without any air sequences" (Asquith) and demonstrated the acting skill of Trevor Howard, John Mills, and Jean Simmons. But the film of the Forties that reflected like a prism the many facets of English life—the humour, the gossip, the odd character, the maliciousness, the shy affection—was *The Demi Paradise*. With Laurence Olivier as a cheerful Russian inventor, and Margaret Rutherford as the embodiment of patriotic fervour, this gentle, tolerant satire displayed Asquith's talent at its self-effacing best. His only other success of the immediate postwar period was *The Winslow Boy* (1948), based,

David Niven and Margaret Leighton in Asquith's CARRINGTON V.C.

like *French without Tears,* on a play by Terence Rattigan. Here Asquith's flair for suggesting the gravity that lies behind politeness, the indomitable spirit that can lurk in the mildest of Englishmen, was brought to bear on the Archer-Shee case of 1912, when a naval cadet was expelled from his college for stealing a 5s. postal order and was defended as far as the House of Commons by his father.

Asquith during the Fifties
The Fifties represented a high plateau of achievement in Asquith's career. *The Browning Version* (1951) focussed on the plight of a schoolmaster (brilliantly portrayed by Michael Redgrave) suffering both from ill-health and a nagging wife. Asquith's direction brought to life the class-room encounters and Terence Rattigan's dialogue moved with ease from soliloquy to priggish badinage on the playing fields. This essentially downbeat film was followed by Asquith's major box-office success of the period—*The Importance of Being Earnest* (1952), a screen version of the Oscar Wilde play notable for its colour (art direction by Carmen Dillon), and the performance of Edith Evans as Lady Bracknell, her tone forever interrogatory, her comportment forever regal.

Two other films were outstanding under Asquith's direction. *Carrington V.C.* (1954, *Court Martial* in the U.S.A.) was one of the cinema's few distinguished court-room dramas, with David Niven as the Major whose personal integrity and honour are at stake. *Orders to Kill* (1958) can be described in retrospect as Asquith's masterpiece. He had more to do with the creation of the film than with any previous production. Within the framework of a thriller about an ex-pilot sent to Paris in 1944 to "remove" a traitor, Asquith created a profound character study. The guilt that slowly overwhelms Gene Summers (Paul Massie) is registered in several telling vignettes—his meetings with a bitter, gallant Resistance agent (Irene Worth), his visit to the Montparnasse cemetery, and finally his drunken wandering through the city streets.

The remainder of Asquith's work was an anti-climax, although his ability to inspire a large cast and his respect for production values led to pleasing adaptations of two Shaw plays, *The Doctor's Dilemma* (1958) and *The Millionairess* (1960), and to his final two pictures, *The V.I.P.s* (1963), a sprawling, episodic melodrama in the tradition of *Grand Hotel,* and *The Yellow Rolls-Royce* (1965), another portmanteau film starring Rex Harrison, Ingrid Bergman, Shirley MacLaine and others. *pdc*

Basil Dearden (1911–1971) began as assistant to Basil Dean, and shared with him an enthusiasm for music hall personalities, but eventually proved himself an accomplished director in many different *genres.* In *The Captive Heart* (1946) and *Frieda* (1947) he showed his feeling for the emotional side of wartime adjustments, while *Saraband for Dead Lovers* (1948) was an exploration into a baroque romanticism.

84

He was not a man to be pinned down, and continued to be unpredictable, moving from *The League of Gentlemen* (1960), an ironical comedy-thriller, to *Life for Ruth* (1962), a study of conscience; from *The Mind Benders,* probing the foundations of personality, to *Woman of Straw,* a straight-forward thriller (both 1963); from *Khartoum* (1966), a full-scale epic remarkable for Charlton Heston's portrayal of General Gordon, to *Only When I Larf,* an ironical, rueful thriller, and *The Assassination Bureau* (both 1968), which combined organisational excitement with a period elegance and stylish irony.

In 1947, the year of *Hue and Cry,* an Oxford magazine, *Sequence,* appeared, heralding a movement which was to turn the whole current of British film-making. The real impetus came from the theatre. *Look Back in Anger* (1956) expressed a bitter dissatisfaction with postwar life, its lack of inspiration, the false values of class, and Southern English domination. It was, however, not a theatre man who made the first film in this mood. **Jack Clayton** (*b* 1921) grew up in the industry, working under Korda at Denham, in documentary during the war, and later as assistant to Asquith. In 1958 he made *Room at the Top,* a film about class, sex, money, and ambition; it was an overwhelming success and opened up a new world. The main inspiration was North Country and Midland, and a group of writers were ready who shared the postwar experience of disillusionment and bitterness, class resentment and frustrated aspiration. Clayton himself refused to repeat *Room at the Top,* and in 1961 made *The Innocents,* based on Henry James's *Turn of the Screw.* It was an elegant and coolly intellectual film, with the same emotional precision which had distinguished *Room at the Top,* and which came into full flower in *The Pumpkin Eater* (1964). In this, Clayton controled a surging emotion in such a way as to invite an attentive sympathy and at the same time a cool, balanced, appraisal. With *Our Mother's House* (1967) he changed again. He has steadfastly refused to copy his own successes, and has made the films that have interested him. He stands out as an individual talent, even though his talents are given unpredictable expression.

Tony Richardson (*b* 1928) came into films with the Free Cinema movement, but was basically of the theatre, and directed his first feature, *Look Back in Anger* (1959) at John Osborne's insistence. The film confirmed the new realist trend, while the financial success of the Richardson-Osborne company, Woodfall, combined with a timely relaxation of censorship, established it as viable. *A Taste of Honey* (1961) introduced the forlorn little couple that was to become so familiar, while *Tom Jones* (1963), a robust, cheerful adaptation of the Fielding novel, reaffirmed Richardson's international reputation. His later films have included some strange and unsuccessful ventures, but with *The Charge of the Light Brigade* (1968) he again came to the fore, though the film was an odd mixture of leisurely romance and

New British Talents

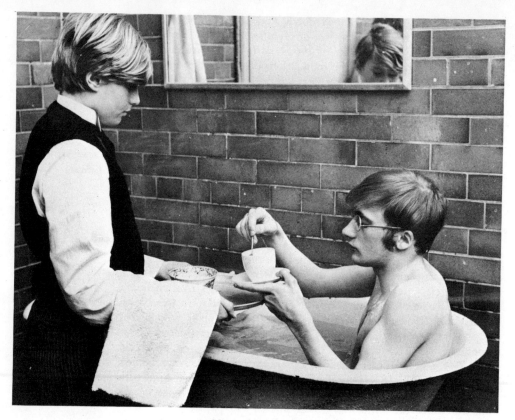

Public school traditions in Lindsay Anderson's IF . . .

muddled battle scenes. His career has not shown a clear sense of direction, but has been varied enough to suggest that he may find it difficult to concentrate his choices.

Lindsay Anderson

Lindsay Anderson (*b* 1923) is one of a group whose interest in the cinema started with a new approach to film criticism. He demanded a personal commitment from both the film-maker and the critic, and claimed that the cinema should reflect social truth. He was a key figure in the Free Cinema movement, whose initiators aimed at cheap, non-studio films by creative people, and claimed to be the first generation of British film-makers to be in control of their material. They concentrated on the working-class and tried to reflect contemporary society.

Anderson's first feature was custom-built to these specifications. *This Sporting Life* (1963) was remarkable for a candid truthfulness of brutality and for its recognition that feelings are not enough but must, to be effective, issue in appropriate behaviour. *The White Bus* (1967) was not distributed, but *If . . .* (1969) was widely shown. Recalling both

James Fox and Dirk Bogarde in Joseph Losey's THE SERVANT

Zéro de Conduite and Kipling's novel *Stalky and Co.,* it is a study of
social revolt epitomised in the life of a boys' school; here too there is
a recognition of brutal cruelty as an element in social conduct.

Also closely associated with Free Cinema was **Karel Reisz** (*b* 1926).
He made a number of commercial and information films for Ford,
who also sponsored *We Are the Lambeth Boys* (1958); this confirmed
his documentary approach, as evidenced by his first feature, *Saturday
Night and Sunday Morning* (1960), which established Albert Finney
as the imaginative embodiment of the *genre.* With *Morgan, a Suitable
Case for Treatment* (1966), he achieved a subtlety which had previously eluded him, fusing together documentary observation, humour
at different levels, and a complexity of motivation and feeling. As with
Finney, so with Vanessa Redgrave, he sensed an intense contemporary
quality. This, in *Isadora* (1969) led to some confusion in the basic conception, but gave to the portrait a resonance of ambiguity.

A surprising addition to the British scene is the American, **Joseph**

Karel Reisz

Losey (*b* 1909), who left the U.S.A. during the McCarthy persecutions. In contrast to most British films, in which the content, and of late especially the social content, is all-important, Losey is first and foremost a stylist. He is concerned with destructiveness in sexual relationships and the havoc wrought by hypocrisy, and claims that individual comment alone can be true and generally applicable. He studied medicine and literature, then worked in the theatre for a number of years. Among his earlier films in this country, *Time without Pity* (1957), *Blind Date* (1959), and *The Criminal* (1960) struck a disquieting note, while *Eve,* shot on the continent and released in a confused commercial version in 1962, presented a baroque image within which to explore sexual relationships. But it was *The Servant* (1963) that really established his reputation. Written by Harold Pinter, the film expounded the hypocrisies of class with a sensuous, excited, use of the medium, rare in British films. *King and Country* (1964) reaffirmed Losey's stature as a stylist and as a director of actors; it is remarkable for its use of naturalistic material in a highly stylised and formal combination; it has a quality of classicism shot through with naked emotional detail. He did not seem at home with *Modesty Blaise* (1966), but in 1967 he again worked with Pinter, this time on *Accident,* a less wholly achieved work perhaps than either *The Servant* or *King and Country,* though thought by some to be his masterpiece.

Clive Donner (*b* 1926) is, like Clayton, a product of the industry, and has had considerable experience in television. He has been successful with adolescents, and made a sympathetic study of them in *Some People* (1962), a film about the Duke of Edinburgh's award. *The Caretaker* (1963), from Pinter's script, showed understanding and humanity, controlled by great professional skill, so that the very small cast and limited space seemed to contain an infinity of feeling and significance. In the same year, *Nothing but the Best,* a cheerful, heartless, comedy, with black undertones, reaffirmed Donner's skill with actors, and his precise, intelligent, awareness of social areas. He has worked in Hollywood, but seems to have been less at ease there, though successful at the box-office with *What's New, Pussycat?* (1965). With *Here We Go Round the Mulberry Bush* (1967) he returned to 'teenagers in a lively, fast-moving picture of adolescence. In *Alfred the Great* (1969) he launched into full-scale epic, but seems to have lost some of his firmness in a film which denied him an accurately known social context.

Social context is the predominant influence in the work of **John Schlesinger** (*b* 1926). He started with BBC documentaries, and attracted attention with *Terminus* (1960). His first feature, *A Kind of Loving* (1962), epitomised the new British film; it was set in a dingy, featureless, town, and aimed at portraying the dullest of its citizens in all their narrow-minded self-interest, and the seeming hopelessness of their situation in their one cramped corner of the world. *Billy Liar,* made in the following year, was very different. The documentary observation was put at the service of a clearly-imagined concept, and the two worlds that Billy inhabited dovetailed into one another with an ease and precision which matched the agile subtlety of Tom Courtenay's performance. Schlesinger caught, too, in Julie Christie, a quality of sexual magnetism and exhilaration unique in British cinema. He was not to repeat this in *Darling* (1965); less at ease with international opulence, the film is at its best in its documentary approach to the English sequences. In *Far from the Madding Crowd* (1967) he brought his feeling for the English scene to Hardy country, and scored a triumphant success. It is a landscape film, in which the narrative takes its place in a natural organic development. *Midnight Cowboy* (1969), filmed in America, was the most polished work of Schlesinger's career and brought the seamy face of Manhattan to life with considerable verve and sympathy. *sb*

In the late Sixties a new crop of British directors appeared. Two of them, **Peter Yates** (*b* 1929) and **John Boorman** (*b* 1933), helped by the sophisticated craftsmanship of Hollywood, consolidated their careers in the U.S.A. Yates, a former assistant to Tony Richardson, shot a pleasantly watchable musical with Cliff Richard, *Summer Holiday* (1963), but only made his mark as a director of pace and panache with *Robbery* (1967), which was loosely based on the "Great Train Robbery" of 1963. *Bullitt* (1968), Yates's first Hollywood picture, represented much his most assured work to date. The sheer professional expertise of this thriller, with an explosive car chase through San Francisco at its heart, compelled admiration from critics and audiences alike. *John and Mary* (1969) showed Yates still eager to experiment with film rhythm, and emphasised his gift for conveying the feel of a large city (New York).

John Boorman entered the industry much later than Yates, although he had joined the BBC as a television producer in 1962. His first film was a musical, *Catch Us if You Can,* quite out of the rut, and when he moved to Hollywood for *Point Blank* (1967) he revealed an exciting, off-beat talent. With Lee Marvin as a vengeance-ridden gangster determined to retrieve his share of a robbery, the film was clothed in violence and Boorman's fragmentation of the plot was convincing if also confusing. *Hell in the Pacific* (1969) chronicled the derisive struggle for survival between a Japanese and an American soldier marooned on a remote island. *Leo the Last* (1970) was at once more ambitious and less satisfying than Boorman's previous work. A tangled plot described the efforts of an expatriate Italian prince to immerse himself and his ideals in a Notting Hill Gate milieu.

Anthony Harvey (*b* 1931) was recognised as one of the best British editors before shooting a screen version of the LeRoi Jones play,

Dutchman (1967). This immaculately controlled movie lasted a mere fifty-five minutes, and, using a single set (the inside of a Manhattan subway car), Harvey built up an atmosphere of extraordinary tension, as the antagonism between a white girl (Shirley Knight) and a passive Negro (Al Freeman jr.) was inexorably brought to a climax.

Harvey's next film, *The Lion in Winter* (1968), was made on a vast budget by comparison, but it was no more effective than *Dutchman*, merely stressing the director's adroitness at handling dialogue exchanges. **Desmond Davis** (*b* 1928) has made more features than Harvey, but none of them has enjoyed much success. Even the critics were reserved about the casual pace and sentimental leanings of *Girl with Green Eyes* (1964) and *I Was Happy Here* (1966), both set in Eire. But Davis, a former camera operator in Tony Richardson's team, has an undeniable feeling for landscape and timid personalities.

Other film-makers who may develop well during the Seventies include Jack Gold, who has made *The Bofors Gun* (1968) and *The Reckoning* (1970), Kenneth Loach, whose *Poor Cow* (1968) and *Kes* (1970) were unorthodox descendants of the "neo-realist" trend in British cinema, and Ken Russell, a flamboyant figure who has moved from farce to D. H. Lawrence (*Women in Love*, 1969) via a Len Deighton thriller with varying degrees of facility and success. *pdc*

3. France

WITH FEYDER, RENOIR, DUVIVIER AND CLAIR all abroad, Marcel Carné and Jean Grémillon were the only leading directors of the Thirties active in occupied France. Both took the opportunity to make works of quite outstanding merit. Carné and his scriptwriter Jacques Prévert left the pseudo-naturalistic setting of *Le Jour se lève* to return to a world of medieval legend for *Les Visiteurs du Soir* (1942). Here, aside from contemporary pressures, the battle between good (the lovers) and evil (the devil, Jules Berry), is fought out again. But this time the outcome is more nearly optimistic and the devil's triumph is shown to be limited. Despite the very sparse means at his disposal Carné achieves in *Les Visiteurs du Soir* a remarkable visual opulence. This particular quality is even more pronounced in his next film, the huge and resplendent portrait of the Romantic theatre, *Les Enfants du Paradis* (1944–5). Against a lively and vividly drawn background the film follows the interweaving loves of a group of outsize characters: the actor Frédérick Lemaître (Pierre Brasseur), the mime Debureau (Jean-Louis Barrault) and the murderer Lacenaire (Marcel Herrand) and the woman they all love, Garance (Arletty). The acting under Carné's direction is as dazzling as Jacques Prévert's dialogue and the film remains the pair's most brilliant success. These two films made during the Occupation represent the most extreme examples of the turning away from the contemporary scene which characterises much of the French cinema under German domination, for example Marcel L'Herbier's *La Nuit Fantastique* (1942) and the Delannoy-Cocteau film *L'Eternel Retour* (1943).

Though Prévert is best known for his collaboration with Marcel Carné, he has also worked with other directors, including Renoir and Grémillon. Together with his brother the director **Pierre Prévert** (*b* 1906) he was responsible for three remarkable comedies. The first, *L'Affaire est dans le Sac,* was made as early as 1932 but it was not until the Forties that the brothers were able to follow it up with two further absurd and totally incalculable works: *Adieu Léonard* (1943) and *Voyage Surprise* (1946). Unfortunately Pierre Prévert never fully established himself as a director and no further feature films ensued. More recently Jacques Prévert has also been active in a very different field, collaborating with **Paul Grimault** (*b* 1905) on the cartoon films *Le Petit Soldat* (1947) and *La Bergère et le Ramoneur* (1952).

The Occupation years were also a time of opportunity for Jean Grémillon, who was finally able to find an adequate outlet for his talents. *Lumière d'Eté* (1943), made from a script by Jacques Prévert and Pierre Laroche, is in a sense a reply to Renoir's *La Règle du Jeu*. Again we find a contrast between the idle rich and the workers and a set of personal conflicts which are clarified and brought to explosion point during a fancy dress ball. Grémillon handles his complex plot with its symbolic overtones (the crumbling mountain and the literary associations of the fancy dress costumes the characters adopt) with great skill, and he and his writers come down firmly on the side of the workers and in condemnation of a frivolous society. *Le Ciel est à Vous* (1944), written by Charles Spaak and widely regarded as Grémillon's masterpiece, tells of the effect on their family and friends of their shared passion for aviation which is eventually crowned with success when the wife beats a world record. Based on an authentic incident, the film was generally taken to be a work exalting Resistance values, but in fact Grémillon's interest probably lay less in this kind of explicit commitment than in the motivation of the couple (admirably played by Charles Vanel and Madeleine Renaud, the latter appearing in her fourth successive Grémillon film).

Pierre Renoir, Arletty, and Marcel Herrand in LES ENFANTS DU PARADIS

Pierre Fresnay in a production shot for LE CORBEAU

The early Forties also saw the emergence of a varied and talented new generation of directors, virtually all of whom had been working within the industry in the Thirties as scriptwriters or assistant directors. Some of these new directors—**André Cayatte** (*b* 1909), **Yves Allégret** (*b* 1907), and **Louis Daquin** (*b* 1908)—had merely routine assignments, but others were able to express their personalities more fully. **Robert Bresson** (*b* 1907), for example, made two films, *Les Anges du Péché* (1943) and *Les Dames du Bois de Boulogne* (1944–5), in which the dominant themes of his work are already apparent. The latter film in particular, for which Jean Cocteau wrote the dialogue, was a most accomplished treatment of the theme of feminine revenge, with an exceptional performance by Maria Casarès. **Henri-Georges Clouzot** (*b* 1907) was another director who gave a clear demonstration of his power as a director. His second film, *Le Corbeau* (1943), was a characteristically black portrait of a French provincial town terrorised by a writer of anonymous letters. It achieved wide notoriety and after the liberation it was (unjustly) accused of being anti-French propaganda, with the result that Clouzot was barred from directing for several years. In a very different vein, **Jacques Becker** (1906–1960) made perceptive and sympathetic studies of both peasant life, in *Goupi-Mains Rouges* (1943), and the Parisian fashion houses, in *Falbalas* (1944–5).

The Occupation years also allowed two other directors, whose work had made little impact in the late Thirties, to come to the fore. **Claude**

Autant-Lara (*b* 1903) had in fact made his first feature *Ciboulette* as early as 1933, but it was not until 1937 that he established himself as a director in France. During the Occupation years he made a number of sensitive and delicate period films with the actress Odette Joyeux— *Le Mariage de Chiffon* (1942), *Lettres d'Amour* (1942), *Douce* (1943). His first postwar film, *Sylvie et le Fantôme* (1945), was in the same vein. These works are important chiefly in that they allowed Autant-Lara to begin building the team of collaborators on which his later postwar successes were based. **Jean Delannoy** (*b* 1908) also established his reputation during the war years and *L'Eternel Retour* (1943), his version of Jean Cocteau's adaptation of the Tristan and Isolde myth, laid the foundation of his mature style.

The late Forties belong almost entirely to these newly emerged directors who were soon to be joined by **René Clément** (*b* 1913), **Jacques Tati** (*b* 1908) and **Georges Rouquier** (*b* 1909). The veterans of earlier days seemed much less at home in the changed atmosphere of postwar France. René Clair returned from Hollywood to make *Le Silence est d'Or* (1947), a reflective work which sets the tone for his subsequent output but very clearly looks back nostalgically to the past. Clair had to go to Italy to make his only other film of the Forties, *La Beauté du Diable* (1949), a version of the Faust legend. Jean Grémillon saw his documentary on the Normandy landings—*Le Six Juin à L'Aube* (1945)—mutilated by distributors and had to wait until 1949 to direct a feature. *Pattes Blanches,* the resulting film, was a none too happy amalgam of the director's skill and that of the author, Jean Anouilh. Julien Duvivier with *Panique* (1947) and Marcel Carné with *Les Portes de la Nuit* (1946) both seemed content to continue the styles and attitudes of the prewar years and neither director was to achieve his old eminence again, though both made films which were highly successful commercially.

The real inheritors of the Thirties tradition were men like Clouzot and Allégret. Clouzot produced a superbly economical detective story, *Quai des Orfèvres* (1947), which gave Louis Jouvet one of his best roles, and then made an ambitious and flawed modernisation of a classic novel *Manon* (1949). Yves Allégret, working with the scriptwriter **Jacques Sigurd** (*b* 1920), made three equally black studies of tormented passion. *Dédée d'Anvers* (1948), *Une si jolie petite Plage* (1949), and *Manèges* (1950) were extremely tightly scripted atmospheric evocations of defeat. Neither Allégret nor his writer achieved equal success with later and more "positive" themes.

Attempts at a genuine realism akin to those of the Italian neo-realists remain isolated efforts never integrated into a collective movement. René Clément made the semi-documentary *La Bataille du Rail* (1946) about the resistance to the German occupiers shown by the French railways workers, but he was unable to make other films in similar vein.

Instead, his other works of the Forties are a Resistance drama built around the talents of a popular actor (*Le Père Tranquille*, 1946), a melodramatic story of Nazis in defeat (*Les Maudits*, 1947) and a last sad flutter of the prewar Gabin myth (*Au Delà des Grilles*, 1949). Georges Rouquier made *Farrebique* (1946), a sensitive evocation of a year's life on a farm in the Massif Central, but was unable to establish himself as a feature director. Roger Leenhardt's study of childhood merging into adolescence, *Les Dernières Vacances* (1947), likewise remained a work without immediate successors. Jacques Becker was more fortunate and his two films of the late Forties set the pattern for his subsequent work. *Antoine et Antoinette* (1946), a study of a working class marriage, and *Rendez-Vous de Juillet* (1949), an investigation into the behaviour of young people, were affectionate works accumulating a multitude of tiny details and avoiding the major problems and social issues. All these were works in a recognisably realist tradition but Jacques Tati, though he has at times been compared with the neo-realists, is in fact quite unclassifiable. *Jour de Fête* (1949) revealed him to be the most brilliant French comic since Max Linder and earned him an international reputation. In François, the rural postman who tried to emulate American methods, Tati created one of the great comic figures of the screen.

As dominant a force as the realist tendency was the literary cinema of the postwar years. In this a key figure was Jean Cocteau, who followed his scriptwriting of the Occupation period by directing a series

Jacques Tati in his own comedy,
JOUR DE FETE

95

of striking films. *La Belle et la Bête* (1946) had a striking visual style based on Dutch painting (particularly Vermeer) and was a sophisticated retelling of the classic fairy tale. Cocteau followed this venture into the "realism of the unreal" with two adaptations of his own plays, the Ruritanian melodrama *L'Aigle à Deux Têtes* (1947) and the far more telling and compressed family drama *Les Parents Terribles* (1948). At about this time too Cocteau worked on an adaptation of his novel *Les Enfants Terribles,* which was directed in 1949 by **Jean-Pierre Melville** (*b* 1917), who had already made a striking *début* with the adaptation of a Vercors story *Le Silence de la Mer* (1947). Melville's work passed unnoticed at the time, but ten years later his influence could be felt in the production methods chosen by the "new wave" directors. Cocteau's own major achievement in the cinema was *Orphée* (1950), his personal version of the mythical relationship of the poet and death. Making full use of verbal paradox and the cinema's capacity for conjuring, Cocteau designed *Orphée* as the full orchestration of the themes already set out in *Le Sang d'un Poète* twenty years before.

Adaptations
The late Forties also saw the establishment of another kind of literary cinema which was to dominate the French cinema in the early Fifties. This was the adaptation of celebrated works of literature by professional scriptwriters. The key figures here were **Jean Aurenche** (*b* 1904) and **Pierre Bost** (*b* 1901) who, as a team, were responsible for some of the greatest successes of the period. For Claude Autant-Lara they wrote an adaptation of Raymond Radiguet's novel, *Le Diable au Corps* (1947), which gave the director his first international success, and a version of the Feydeau farce *Occupe Toi d'Amélie* (1949). They also adapted André Gide's novel *La Symphonie Pastorale* (1946), which was directed by Jean Delannoy with the cold, academic precision that has become his hallmark. Delannoy was markedly less successful when he filmed an original script by Jean-Paul Sartre, *Les Jeux sont Faits,* in 1947.

French Cinema
in the Fifties
The Fifties are a difficult period to evaluate objectively, since they have been the subject of much pleading and polemic on the part of the *Cahiers du Cinéma* critics as they prepared to become directors. In fact the decade is a particularly rich one, though falling into two quite distinct halves. The early Fifties belong to the newcomers of the war and immediate postwar years, generally solid craftsmen with a lengthy experience of the industry, who reach new heights in these years. But there are no new directorial *débuts* in this period until the timid emergence of Agnès Varda with the medium-length *La Pointe Courte* and Alexandre Astruc with his first feature *Les Mauvaises Rencontres* in 1955. After that date, however, the atmosphere of stolid routine was shattered as more and more new directors arrived on the feature film scene with fresh ideas and an uninhibited technique.

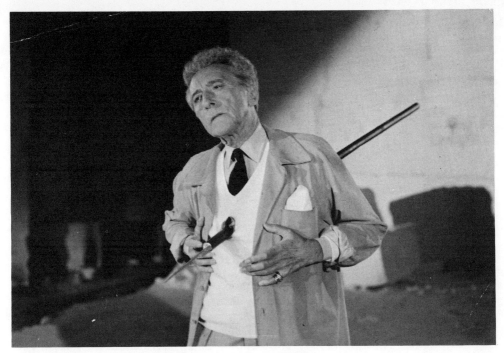

Jean Cocteau in his own LE TESTAMENT D'ORPHEE

For the veteran directors of the prewar cinema the Fifties were a
time of very mixed achievement. For Jean Cocteau with *Orphée*
(1950) and *Le Testament d'Orphée* (1959) this period is the culmination of a long involvement with the cinema, a time when a lifetime's
concern with the myth of the poet's relationship with death could
achieve full cinematic expression. Max Ophuls too returned to France
after a decade in the U.S.A. and was able to make a series of films that
are his crowning achievement. *La Ronde* (1950) wove the material of
Arthur Schnitzler's play into a witty and cynical pattern of encounter,
seduction and desertion, linking the twelve episodes with an Oscar
Straus waltz. In *Le Plaisir* (1952) Ophuls took three stories by Maupassant to illustrate the idea that pleasure is a far from simple or
enjoyable thing. *Madame de . . .* (1953) too furnished the opportunity
for a further excursion into the Ophuls world of uniforms and evening
dress, all-night balls and duels in the dawn. *Lola Montès* (1955),
Ophuls's last film before his death at the age of fifty-five, is in every
way a culmination: intricate in structure, elaborate in technique, made
with the full resources of a large budget, colour CinemaScope and international stars. The film was hacked to pieces by its producers but the
full version exists for future generations to marvel at.

The Veterans

Clair and René Clair and Jean Renoir both achieved striking successes too in
Renoir this period. Clair followed his frenetic comic version of *Intolerance,
Les Belles-de-Nuit* (1952) with two works of a more reflective nature.
Les Grandes Manoeuvres (1955) was an exquisitely told tale of an
habitual Don Juan finally ensnared by the words and feelings he has
exploited so long. An added dimension was given by the setting of a
French provincial garrison town on the eve of the First World War.
Porte des Lilas (1957) was a story of male friendship disrupted by the
intrusion of a violent criminal on the run, set in a Parisian environ-
ment nostalgically reminiscent of *Sous les Toits de Paris.* Jean Renoir
returned to France in 1954 to continue the concern with colour and
spectacle already apparent in *The River,* made in 1950 in India and
The Golden Coach, his Italian produced film of 1952. Both *French
Cancan* (1954) and *Elena et les Hommes* (1956) were in this vein.
His two films of 1959, *Le Déjeuner sur l'Herbe* and *Le Testament du
Docteur Cordelier* on the other hand show the influence of television
methods, such as the use of several cameras and shooting in sequence.
For Marcel Carné the Fifties were a less happy period, and he achieved
greater success with a straightforward adaptation of Simenon, *La Marie
du Port* (1950) than with his extremely ambitious *Juliette ou la Clef
des Songes* (1951). His best film of the Fifties is no doubt his version
of *Thérèse Raquin* (1953) but more successful commercially was *Les
Tricheurs* (1958), an attempt to come to terms with the younger generation which showed a number of bright young players in the somewhat incongruous context of the Carné fatalistic universe.

For those who had made their reputations in the Forties the two
dominant sources of inspiration continued to be the *film noir* and the
literary adaptation. André Cayatte gave the former a new lease of life
in the early Fifties with a series of legal studies: *Justice est Faite*
(1950), *Nous Sommes Tous des Assassins* (1952), *Avant le Déluge*
(1953), *Le Dossier Noir* (1955). These films attacked conventional
social attitudes on such subjects as capital punishment and juvenile
delinquency with all the fervour that Cayatte, himself an ex-lawyer,
could muster. The quality of Cayatte's work is very dependent on the
force and coherence of his scripts and the contribution of Charles Spaak
to these films is as decisive as that of Jacques Prévert to Cayatte's earlier
Les Amants de Vérone (1948). In the same black mood is Henri-
Georges Clouzot's masterly *Le Salaire de la Peur* (1953), made after
a break of four years. The film combined a brilliant evocation of life
in a squalid little South American township totally dominated by a U.S.
oil company with a finely contrived piece of suspense involving two
lorries loaded with T.N.T. This kind of sordid realism is clearly
Clouzot's *forte* and was widely imitated, for example by Yves Allégret
in *Les Orgueilleux* (1953) and Yves Ciampi in *Les Héros sont*

Fatigués (1955). Clouzot's own taste is for a more Kafkaesque blend of realism and fantasy, seen in *Les Diaboliques* (1955) and, more especially, in *Les Espions* (1957). In a very different vein, Clouzot made the entertaining art film *Le Mystère Picasso* (1956). Jacques Becker continued his Forties style with two very agreeable comedies of domestic life *Edouard et Caroline* (1951) and *Rue de l'Estrapade* (1953), but his most striking film of the Fifties is *Casque d'Or* (1952), a tale of passion and crime in a beautifully reconstructed period setting. With *Touchez pas au Grisbi* (1954) Becker gave Jean Gabin a chance to break with his Thirties image of a defeated man vainly trying to avoid the blows of fate. The film also set something of a fashion in thrillers, beginning a series typified by works like *Du Rififi chez les Hommes* (1955) by Jules Dassin, a Hollywood *émigré*, and *Razzia sur la Chnouf* (1955) by veteran Henri Decoin.

The literary tendency of the French postwar cinema is exemplified by the work of Claude Autant-Lara. Like most of his contemporaries at this period he worked largely within the studios and with a regular team of collaborators to create works which are models of craftsmanship if not of artistic originality. Virtually all his postwar work has been scripted by Jean Aurenche and Pierre Bost whose methods tend, however, to reduce all material, literary or non-literary, to the same level and all styles to the same pattern of construction and dialogue. Autant-Lara's first work of the Fifties, *L'Auberge Rouge* (1951), broke somewhat with this tradition, being made from an original script by Aurenche. Significantly it is one of the director's very finest works, a wittily blasphemous study of murderous hypocrisy and priestly cowardice which gives Fernandel one of his finest roles. Autant-Lara followed this with adaptations of Colette (*Le Blé en Herbe*, 1954), Stendhal (*Le Rouge et le Noir*, 1954) and Dostoievsky (*Le Joueur*, 1958) as well as Simenon (*En Cas de Malheur*, 1956) and Marcel Aymé (*La Traversée de Paris*, 1956, and *La Jument Verte*, 1959). In *Marguerite de la Nuit* (1956), a version of the Faust legend, he experimented with colour and *décor* in a way reminiscent of the Twenties when he first entered the industry as costume and set designer.

René Clément has also worked extensively with Aurenche and Bost. After the weak and unconvincing *Le Château de Verre* (1950), he made a remarkable study of children corrupted by the war, *Jeux Interdits* (1952), and an adaptation of Zola's *L'Assommoir, Gervaise* (1956), which was a most painstaking evocation of Nineteenth century Paris, its poverty and its alcoholism. Between these last two works Clément went to London to make *Monsieur Ripois* (1954) with methods of location shooting very close to those followed later by directors like Jean-Luc Godard. All Clément's work is characterised by a sharp visual sense (he was trained as an architect) and an almost obsessive

Autant-Lara

concern with detail. The same eclecticism, but combined this time with a more academic style and more superficial approach is to be found in the films of Jean Delannoy. Works like *Dieu a besoin des Hommes* (1950) and *Chiens Perdus sans Colliers* (1955) show the limitations of the Aurenche and Bost approach when it is not enlivened by a director with the forcefulness of Autant-Lara or Clément.

The works of this Forties generation in the first postwar decade are solid and impressive, if not revolutionary, and they helped maintain France's reputation as a major film producing country. By the mid-Fifties, however, it was possible to feel that the majority of these film-makers were losing their originality. Victims of their own success, they began to work more and more on co-productions made with colour and big budgets and which, for this reason, often became inconclusive and impersonal works. Examples of this trend are Becker's *Ali Baba et les Quarante Voleurs* (1954) and *Arsène Lupin* (1957), Clément's *Barrage contre le Pacifique* (1958), Autant-Lara's *Vive Henri Quatre, Vive l'Amour* and *Le Comte de Monte Cristo* (both 1961), Cayatte's *Le Passage du Rhin* (1960) and Delannoy's *Marie Antoinette* and *Notre Dame de Paris* (both 1956). There was clearly a need for film-makers with a more personal and intimate style.

Two directors alone stood out against these trends and these are the two greatest of the period, Robert Bresson and Jacques Tati. Tati made only two films in the Fifties but both were strikingly original works. In *Les Vacances de Monsieur Hulot* (1953) he created a successor to François the postman in Monsieur Hulot, a kind of comic Everyman who unwittingly brings chaos to the holiday hotel in which he is staying. Into his very loose framework Tati fits both a whole gallery of closely observed types and a sequence of classic gags. His own training as a mime is apparent both in his own performance as Hulot and in his visual conception of humour. *Mon Oncle* (1958) had a more serious subject, being an examination of the soullessness of modern life rather in the manner of René Clair's *A Nous la Liberté*. It is based on a pattern of contrast, setting the imperturbable pipe-smoking Hulot against his materialistic bourgeois brother-in-law Arpel and comparing Hulot's quaint old home in the old quarter of the town with the empty and gadget-ridden interior of the Arpels' house. The gags are carefully worked out in *Mon Oncle* but are amusing rather than hilarious, the whole film being filled with a kind of nostalgia and warm regard for humanity. Tati's perfectionism and method of painstaking preparation have prevented him from making more than a tiny handful of films, but these are masterpieces of observation and comic art.

An equal austerity is shown by Robert Bresson. It was not until 1951 that he was able to make his first postwar film, a version of Bernanos's novel *Journal d'un Curé de Campagne*. The first adaptation was written by Aurenche and Bost, but Bresson scrapped this and fashioned his

Jacques Tati

own script, keeping as close as possible to the original. His film is far
from being a conventional dramatisation—all the minor dramatic high-
lights are missing and emotions are constantly understated. The film
was shot with considerable surface realism, but Bresson's true interest
was elsewhere: in the depiction of the spiritual struggle of the young
priest. *Un Condamné à Mort s'est échappé* (1956) was an equally dis-
tinctive handling of the theme of a prison escape. A sharp contrast to
the more melodramatic methods of Clouzot or Cayatte is furnished by
Bresson's use of greys and blacks and his concentration on details of
hands and faces. The performances of the non-professional cast all bear
the stamp of the director's own personality and the whole story is
pruned down to a bare thread of narrative, implication being used
where any other film-maker would turn to direct statement. Again the
theme is the working out of divine grace—the spiritual undertones
being hinted at by the Mozart C Minor Mass which accompanies
scenes of humdrum activity. *Pickpocket* (1959) forms an interesting
contrast to the two earlier films. Unlike them it was not the product
of a long period of planning and reflection and, for the first time,
Bresson was working from original material (though the influence of

Robert Bresson

The final scene of Bresson's PICKPOCKET

Dostoievski is strong). Michel, the Pickpocket, is a man who deliberately turns his back on God and becomes a criminal, only to find in the end that his life of crime is merely a long detour that brings him back to God. Again, Bresson's film proceeds with a calm, reflective rhythm, giving as much attention to silences and inscrutable faces as to moments of drama.

Bresson and Tati offer the succeeding generation a lesson in the possibilities of the cinema as a medium for personal expression, but their approaches are too individual to be a direct source of inspiration. The new directors have their roots more in the documentary and in the styles of film-makers working in an independent way on the fringes of commercial production. The documentary was a vital field of experiment in the French cinema throughout the Fifties and as early as 1948–9 Georges Franju and Alain Resnais were achieving a wide reputation in this area. The predominance of documentary is due in part to a finance and production set-up that encouraged works of quality to be made and in part to the existence of a few enlightened producers (notably Pierre Braunberger). There were also a number of major directors unable to make features who turned to the short film as a means of expression. Georges Rouquier followed his remarkable *Farrebique* with several splendid documentaries showing man's triumph over his environment (*Le Sel de la Terre,* 1950, and *Malgovert,* 1952) and an admirable objective study of faith healing: *Lourdes et ses Miracles* (1955). Jean Grémillon, as well as making two feature films that were poorly received—*L'Etrange Madame X* (1951) and *L'Amour d'une Femme* (1954)—directed several studies of art, culminating in *André Masson et les Quatre Eléments* (1958), his final testament as film-maker. **Roger Leenhardt** (*b* 1903) also made numerous films, most notably a series on great men, such as Hugo and Mauriac, Rousseau and Valéry.

Georges Franju **Georges Franju,** (*b* 1912), synthesising the anarchist spirit of Jean Vigo and the stylistic perfection of Marcel Carné, made a remarkable series of documentaries in the Fifties. He followed his staggering film on the Parisian slaughterhouses, *Le Sang des Bêtes* (1949), with a study of the steel works seen as a fiery hell amid the peaceful cornfields, *En Passant par la Lorraine* (1950). He managed to turn a seemingly innocuous study of the museum *Hôtel des Invalides* (1951) into a masterpiece of anti-militarist propaganda, and then made two studies of men struggling against overwhelming odds in *Le Grand Méliès* (1952) and *Monsieur et Madame Curie* (1953). All Franju's documentary work is marked by a fusion of cruelty and tenderness, polemic and nostalgia. He continued making short films for a further five years, making films on a wide range of subjects, but finally he was able to make his feature *début*. For his first film he chose *La Tête contre les Murs* (1958), which combined a plea for love and freedom with a

striking semi-documentary reconstruction of the atmosphere in a French mental hospital. By contrast *Les Yeux sans Visage* (1959) was a horror film about a doctor who kidnaps and kills young girls so as to be able to transplant their faces on to his own disfigured daughter.

Alain Resnais

The other key figure in the French documentary of the Fifties is **Alain Resnais** (*b* 1922), who began with a number of art films— *Van Gogh* (1948), *Gauguin* (1950), *Guernica* (1950) and continued making short films until 1958. In *Les Statues meurent aussi,* made with Chris Marker in 1953, he studied the decline of African culture with a forcefulness which caused the film to be banned for ten years. *Nuit et Brouillard* (1954) accomplished the incredible feat of encompassing the worst horrors of the Nazi *régime* in a work of art. With *Hôtel des Invalides* it is perhaps the greatest of all French documentaries of the period. In contrast to the sobriety of this work Resnais's last two documentaries were free and flowing works constructed as virtual symphonies of tracking shots. *Toute la Mémoire du Monde* (1956) studied the French national library, while *Le Chant du Styrène* (1958) dealt with the Péchiney plastics factory. In these seven films Resnais treated some of the key issues of Twentieth century intellectual life (total war, the concentration camps etc.) and adopted a series of strikingly original formal patterns. He also developed his characteristic method of working with a literary collaborator (*Guernica* was made with Paul Eluard, *Le Chant du Styrène* with Raymond Queneau, for example) and elaborated his basic conception of the film as a synthesis of image, word and music.

Interesting films were also being made in the Fifties by some of Resnais's associates. **Chris Marker** (*b* 1921), a poet, essayist, traveller and critic, followed his work on *Les Statues meurent aussi* with films on China (*Dimanche à Pekin,* 1955) and Russia (*Lettre de Sibérie,* 1957). He also collaborated with the Polish born Walerian Borowczyk on the animated film *Les Astronautes* (1959). Marker's literary origins are clearly apparent in the importance placed on the commentary in these, and indeed all his films. **Agnès Varda** (*b* 1928), who had previously been a photographer, made several documentaries: *O Saisons O Châteaux* (1957) on the Loire valley and *Du Côté de la Côte* (1958) on the Riviera. *Opéra Mouffe* (1958) combined a study of the sensations of a pregnant woman with a view of a poor district of Paris. More interesting and influential, however, was Varda's first film, the feature length *La Pointe Courte* (1955), made independently of the commercial system and without any prior knowledge of the cinema, and edited by Alain Resnais. Many of the qualities of this film, especially the device of setting a pair of unindividualised lovers against an alien background, are to be found in Resnais's own first feature *Hiroshima Mon Amour* (1959). Here the director used Marguerite Duras's script as a composer might use a libretto, setting it to images, as it were, rather than merely filming it. Resnais combines a documentary on the atomic bomb with a passionate love story, bridges the gap between wartime France and contemporary Japan and builds his film out of the interplay of thought and action, memory and desire. The acting of Emmanuelle Riva and Eiji Okada and the technical contributions of Resnais's collaborators are excellent and *Hiroshima Mon Amour* is one of the most strikingly original films in the history of the cinema.

Franju and Resnais were preceded in feature film-making by several other young directors whose backgrounds were rather different from theirs and whose conception of the cinema was more conventional. As early as 1952 **Alexandre Astruc** (*b* 1923) made his striking fictional short *Le Rideau Cramoisi,* which revealed both his own technical skill and the beauty of Anouk Aimée. His attempt at a feature film with the same star, *Les Mauvaises Rencontres* (1955), was less original and less successful. But in 1958 he made an extremely beautiful version of a Guy de Maupassant story *Une Vie* in colour and starring Maria Schell. In terms of pure visual effect Astruc has never surpassed this version of his characteristic subject matter, the difficulties of personal relationships. A more startling feature *début* was that of **Roger Vadim** (*b* 1928) who, in 1956, starred his young wife Brigitte Bardot in an uninhibited colour film, *Et Dieu Créa la Femme.* Vadim had, like Astruc, served an apprenticeship as a writer in the commercial cinema and his first film shows a clear appreciation of the requirements of a popular success. He followed this film, which made an international star of his wife, with two other films in which colour and setting were

Roger Vadim

Opposite: Jean-Louis Trintignant and Brigitte Bardot in ET DIEU CREA LA FEMME

more important than plot: *Sait-On Jamais* (1957), made in Venice, and *Les Bijoutiers du Clair de Lune* (1958) set in Spain. A more ambitious film was his modernisation of the French literary classic *Les Liaisons Dangereuses* (1959) starring his new wife Annette Stroyberg. With Laclos's literary style lost in the transposition, the film emerged as no more than a fairly conventional exploration of sexual manoeuvring. A third director sharing Astruc and Vadim's distaste of sordid realism and interest in female stars is **Louis Malle** (*b* 1932). His two films of the Fifties, *Ascenseur pour L'Echafaud* (1957) and *Les Amants* (1958) both exploit the charm and personality of Jeanne Moreau. While the first of these was a fairly conventional, if smoothly handled thriller, *Les Amants* was a lyrical and romantic evocation of physical desire, depicting with great frankness the night of love which makes a bored socialite leave her dull husband.

The way to create films independently in the cinema was shown in France most clearly by Jean-Pierre Melville, who began his career in

Jeanne Moreau (centre) with José-Luis Villalonga

the Forties with two literary adaptations, both independently produced.
With *Quand tu liras cette lettre* (1952) he tried making a film within
the commercial system but the result was his least interesting work.
In the Fifties, Melville, who is an all-round technician, able to act as
his own scriptwriter, director of photography, art director or editor,
also acquired his own little film studio. His next two films show his
interest in the world of detectives and newspaper reporters and his
concern with America. *Deux Hommes dans Manhattan* (1958), the less
successful of the two, was set in New York and featured Melville
himself in a leading role. *Bob le Flambeur* (1955) is his most personal film despite the collaboration on the script of Auguste le Breton
(author of *Touchez pas au Grisbi* and *Du Rififi chez les Hommes*). It
is a nostalgic portrait of Montmartre, coloured by Melville's memories
of the Thirties and predilection for American gangster movies.

The Melville method of independent film-making was the one followed by many members of the so-called "new wave," the critics of
the magazine *Cahiers du Cinéma* who were eager to become directors.
In the late Fifties several of these young men made short fictional
films with actors who were later to become extremely well known.
Jacques Rivette (*b* 1928) made *Le Coup du Berger* (1956), an
elegant study of sexual manoeuvring. In a very different vein **François
Truffaut** (*b* 1932) made a tender and affectionate study of childhood
turning into adolescence, *Les Mistons* (1957). **Jean-Luc Godard** (*b*
1930) applied his characteristic touch to *Tous les Garcons s'appellent
Patrick* (1957), the story of two flat mates who find they are both going
out with the same boy (Jean-Claude Brialy), and *Charlotte et son
Jules* (1958), a long monologue featuring Jean-Paul Belmondo.

The man who led the way into feature film-making, however, was
Claude Chabrol (*b* 1930), who financed *Le Beau Serge* (1958) with
money inherited by his wife. Based on the contrasting styles of its
two leading players, Jean-Claude Brialy and Gérard Blain, the film told
of an attempted rehabilitation of a village drunkard by a former school
friend. The Christian overtones of this film are lacking in *Les Cousins*
(1959) which retains, however, the idea of contrasting two men, making Brialy and Blain students who are cousins and rivals for the love
of the same girl. Achieving wide recognition with these two films,
Chabrol plunged into an international co-production, *A Double Tour*
(1959), and then returned to more characteristic ground with *Les
Bonnes Femmes* (1959), scripted by Paul Gégauff, Chabrol's collaborator on four of his first five films. By his success Chabrol opened
the way for others of his colleagues from *Cahiers du Cinéma*. François
Truffaut made a brilliant *début* with the semi-autobiographical *Les
Quatre Cents Coups* (1959) in which Jean-Pierre Léaud played the part
of a young delinquent driven into petty crime by the indifference of
the adults around him. There are important social implications in the

Jacques Becker's *LE TROU (above, left)*. Jean-Luc Godard's *A BOUT DE SOUFFLE (above, right, with Jean Seberg)*. Alain Resnais's *L'ANNÉE DERNIÈRE A MARIENBAD (below)*

fate of the boy Antoine but Truffaut's own concern is more with painting a true and moving picture of a child and his world. By contrast Jeau-Luc Godard's *A Bout de Souffle* (1959) used the basic pattern of the thriller film to examine themes of involvement and betrayal. With its fluid camera style and jagged cutting the film had a strong impact on the younger generation of film-makers in France and elsewhere. It also contains all the allusions and quirks characteristic of the later Godard. *ra*

The new generation led by Resnais and Godard that emerged in the late Fifties virtually dominated the French cinema in the Sixties. The work of many of the most esteemed of the veterans shows a sad decline. Jean Renoir's *Le Caporal Epinglé* (1962) is no more than a pale echo of *La Grande Illusion* made twenty-five years earlier. Similarly René Clair's work in this last period, *Tout l'Or du Monde* (1961) and *Les Fêtes Galantes* (1965), shows a marked decline in wit and invention. Abel Gance found his achievements in the cinema lauded by the younger generation which re-discovered his silent masterpieces, but his own works of the Sixties, *Austerlitz* (1960) and *Cyrano et d'Artagnan* (1964), though colourful spectacles, are no longer in the forefront of cinematic development. Marcel Carné, on the other hand, has suffered a considerable decline in critical reputation as his films moved further and further away from current taste. Traces of the old Carné can be found in *Terrain Vague* (1960), *Du Mouron pour les Petits Oiseaux* (1963), *Trois Chambres à Manhattan* (1965) and *Les Jeunes Loups* (1968) but they cannot redeem the essential dullness of the works as a whole. More striking was the work of Luis Buñuel, who had made one or two bizarre but uneven French co-productions in the late Fifties (*Cela s'appelle l'Aurore*, 1955; *La Mort en ce Jardin*, 1956; *La Fièvre monte à El Pao*, 1959), then returned to the French studios in the Sixties to make films of great originality. *Le Journal d'une Femme de Chambre* (1964) was a re-make of the Octave Mirbeau novel previously filmed by Renoir in Hollywood in 1946. *Belle de Jour* (1967), the most striking of these later works, was a fascinating and totally enigmatic account of the fantasy life of a beautiful young woman (Catherine Deneuve), while *La Voie Lactée* (1969) attacked Catholic dogma and orthodoxy with a characteristic bite and humour.

Several of the film-makers who made their initial impact in the Forties proved more fortunate and were able to produce films of the first importance. Jacques Becker ended his career with a film that ranks with his best: *Le Trou* (1960), a beautifully controlled study of a failed prison escape. Claude Autant-Lara, amid a great deal of unimportant commercial film-making, produced *Tu ne Tueras Point,* a courageous and outspoken pacifist film, in 1961, after twelve years of struggle. His treatment of the subject of birth control in *Journal d'une*

Femme en Blanc (1965) and its sequel was less striking. Henri-Georges Clouzot, dogged by ill health that made him abandon *L'Enfer* (1964) after a few days of shooting, made only two films in the decade: *La Vérité* (1960), a fairly routine study of criminal procedure and the more interesting *La Prisonnière* (1968), which dealt with the corruption of a young woman and allowed scope for some visual experiments. René Clément's output has been very varied including a farce set in Fascist Italy, *Quelle Joie de Vivre!* (1961) and a further study of the Resistance, *Le Jour et l'Heure* (1963). More startling were the two thrillers starring Alain Delon, *Plein Soleil* (1959) and *Les Félins* (1963), in which Clément's technical prowess was strikingly apparent. The same cannot, unfortunately, be said of *Paris brûle-t-il ?* (1966), a dull and ponderous Franco-American co-production about the liberation of the French capital.

The two most exciting of the older directors have remained Jacques Tati and Robert Bresson, both of whom have vigorously preserved their independence and identity. Tati made only one film in the Sixties, *Playtime* (1967), but this was a major work of great originality, made with all the resources of an international co-production, but remaining a totally personal piece of artistic expression. Turning his back on the traditional notion of the comic actor as the focus of attention, Tati based the whole structure of his film on observation, his own performance as Hulot being given less weight than the portrait of a soulless corner of modern Paris brought to life by the people who undermine its impersonal organisation.

By comparison with Tati, Robert Bresson seemed positively prolific with four films in the decade. *Procès de Jeanne d'Arc* (1962) marked the extreme refinement of the stylistic process begun with *Journal d'un Curé de Campagne*. All irrelevancies are put aside and the film follows Joan's resolute march to the stake, concentrating on her trial and interrogation by Bishop Cauchon. Visually this is Bresson's most austere work, filmed largely in medium shot. After a four year break he returned to film-making with a new and enriched style. *Au Hasard, Balthazar* (1966) has a richness of incident that earlier films had lacked (including violence, nudity and cruelty), masterfully controlled by a structural pattern based on the accumulation of tiny elliptical scenes. The film balances the fate of two individuals in a world where evil seems triumphant. The girl Marie, fascinated by the wicked and cruel Gérard, submits herself to suffering and humiliation, while the donkey Balthazar, originally her pet, follows a parallel course, encountering murder, cruelty, avarice on his travels towards death. *Mouchette* (1967) used the same techniques to adapt a novel by Georges Bernanos (who had already provided the starting point for *Journal d'un Curé de Campagne*). Again as in *Au Hasard, Balthazar*, there is a deliberate mixing of incongruous elements of traditional life and modernity. Unlike

Marie, the fourteen-year-old Mouchette does not have to seek humiliation and pain. All her attempts at human contact are thwarted, her tenderness is rewarded by a brutal rape and she is driven imperceptibly to suicide. To tell this tragic story, Bresson uses a simple but totally stylised visual approach, a fragmentary pattern of incident, sound and dialogue. Bresson has frequently used classical music to counterbalance the realism of the images and here Mouchette's pathetic death is accompanied by portions of Monteverdi's *Magnificat*. The Dostoievskian element in Bresson's work has been particularly apparent since *Pickpocket,* so it was unsurprising when he turned to a story by the Russian novelist to make *Une Femme Douce* in 1969.

In a very different vein the early Sixties also saw the brief flourishing of the *cinéma-vérité* movement in France. The two main figures in this were the documentarists **Jean Rouch** (*b* 1917) and **Mario Ruspoli** (*b* 1925), and a major contribution was also made by Chris Marker with *Le Joli Mai* (1963), a study of Paris in the month of May 1962, containing interviews with a wide range of people. Ruspoli's films, shot with flexible 16mm equipment, set out to capture with truth and spontaneity the lives of peasants in *Les Inconnus de la Terre* (1961) and the inmates of a mental hospital in *Regard sur la Folie* (1962). Rouch himself had made a number of documentaries on African life from 1946 onwards, the most remarkable being *Les Maîtres Fous* (1955). Then he began to work at feature length, beginning with *Jaguar,* shot in the early Fifties but not edited until 1968. This told the cheerful tale of a trio of migrant workers, but *Moi un Noir* (1958) was more complex in that it included the dreams as well as the real life of its stevedore hero. With *La Pyramide Humaine* (1961), about contact between black and white students at the grammar school in Abidjan, fiction began to play a major part, and both *La Punition* (1963) and the short *Gare du Nord* (1964) were improvised fictional stories made on location in Paris with non-actors. Rouch has also worked in more conventional *genres,* making *Chronique d'un Eté* (1961), an inquiry film co-directed with the sociologist Edgar Morin in the manner of *Le Joli Mai,* and the African documentary *La Chasse au Lion à l'Arc* (1965).

The move towards pure fiction to be found in Rouch's work is paralleled by the development of Georges Franju. While his first feature, *La Tête contre les Murs* (1958) had had strong documentary overtones, both *Les Yeux sans Visage* (1959) and *Judex* (1963) were deliberately unreal. The latter was a nostalgic homage to the fantastic 1914 world of Louis Feuillade's serials, which had a formative influence on the surrealists and on Franju himself. A balance between documentary and fantasy was struck in Franju's two beautifully filmed literary adaptations: *Thérèse Desqueyroux* (1962) from a novel by François Mauriac and *Thomas l'Imposteur* (1965), co-scripted by Jean

Cocteau from his own novel. In these films Franju's sense of visual composition and his ability to evoke atmosphere and extract poetry from reality were strikingly apparent.

Resnais   There is a strong literary element too in the work of Alain Resnais, though all his films have been made from original scripts written specifically for the screen. After the highly original *Hiroshima Mon Amour* Resnais turned to another novelist, Alain Robbe-Grillet, for the script of *L'Année Dernière à Marienbad* (1961). Plunging the spectator into a strange world of anonymous characters beyond the reach of time and logic, the two film-makers created an analysis of the ambiguities of love without parallel in the history of the cinema. Technically, Resnais's stylistic approach was impeccable. He maintained the totally stylised pattern of gesture and speech throughout and built a complex rhythm out of the sequence of tracking shots to balance against the verbal patterns of Robbe-Grillet's script. With *Muriel* (1963), made with Jean Cayrol, who had previously written the text for *Nuit et Brouillard,* Resnais returned to the real world but an air of mystery persists in this abruptly edited, elliptical study of the power of the past over a group of closely-knit individuals. *La Guerre est Finie* (1966), Resnais's most committed feature, was the first built around the re-actions of a man, in this case a revolutionary working for the overthrow of the Franco *régime* in Spain. Jorge Semprun's script lacked the literary richness of the preceding work but substituted a remarkable surface realism and closeness to contemporary events. In *Je t'aime, je t'aime* (1968), scripted by Jacques Sternberg, Resnais returned to the exploration of time, following the progress of a man projected by scientists into his past.

In subject at least Resnais's film had similarities with Chris Marker's remarkable venture into science fiction, *La Jetée* (1962–4), composed almost entirely of still photographs. Apart from this film and *Le Joli Mai,* Marker also made in the Sixties a number of documentaries in his highly personal style blending wit and political commitment: *Description d'un Combat* (1960) about the state of Israel; *Cuba Si* (1961), an evocation of Castro's revolution; *Le Mystère Koumiko* (1965) on Japan and *Si j'avais Quatre Dromadaires* (1966) based on still photographs taken in twenty-six countries in the course of ten years. Marker was also one of the principal organisors of the collective film *Loin du Viêtnam* (1967) which united the efforts of Resnais, Godard, Varda, Lelouch, Joris Ivens, William Klein and dozens of technicians.

The influence of Resnais was to be seen clearly in Henri Colpi's first film, *Une Aussi Longue Absence* (1960), from a script by Marguerite Duras, while the preoccupations of *Nuit et Brouillard* were echoed in Armand Gatti's *L'Enclos* (1961). In a wider sense Alain Resnais, with this series of films unsurpassed for their thematic complexity and stylistic innovation, dominates a whole area of world cinema. His efforts

towards achieving a non-naturalistic film style has been ably supported by
Agnès Varda. In the Sixties, she was responsible for *Cléo de Cinq à Sept* (1962), a delicate study of a young woman awaiting a hospital report, *Le Bonheur* (1965), a splendidly decorative study of love and marriage, remarkable for its absence of psychological or moralistic over- tones, and *Les Créatures* (1966), which examined the interaction of fiction and reality in the mind of a novelist at work on a new book. More recently Varda has worked largely in America, making two docu- mentaries and the delightful semi-improvised feature *Lions Love* (1969), starring one of Andy Warhol's "superstars," Viva.

Another by-product of Resnais's work has been the films subsequently made independently by his writers. Jean Cayrol followed his script for *Muriel* with a new feature on related themes, *Le Coup de Grâce* (1964). Marguerite Duras, after co-directing a version of *La Musica* (1967), made the most uncompromising *Détruire Dit-Elle* (1969), a modernist parable on revolution. Jorge Semprun has not turned to directing but the commitment of *La Guerre est Finie* found an echo in his script for *Z* (1969). This film, one of the most successful political films of the decade, was directed by the Greek-born **Costa-Gavras** (*b* 1933) who had previously made a thriller, *Compartiment Tueurs* (1964), and a Resistance melodrama, *Un Homme de Trop* (1966). But the most interesting and intellectually exciting series of films by an ex-colleague of Resnais's has been that produced by **Alain Robbe-Grillet** (*b* 1922). With *L'Immortelle* (1963), *Trans-Europ-Express* (1967) and *L'Homme qui Ment* (1968) he developed further the concern with narrative and the exploration of the working of the mind and the emotions already apparent in *Marienbad*.

From the directors who emerged before the "new wave" phenomenon there came in the Sixties an abundance of polished and elegant films carefully tailored to the requirements of the audience. Jean-Pierre Melville gave up his totally independent film-making style to reach wider audiences with his "star" films *Léon Morin Prêtre* (1961) and *L'Aîné des Ferchaux* (1963), and more especially with his series of outstanding gangster movies *Le Doulos* (1963), *Le Deuxième Souffle* (1966) and *Le Samourai* (1967). In 1969 he showed equal skill with a sombre study of the Resistance, *L'Armée des Ombres*. The eclectic Louis Malle followed an adaptation of Raymond Queneau's inventive and pun-ridden novel *Zazie dans le Métro* (1960) with a glorification of the Brigitte Bardot myth, *Vie Privée* (1961). His best film, *Le Feu Follet* (1963), was about a young man's realisation of the inevitability of suicide, a lucid and faultlessly executed piece of work. The Mexican extravaganza *Viva Maria* (1965) was clearly a reaction to the gloom and introspection of *Le Feu Follet*. He returned to a more serious sub- ject with *Le Voleur* (1967), then went to India to make the docu- mentary *Calcutta* (1969). Alexandre Astruc was more successful with

Varda

113

his studies of emotional life—*La Proie pour l'Ombre* (1960) from an original script and *L'Education Sentimentale* (1961), a modernisation of Flaubert—than with his subsequent war films, *La Longue Marche* (1968) and *Flammes sur l'Adriatique* (1968). Roger Vadim directed half-a-dozen beautiful and totally insignificant films exploiting the charms of his leading ladies before making his most enjoyable work of the decade, the spoof science fiction *Barbarella* (1968).

Jean-Luc Godard

With about twenty feature films and sketches in the course of ten years Jean-Luc Godard is the most prolific as well as (with Resnais) the most audacious and influential of the younger French film-makers. The mere enumeration of his films gives some indication of his enormous range. *Le Petit Soldat* (1960), banned for three years because it commented on violence and the Algerian war, was followed by the pseudo-musical comedy *Une Femme est une Femme* (1961), a touching homage to the American cinema. *Vivre sa Vie* (1962) studied prostitution in clinical terms and its heroine, Godard's wife Anna Karina, in loving detail, while *Les Carabiniers* (1963) was a de-mystification of war. If in *Le Mépris* (1963) Godard ventured into the unaccustomed area of international co-production, he returned to Paris and its suburbs with the touching *Bande à Part* (1964), a transmutation of pulp-fiction material, and with *Une Femme Mariée* (1964), the study of a woman torn between husband and lover. In *Alphaville* (1965) Godard took a look at the world of the future, making uncharacteristic use of Eddie Constantine and building his city of the future out of the elements of present day Paris. A quite new note of bitterness, almost despair, was to be found in Godard's last two a-political films *Pierrot le Fou* (1965) and *Masculin-Féminin* (1966). In the former the Robinson Crusoe style idyll proved all too transitory, while in the latter the hero wandered through a Paris full of squalid sex and violence. With *Made in USA* (1967) a new note of political involvement entered Godard's work, and though he still based his work on thriller material, the narrative thread had now become virtually non-existent. In *Deux ou Trois Choses que je sais d'elle* (1967), made simultaneously, the concern with prostitution already apparent in *Vivre sa Vie* is now broadened with an indictment of our whole civilisation, and in *La Chinoise* (1967) the political inspiration is obvious in the lengthy discussion of Maoist ideals and methods. The climax of this trend is *Weekend* (1967), an incredibly bitter look at civilisation seen as typified by mindless slaughter on the roads on the part of the bourgeoisie and cannibalism among those who opt out of it. By comparison with this major film Godard's English feature *One plus One* (later renamed *Sympathy for the Devil*, 1968) and the television film *Le Gai Savoir* (1968) seem pale and timid. Godard, as these films show, has gradually moved to a position in which feature film-making in the traditional sense is no longer possible for him. But despite the

Eddie Constantine and Anna Karina (left) in ALPHAVILLE. Catherine Deneuve and Nino Castelnuovo in LES PARAPLUIES DE CHER-BOURG (below)

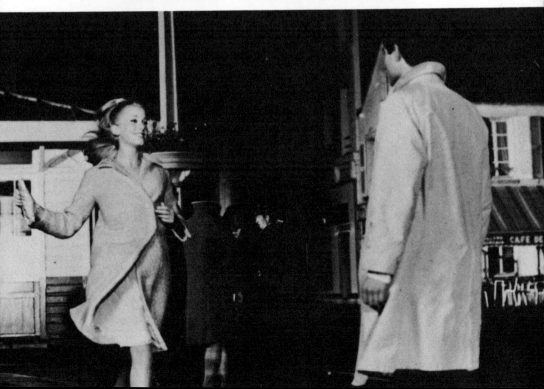

dead end into which the logic of his development has brought him, Godard more than any other film-maker of his generation has made audiences and film directors re-examine the basic qualities of the medium.

Truffaut　　None of Godard's former colleagues on the staff of *Cahiers du Cinéma* can match his prolific outpouring of original works. François Truffaut's films in the Sixties show an interesting blend of the purely personal tone of *Les Quatre Cents Coups* and a concern with contrivance and effect in the manner of Hitchcock, the subject of a book published by Truffaut in 1967. *Tirez sur le Pianiste* (1960) and *Jules et Jim* (1961) were both adapted from novels but filled with a wealth of charming and inconsequential detail invented by the director. In *La Peau Douce* (1964) Truffaut tried to deepen his approach with a study of adultery in a contemporary setting, but his taste for bad novels was clearly revealed by the contrived and unnecessary ending. Most of his later works are remoter stylistic exercises. *Fahrenheit 451* (1966), which he made in England, was a watered-down version of Ray Bradbury's science fiction novel, while both *La Mariée était en Noir* (1967) and *La Sirène du Mississipi* (1969) were virtual pastiches of Hitchcock. By contrast, with *Baisers Volés* (1968) and *Domicile conjugal* (1970) Truffaut returned to the semi-autobiographical tone of his first feature, giving further adventures of his diffident but enterprising young hero Antoine (Jean-Pierre Léaud).

Harry Max and Jean-Pierre Léaud in Truffaut's BAISERS VOLES

Claude Chabrol began the Sixties with a number of idiosyncratic and rather bitter and uneven films—*Les Godelureaux* (1961), *L'Oeil du Malin* (1962), *Ophélia* (1962)—which bore the unmistakable mark of his personality but achieved little success. With *Landru* (1963) and a series of trivial spy films he worked to recover the favour of producers and in 1968-9, with *Les Biches* (1968), *La Femme Infidèle* (1969) and *Que la Bête Meure* (1969), he was able to return to the kind of film-making he does best: the cold and elegant dissection of the tangled emotional problems of a handful of characters and the crimes of passion to which they are driven. **Jacques Rivette** (*b* 1928) has proved himself the most austere member of the group with only three films in ten years. Both *Paris Nous Appartient* (1960) and the four-hour-long *L'Amour Fou* (1968) showed the disintegration of personal relationships in a theatrical setting with, in each case, the production of a play serving as a catalyst in the lives of the characters. Rivette's most publicised film was *Suzanne Simonin, la Religieuse de Diderot* (1966), a sober adaptation inexplicably banned for several years by the French censor. **Eric Rohmer** (*b* 1920) who had almost disappeared from professional film-making after the failure of *Le Signe du Lion* (1959) returned in the late Sixties with a series of "moral tales" which included *La Collectionneuse* (1967) and the brilliantly witty *Ma Nuit chez Maud* (1969) and *Le Genou de Claire* (1970).

The Sixties in France were dominated by the men who first appeared on the scene in the late Fifties, but there were also a number of younger directors whose work is of interest. The new men had generally not been involved in film criticism and though they may have been influenced by earlier styles of film-making, they are by no means theorists. Intellectual depth is often replaced by a simple desire to entertain. There are a few isolated film-makers of real distinction. **Jacques Rozier** (*b* 1926) made a single very agreeable feature, *Adieu Philippine* in 1961 and **Alain Jessua** (*b* 1932) showed an original approach in *La Vie à l'Envers* (1963) and *Jeu de Massacre* (1967). **René Allio** (*b* 1924) adapted a Brecht story in *La Vieille Dame Indigne* (1965) and then went on to make two studies of personal disintegration, *L'Une et l'Autre* (1967) and *Pierre et Paul* (1969). The year 1968 saw the feature *début* of **Walerian Borowczyk** (*b* 1923) who, with films like *Dom* (1958), *Le Concert de M. et Mme. Kabal* (1962), *Renaissance* (1964) and *Les Jeux des Anges* (1964), had shown himself the most brilliant short film-maker since Franju and Resnais. *Goto, l'Ile d'Amour* (1968) was a totally original film, a fairy-tale remarkable for its bitter force and cold irony.

Other characteristic film-makers of the Sixties were **Jacques Demy** (*b* 1931), **Pierre Etaix** (*b* 1928) and **Claude Lelouch** (*b* 1937). Demy began with two films built around the personality of his stars, *Lola* (1960) with Anouk Aimée and *La Baie des Anges* written for Jeanne

Moreau. Then he was able to direct the kind of films he had always wanted to make and, working in close collaboration with the composer Michel Legrand, he made *Les Parapluies de Cherbourg* (1964) and *Les Demoiselles de Rochefort* (1967), colourful and agreeable musicals in which the influence of Hollywood is very apparent. His own first film made in America, *Model Shop* (1969), was, however, a sadly drab and limp affair despite the presence of Anouk Aimée. Etaix, after a number of short films, began his feature career with *Le Soupirant* (1962) in which he appeared in the leading role. His finest and most ambitious film was *Yoyo* (1965) in which a satisfying narrative was combined with a wealth of gags and the humour blended with a genuine melancholy, as in the work of all the great clowns. After the comparative failure of *Tant qu'on a la Santé* (1966), Etaix returned to his best form with *Le Grand Amour* (1969). In a very different vein Lelouch's films, notably *Un Homme et une Femme* (1966), *Vivre pour Vivre* (1967) and *La Vie, l'Amour, la Mort* (1969) have achieved an international success thanks to their mixture of warm sentimentality and a surface gloss equal to that of Vadim at his most self-indulgent. *ra*

Marie-Christine Barrault and Jean-Louis Trintignant in Rohmer's MA NUIT CHEZ MAUD (below). Opposite: Stéphane Audran and Jacqueline Sassard in Chabrol's LES BICHES

4. Italy

THE RENAISSANCE OF THE ITALIAN CINEMA coincided with the re-birth of political activity in Italy. 1942, the year when the political parties came to life again, was the year in which the first films heralding the new cinema appeared—such works as Blasetti's *Quattro passi fra le nuvole,* Rossellini's *Un pilota ritorna* and *L'uomo della croce,* De Sica's *I bambini ci guardano* and Visconti's *Ossessione.* For all its weaknesses as a political system, Fascism had in fact favoured the cinema. The "Centro sperimentale" trained a new generation of film-makers and the magazines *Cinema* and *Bianco e nero* gave them a theoretical grounding. Virtually all the directors of the Forties owe much to one or the other (or both) of these institutions and the hot-house atmosphere of the Italian cinema (three hundred films were made in the years 1940–42) allowed these eager young *cinéastes* to obtain practical experience.

The Realist Tendency Initially the realist tendency (which naturally received little official encouragement) existed alongside a more literary approach, labelled calligraphism by the critic De Santis, which sought to re-invigorate the Italian cinema by adapting late Nineteenth and early Twentieth century novels. The path opened by Soldati, the originator of this approach, was the one followed by two young architects when they became film-makers in turn: **Renato Castellani** (*b* 1913) with *Un colpo di pistola* (1941), adapted from Pushkin, and **Alberto Lattuada** (*b* 1914) with *Giacomo l'idealista* (1942), from a novel by Emilio De Marchi. These films and others like them clearly parallel the works of Carné and Prévert in France during the same period. In them, as in *Les Visiteurs du Soir,* the pursuit of style was adopted as a reply to an oppressive and distasteful system. But it is noticeable that in Italy none of the three truly great directors of the Forties, Rossellini, De Sica and Visconti, indulged in this form of cinema.

For those who wished to achieve a more realistic approach there were several cinematic traditions that seemed to offer the possibility of renewal. One was the popular or dialect comedy, a form in which the actors Aldo Fabrizi and Anna Magnani, as well as the writer Federico Fellini, first achieved prominence. But though these three made a valuable contribution to some of the postwar work of **Roberto Rossellini** (*b* 1906), the form itself produced only minor works. Rossellini's own origins lay in the documentary. The pioneer of this *genre* was **Francesco De Robertis** (1902–1959), whose first documentary *Uomini sul fondo* (1941) made a great impact on the younger generation. He also supervised and co-scripted the film with which Rossellini made his *début, La nave bianca* (1941). The documentary approach obviously has marked affinities with postwar neo-realism in matters of style, but the ethos of the two approaches is quite distinct. De Robertis was a convinced Fascist (he later ran the film industry of the Salò Republic) and Italian documentary of the Forties lacks the element of confrontation and questioning essential to neo-realism. Another form of cinema in which some of the roots of neo-realism lie is middle-class comedy, pioneered by Mario Camerini with *Gli uomini che mascalzoni* in 1932 and renewed by Alessandro Blasetti with *Quattro passi fra le nuvole* ten years later. It was in this form that **Vittorio De Sica** (*b* 1901) made his reputation as an actor and his first films as a director were direct imitations of Camerini. *I bambini ci guardano* (1942), the film with which De Sica began his collaboration with the writer **Cesare Zavattini** (*b* 1902), shows the limitations of this approach: the sentimentality and ultimate refusal to confront adult problems in adult terms.

There were also outside influences which served to counteract the shortcomings of the Italian film tradition. One of these was the influence of foreign films widely known through the critical writings of men like **Giuseppe De Santis** (*b* 1917). Several Italians worked in France during the Thirties and early Forties, including Visconti and Michelangelo Antonioni, and the prestige of French "poetic realism" was enormous. To counterbalance it there was the literary influence of the American naturalistic novel—Faulkner, Hemingway, Steinbeck, and Caldwell. Most of the Italian Forties film-makers were scriptwriters before becoming directors and many were journalists as well, so the influence of literature was naturally strong. It would be wrong to think that they were seeking something exotic in concerning themselves with France or America: it was through these foreign sources alone that they could discover themselves. In their own Italian tradition they had to look back to the Nineteenth century realism of the novelist Giovanni Verga to find a style free from rhetoric and "d'Annunzianism." There is one film which unites all these divergent sources and yet remains essentially Italian—*Ossessione* (1942) directed by **Luchino Visconti** (*b* 1906). This fatalistic tale of passion and betrayal was directed from an American pulp fiction source by an ex-assistant of Renoir for whom the novels of Verga are something of an obsession (a Verga novel is at the root of *La terra trema*). *Ossessione* shows the kind of realist cinema—honest, direct and technically virtuoso—which might have developed in Italy. It was only the war which raged throughout the length of Italy between 1943 and 1945 that brought about the sense of actuality and commitment, the basic optimism and social concern that characterise neo-realism.

In 1945 it was Roberto Rossellini who showed the Italian cinema the way. That year he made *Rome—Open City* (*Roma città aperta*),

Clara Calamai and Massimo Girotti in Visconti's OSSESSIONE

Rossellini

the first authentically neo-realist work, begun a mere two months after the liberation of Rome by allied forces. Set in the winter of 1943–44, the film depicts the ruthless hunting down of a Communist Resistance leader by the Gestapo. As he vainly seeks to escape, the man (Marcello Pagliero) succeeds only in bringing death to his friends, including Pina, the *fiancée* of his best friend (played by Anna Magnani) and the priest, Don Pietro (Aldo Fabrizi). *Roma città aperta* was a story of political enlightenment and the evolution of the characters presumably paralleled Rossellini's own, for by 1944 he had left behind the ideology of De Robertis and aligned himself firmly with the Committee of National Liberation. *Roma città aperta* was a striking, if uneven, work, based partly on events widely known in Rome (such as the execution of a priest Don Morosini by the Germans) and partly on the personal experiences of the film-makers: Rossellini, Fabrizi and the scriptwriter Sergio Amidei. The latter's wartime adventures formed the basis for the treatment of the Communist, and it was in his flat that part of the film was shot. Deliberately playing down the heroics, but emphasising the reality of German torture, the film managed to combine brutality with an abrupt whimsical humour. In its production methods (location shooting, post-synchronisation etc.) the film inaugurated the neo-realist style, but at the same time it retained a strong story line and a reliance on dialogue to make its message explicit. *Paisà* (1946), Rossellini's second postwar film, covered a wider scope, dealing with six episodes in the liberation of Italy and ranging from Sicily to the Po valley. The strong story line of *Roma città aperta* gave way to the episodic structure, each of the little tales showing an instance in the interaction of Italians and Americans. In Sicily a girl seems to betray the American invaders, in Naples a boy robs a Negro military policeman, in Rome a GI meets a whore who was once the pure young girl of whom he preserves a romantic dream. In Florence Fascists and partisans fight a bitter struggle for supremacy, but in the remote Apennines the life of the monks is troubled only by the need to convert the "heathen" (Jewish and Protestant army chaplains). In the final episode, set in the Po valley, partisans are rounded up by superior German forces in one last mopping up operation before the collapse of the Nazi Reich. The tone varies widely from one episode to another, but all are basically individual stories and the wider issues are virtually ignored. *Paisà* was not about war or ideology, but about people caught up, uncomprehending and against their will, in the turmoil of war. The third episode in Rossellini's war trilogy was *Germania anno zero* (1947), which was set in Berlin and studied the corrupting effect of Nazi ideology on a young boy who poisons his sickly father and then commits suicide. Much of the film was wordy and contrived, but the final sequence of the boy wandering through the ruins of Berlin had a power which Rossellini has never surpassed.

An interesting comparison with the war films of Rossellini is furnished by the two films financed by the partisan organisation, Vergano's *Il sole sorge ancora* (1946) and De Santis's *Caccia tragica* (1947). **Aldo Vergano** (*b* 1891), ex-scriptwriter (about thirty scripts for commercial films between 1929 and 1943) and active fighter in the partisan struggle, made only one notable film. This no doubt owed much to its writers, the future directors De Santis and **Carlo Lizzani** (*b* 1922) and the critic Guido Aristarco (who with Umberto Barbaro contributed largely to the theoretical basis of neo-realism). *Il sole sorge ancora,* a rather conventional story of a young man's political enlightenment, was most notable for a number of striking, almost theatrical scenes. It equated Fascism with the corrupt ruling classes and stressed the unity of Catholic and Communist in the resistance struggle. *Caccia tragica* showed the fate of this partisan spirit in the postwar world. The tragic pursuit of the title is that organised by the workers on a collective farm to track down the bandits who have stolen their money. An impassioned and totally committed work, *Caccia tragica* resorted in places to verbal rhetoric to put across its message, but De Santis managed to endow his characters with the kind of earthy reality that Visconti had discovered in *Ossessione* (for which De Santis was one of the writers). In both *Il sole sorge ancora* and *Caccia tragica* elements of melodrama were never far below the surface as conflicts were pushed to their extreme limits. This tendency was even more strikingly apparent in the more commercial films of Alberto Lattuada. Lattuada had a cultured artistic background and a deep love of opera (he is the son of the composer Felice Lattuada) and his earliest film work was in the calligraphist style. This tendency persisted too in the postwar era (he adapted a D'Annunzio novel to make *Il delitto di Giovanni Episcopo* in 1947) but was counterbalanced by a search for realism. This was at the roots of *Il bandito* (1946) and *Senza pietà* (1948) in which he dealt with contemporary crime and corruption in a vivid manner, tackling social evils without adopting the limitations of explicit political commitment and working inventively but never losing touch with the mass audience.

One of the major achievements in world cinema in the Forties was

The fishermen of Sicily in Visconti's LA TERRA TREMA

La terra trema (1947), Luchino Visconti's mammoth study of the south.
It is in many ways a paradoxical work, for Visconti, an aristocrat by birth and temperament, chooses illiterate peasants as his protagonists, adapts a novel published in 1881 and yet makes a film of great contemporary relevance; adopts a Marxist perspective, yet makes a study of family pride and independence. In part this complexity derives from the double source of Visconti's inspiration. On the one hand is the vision of the novelist Verga, who died in 1922 but whose best work dates from the 1880s. It was he who aroused Visconti's interest in the South seen as an almost mythical land of primitive splendour. He also gave an example of a direct approach to reality, attempting to recapture the words and intonations of the poor and to present the truth with as great a spontaneity and objectivity as possible. To bring this Nineteenth century world into focus, Visconti uses the writings of Antonio Gramsci, the founder of the Italian Communist Party, who analysed the South in terms of economic development and class exploitation. Originally Visconti planned a trilogy on Sicilian themes, dealing with fishing, mining and agriculture, but only the first and most pessimistic of the three, the *episodio del mare,* was completed, so that a work planned as progressive and revolutionary finally emerged as a story of defeat. *La terra trema* unfolds with the slow, ordered rhythm of a Nineteenth century novel. In the first phase the hero 'Ntoni achieves a remarkable success when he leads the young men in a spontaneous revolt against the wholesalers' system of buying fish. The act is purely negative, but it teaches 'Ntoni much about his place in the community. What he fails to appreciate, however, is the extent to which success was a product of the solidarity of all the workers. He thinks that his family can beat the system on its own and unsupported. At first they seem to succeed, then a single night's storm destroys their boat and nets. With the failure of 'Ntoni's project the slow disintegration of the family begins: 'Ntoni loses his girl and his sister has to renounce the man she loves. When the grandfather dies, his younger sister is seduced and his brother emigrates to the mainland. 'Ntoni takes to drink to drown his sorrows. At last, however, he comes to see the error of his ways and, facing up to the taunts and humiliations of the wholesalers, he returns to work and to the sea. *La terra trema* is a masterly film, carefully structured and shot with a sense of depth and movement reminiscent of Jean Renoir at his best. The photographic texture is closely linked to the mood of the film, the bustle and flow of the earlier scenes giving way to the claustrophobic black of the family's defeat. Music is sparingly used, but the sound of voices is vital to the impact of the film. The non-professional Sicilian cast improvised its own dialogue with the framework provided by Visconti and local dialect was used throughout, though this made the film virtually incomprehensible to the Italians on the mainland.

Visconti's action in going to Sicily to make a film was typical of the revival of interest in the peasant and in the problem of the South to be found in both Italian literature and Italian cinema of the late Forties. With the important exception of Vittorio De Sica, neo-realist directors, though themselves largely town-bred and middle class in origins, shared the Communist party's growing concern with the peasants. Films with urban settings, such as Visconti's *Bellissima* (1951) or Giuseppe De Santis's *Roma ore undici* (1952), were minor works compared with the films dealing with agrarian problems. De Santis himself followed *Caccia tragica* with two films with rural settings. *Bitter Rice* (*Riso amara*, 1948) seems to have been originally conceived by the director and his scriptwriters as a study of the exploitation of casual workers in the rice fields of the Po valley, but somehow developed into an unashamed piece of eroticism, making full use of the physical charms of Silvana Mangano, who achieved international fame with this film. *Non cé pace tra gli ulivi* (1949) was a less compromising work and is generally considered De Santis's masterpiece. Like his other films it combined a strong line of passion and betrayal with elements of melodrama and a consciously elaborated stylistic pattern. Alberto Lattuada's *Il mulino del Po* (1948) had a historical setting but it was perhaps even closer to contemporary events than De Santis's work. For while Lattuada was here filming the first peasant revolt of 1876, real strikes and disorders were breaking out all over the South. Like all the director's work *Il mulino del Po* showed social conflict without direct political moralising. Lattuada's sympathies would seem to be more with the peasants torn between capitalist modernisation and socialist calls for labour solidarity. The ending inevitably is one of defeat. A more optimistic vision of the hopes of the peasant emerged from Pietro Germi's two Sicilian films. *In nome della legge* (1948), the story of a young judge who singlehandedly defeats the Mafia in a remote Sicilian township has been widely praised. But, despite its visual beauty, it was a work of compromise, glorifying rather than exposing the Mafia killers. *Il cammino della speranza* (1950), the story of a group of workers who emigrate to France in search of a new life, was an infinitely superior work, reminiscent in some ways of John Ford's *The Grapes of Wrath*. Germi's epic style also has marked similarities with the American Western: an open air setting, a clear division of good and evil, a simplified pattern of moral choices and a solution obtained in face to face conflict.

While the majority of the Marxist directors turned to the peasant and his problems, Vittorio De Sica and his scriptwriter Cesare Zavattini remained to confront the urban problems of postwar Italy. They began by developing further the more novel aspects of *I bambini ci guardano*. Like this film, *Sciuscia* (1946) traced the end of innocence. The two shoeshine boys, linked by a pure friendship, are separated and corrupted

The man and his son in De Sica's BICYCLE THIEVES

De Sica

by the adult world around them. The world of officialdom is roundly condemned in the film, but the link with specific conditions of the late Forties is tenuous. Much greater weight is placed on the theme of friendship, symbolised by the splendid white horse the two boys buy with their hard earned savings. *Sciuscia* has its importance in De Sica's development from *matinée* idol to realist film-maker, but it is only one step and true mastery was not to be achieved until he and Zavattini made *Bicycle Thieves* (*Ladri di biciclette*) two years later. Remotely based on a novel, this film had a skilfully and elaborately fashioned script which showed the consequences for a workman and his family of the loss of his bicycle. Though the film is intimately linked with the economic conditions of Italy in the late Forties (1948 was a year of peak unemployment), its emotional core is the relationship of the workman and his young son. This allows the film to have a satisfying development and resolution, (the gaining, loss and recovery of the boy's confidence and trust), even though the workman's plight is hopeless. Again, as in all his work of this period, De Sica obtained excellent performances from his non-professional actors and recaptured the background with convincing detail. In the work of De Sica and Zavattini *Miracolo a Milano* (1950) formed a kind of interlude, being a fantastic satirical comedy based on material that had obsessed the writer for a dozen years or so. With *Umberto D* (1951) they returned to the mode of neo-realism proper, giving the movement its final masterpiece. The film tells of a retired official and his pathetic attempts to maintain his personal dignity amid poverty and indifference. Its method is to break the action down into a succession of tiny incidents without a conventional dramatic structure, the emotional core being given by the relationship of the old man to his dog. In a sense this latter blinds him to everything else, particularly to the problems of the maid working in the house where he has his room. Never again did De Sica achieve such stylistic purity as in this film.

Neo-realism lasted from *Roma città aperta* in 1945 until *Umberto D* in 1951, then petered out under the influence of governmental pressure and the film-makers' natural desires to make different kinds of films. Alongside it ran a vein of semi-realist comedy exemplified by *Vivere in pace* (1946), directed by **Luigi Zampa** (*b* 1904), *Domenica d'agosto* (1949) by **Luciano Emmer** (*b* 1918) and by a trilogy of films by Renato Castellani: *Sotto il sole di Roma* (1947), *E Primavera* (1949) and *Due soldi di speranza* (1951). In these agreeable yet minor works reality presents no problems that cannot be brushed aside and the whole dimension of criticism and confrontation essential to neo-realism is lacking. These films were the ancestors of a series of glossy and trivial works of the Fifties, which, despite their authentic settings, are as artificial as any product of the "white telephone" era of the Fascist cinema.

The Essence of Neo-realism   A major cinematic movement like neo-realism is impossible to sum up in a few words. Essentially a contemporary cinema, dealing with problems and aspirations, its fortunes were closely linked to those of the left-wing parties in Italy without the film-makers ever becoming blinkered by commitment to rigid political dogma. The link with real life was a close one but one was always offered a reconstruction, not a simple transcription, of reality. Never was there an attempt to film a story with those who had inspired it or for the cinema to record the purely autobiographical experiences of the film-maker.

By the time these things were done in the Italian cinema, neo-realism was already dead as a unified movement. Essentially, neo-realism was a discipline. Stylistically it implied stripping away the outmoded conventional uses of actors and studio settings while still maintaining a basically Nineteenth century approach to narrative. For the directors themselves it implied a voluntary renunciation of mass popularity or the use of spectacle. It decisively marked the whole subsequent pattern of Italian realism and the very different achievements of men like Fellini and Antonioni. *ra*

The most influential Italian film-maker of the postwar period has been **Michelangelo Antonioni** (*b* 1912). But it was not until 1960, when *L'Avventura* was screened at the Cannes Festival, that he was recognised by his peers and by the critics as a pioneer of the first degree. The distinctive flavour of Antonioni's films lies in their ruthless scrutiny of the characters' emotions, and in their tacit ridicule of the pretensions of a moribund society. The principal inhabitants of his cinema are dissatisfied with their lives, despite the luxury surrounding them. From Paola in *Cronaca di un amore* (1950) to Thomas in *Blow Up* (1967), they go about their business with a lugubrious and abstracted air. The failure or lack of love has become the common factor in his films, and if Antonioni seems unduly preoccupied with eroticism it is because he shares the views of his compatriot and admirer Alberto Moravia, who has said, "My interest in sex depends on sex being a way of relating with reality. It is one of the main ways of getting in touch with another person, one of our basic means of communication." Morality is a stranger in Antonioni's world. He takes his position as a contemporary matriarch, for he is desperately concerned with the future as opposed to the fossilised past. Although he was nearly forty when he completed his first feature, he has always been acutely conscious of the problems of a younger generation—or rather with a younger development: the postwar spurt in scientific progress and the sentimental difficulties it has brought in its train. "Show me a hero, and I will write you a tragedy," remarked Scott Fitzgerald, and Antonioni, whose world is very close to Fitzgerald's, also investigates the heroes of the modern age, penetrating the *façade* of opulent formality to reveal the instability and the anguish within.

At Bologna University, Antonioni took a degree in political economy, and produced plays by Ibsen and Pirandello. Although the Fascist government had not at first taken much interest in the Italian cinema, it steadily assumed control of the industry between 1935 and 1940 while the film, as in Germany, came to be regarded as a potent instrument of propaganda. It became virtually impossible for a studio to lose money even if its films were unsuccessful. All foreign films were surreptitiously dubbed by Italian "state" companies, so that anti-Fascist ideology, could be expurgated. Home production increased from 70 films in 1940 to 119 in 1942, most of these being comedies or melodramas. After writing journalism for a time in Ferrara, Antonioni turned his literary skill to screenplays. He collaborated on the script of Rossellini's *Un pilota ritorna* and Fulchignoni's *I due foscari* (1942), and was, briefly, an assistant to Marcel Carné on *Les Visiteurs du Soir*.

His early documentaries are all sharply observant and often critical of their subject. Only about a thousand feet of *Gente del Po,* the first of these 'prentice works, are extant. But the unashamed realism of Antonioni's approach to the life of bargees plying the Po delta marked a significant contribution to the new movement in Italian cinema (see *neo-realism*). The authorities were displeased by this bleak film, and contrived to "remove" the most unflattering sequences, while the negative was being processed in Venice. Other documentaries like *N.U.*

*Early
Documentaries*

and *La Villa dei Mostri* hint at Antonioni's later and increasing pre-occupation with the almost sinister presence of stone and inanimate objects (in this he resembles Georges Franju).

The theme of Antonioni's first feature, *Cronaca di un amore* (1950) is melancholy and uncompromising, and bears an interesting likeness to Zola's *Thérèse Raquin* or Dreiser's *An American Tragedy*. At the centre of the film is a somewhat dislikeable woman, Paola (Lucia Bosé), whose murky past comes to light as a result of an investigation organised by her husband. Paola is as unhappy as Lidia in *La notte,* attracted to a car salesman several classes beneath her and yet repulsed and fright-ened by the furtive squalor of the affair. The person unsure of his place and level in society is familiar in Antonioni's cinema. In the French and British episodes of *I vinti* (1953), petty ambition leads to murder; and Clara Manni (Lucia Bosé), the starlet hoisted to temporary success by her producer in *La signora senza camelie* (1953) lacks the sophistication required to survive the experience.

Le amiche   In 1955 Antonioni made his first major work, *The Girl Friends* (*Le amiche*), based on a novel by Cesare Pavese, a writer who expressed in his novels the same desolate philosophy that dominates so many of Antonioni's films. Clelia (Eleanora Rossi Drago) returns to her native Turin to launch a fashion salon and quickly becomes involved in a group of wealthy but disorientated young women. Their encounters are frivolous, superficial, and frustrated by inhibitions. But they are surely representative of a certain type and a certain period, and An-tonioni is content to watch them and their foibles. His style is not just formally attractive and supple; it respects the duration of real time on the screen, and attempts to catch the reflection of the characters' inner thoughts and feelings without forcing them to unmask them-selves with dialogue. The pressures of the city become forceful and realistic as Antonioni dwells for a moment on some bystanders or an architectural outcrop before panning round to discover his men and women like aliens in the sombre environment.

Il grido   Alain Resnais has commented, "In Antonioni's *The Cry* (*Il grido,* 1957), where the main character ends by committing suicide, the very intensity of the suffering bears witness to the grandeur of Man." Aldo (Steve Cochran), the factory worker who stumbles off on a doomed voyage into the illimitable wastes and horizons of the Po valley, emerges ultimately and paradoxically as a person of strength, unwilling to compromise his life. None of the women he meets can attune herself to his ill-expressed need for companionship. Antonioni's films as a whole analyse the failure of anachronistic morals and sentiments to keep pace with advances in other spheres of life, and the bulldozers, poised at the end of *Il grido* to destroy the flimsy houses in preparation for a jet airbase, symbolise the inexorable march of science as much as they foreshadow the death of Aldo.

Monica Vitti with Dominique Blanchar in L'AVVENTURA,
one of the most influential films of the Sixties

For all the subtlety of *Il grido*, it was only with *L'avventura* (1960)
that Antonioni found a successful means of dovetailing his social comments into the fabric of a film. *L'avventura* also inaugurated his great
partnership with Monica Vitti, whom he had met while she was dubbing
for Dorian Gray on *Il grido*. Antonioni's male characters have always
been undermined by indolence, vanity, and cowardice. But in *L'avventura* a new kind of sufferer is exemplified by Miss Vitti, a victim of
the casual amorality of the Sixties. At the outset of the film, her
Claudia is a marginal figure, caught discomfited in the reflection of
the erotic relationship between Sandro and Anna. But in the atmosphere
of anticipation, fear and guilt aroused by Anna's disappearance on Lisca
Bianca, a new love germinates between Sandro and Claudia; but it
remains an affair that cannot disengage itself from the uncertainty
and the melancholia in which it has its origins. Claudia resists the
impulse to forget her friend; Sandro does not; and this contrast in
behaviour forms the nucleus of the film. At the end, Sandro and
Claudia, their preconceptions of emotional commitment irrevocably

destroyed, arrive at an acceptance of human weakness and folly. They
are bound together by a dread of the world that can be suppressed only
by mutual dependence.

La notte   The dispute over Antonioni's work a decade ago contributed sizeably
to the debate concerning form and content in modern cinema, and
while in *L'avventura* Antonioni's style, as unusual and taxing as it may
at first appear, is discreetly "superimposed" on the predicament of the
major personalities, his technique in *The Night* (*La notte*, 1961) taps
repeatedly on the viewer's conscious response to the film, creating a
screen through which Lidia (Jeanne Moreau) and Giovanni (Marcello
Mastroianni) may be seen to move in a complex pattern of weariness
and disillusionment. For this couple, marriage is a fractious, living
death among the cruel, overwhelming buildings of Milan. Antonioni is
less sympathetic towards them than he is towards the idle rich of
L'avventura. But it is this absence of a positive, forward thrust, com-
pounded by the precise calculation of each scene, each interplay of
light and shadow, that denies *La notte* the stature of the previous film.

L'eclisse   For Antonioni, the smugness of the *haute bourgeoisie* and the nihilism
of the intelligentsia are equally contemptible. Vittoria (Monica Vitti)
in *The Eclipse* (*L'eclisse*, 1962) tries to chart a course away from both
these conditions. She feels outstripped by the "sick hurry and divided
aims" of urban existence. The lassitude that pervades Antonioni's
earlier characters gives place here to a restlessness, an inner confusion
reflected in the visible chaos of the *Borsa*, where Piero (Alain Delon)
works. Yet there are many intervals of stillness and reticence, and the
literary dialogue that threatens to paralyse much of *La notte* and *Le
amiche* is entirely absent (the first and last seven minutes of *L'eclisse*
are stripped of conversation). By far the strongest impression yielded
by the film is of man's feebleness beside the forces of nature. The

*Alain Delon and
Monica Vitti in
L'ECLISSE*

abstract despair of the film's closing shots emphasises this. Stones and trees, water and light—these have an unfathomable life and logic of their own, and only a vague reminiscence lingers of Vittoria and Piero.

In 1964 Antonioni completed his first colour film, *The Red Desert* (*Deserto rosso*) and it won the Leone d'Oro at the Venice Festival. The colour is used with acute skill; it is at once unprecedentedly *real* and consciously artificial. There is the disturbing yellow of the poison gas flaming up from the tangle of factories outside Ravenna where Giuliana (Monica Vitti) moves neurotically out of step with her husband and a handsome newcomer, Corrado (Richard Harris). Grey ships drift like preternatural monsters through the misty estuaries; even the gum trees in a hotel foyer are whitened for clinical effect. Such imaginative touches are more memorable than the film's drama, in which none of the leading players seems to have much confidence. *Deserto rosso*

The love and sympathy sought so keenly by Giuliana in *The Red Desert* are also lacking in *Blow Up* (1967), a film shot by Antonioni in London and in English, starring David Hemmings as a nameless young photographer (referred to as "Thomas" in the script). Thomas's neighbour is a painter. He is troubled by his abstracts, he says, until he finds "something to hang on to . . . like finding a clue in a detective story." Thomas searches similarly for a clue in the roll of film he exposes during his visit to Maryon Park, where a man's corpse appears to lie beside a tree. When the pictures are magnified to excess they resemble, with their massive grains and flecks of light, the paintings in the artist's studio. At the end of the film, lacking the moral fibre to pursue his conjectures, Thomas withdraws to a safe distance, so that the clues are buried again in the mass of forms before him. He has learned that contemporary life is against interpretation; the spontaneous reaction, the happening (like the beat concert) are all that count. As always, Antonioni makes this shameless surrender look meaningful. *Blow Up* is shot through with a dormant violence. Perspectives and colours seem as unpredictable as the photographer's dashes of movement. Thomas responds to chromatic metaphors, like the bright, unexpected green of the park. The abstract, kinetic *décors* are a significant factor in his environment. *Blow Up*

Blow Up is as impressive as any of the Italian films in its control of pace and atmosphere. Like them it develops with the irregular tempo of daily life. The length of a scene is dictated by its psychological importance rather than by conventional editing tactics.

Zabriskie Point (1970) was an even more controversial picture. Shot principally in Death Valley, it encompassed Antonioni's view of American youth and American landscape, in a virtually plotless skein of beautiful sequences, with the leading personalities (played by Daria Halprin, Mark Frechette, and Rod Taylor) purposely undeveloped; and concluding with a lyrical explosion in slow-motion. *pdc*

133

Luchino Visconti (*b* 1906) had played a crucial part in the development of the Italian cinema in the Forties, though he had made only two films during this time: *Ossessione* (1942), which in retrospect can be clearly seen as the major achievement of the Italian cinema under Fascism and *La terra trema* (1948), one of the three or four supreme works of neo-realism itself. His work in the Fifties and Sixties has been equally significant. *Bellissima* (1951) and the episode in *Siamo Donne* (1953) were starring vehicles for Anna Magnani, and essentially minor works but with *Senso* (1954) Visconti showed conclusively that he could go beyond the confines of neo-realism and create works that combined his cinematic realism with his taste for opera. Until *Senso* the two attitudes ran side by side with only a minimum of interplay: a mere few months separate *La terra trema* from the theatrical experiment of a production of *As You Like It* with sets by Salvador Dali. But in 1954 the fusion was achieved in the cinema and from this date onwards Visconti's work cannot be considered from a purely realistic standpoint.

Senso   The tone of *Senso* is set in the opening sequence in the Fenice Theatre at Venice in 1866 when, against a background of a Verdi opera, Italian patriots shout their defiance of the Austrian occupying forces and the Countess Serpieri (Alida Valli) comes face to face with the handsome Austrian lieutenant Franz Mahler (Farley Granger). From this point the two stories run side by side: the struggle for Italian freedom serving as a counterpoint to the tragic passion of the Countess and Franz, whose love ends in mutual betrayal and in his death. The tone of the film is set by the succession of key confrontations, such as the tender seduction of the Countess in her country house when Franz persuades her to betray the partisan cause, and her humiliation by Franz in front of the whore with whom he is living. Equally impressive are the scenes of battle—all blood, chaos and confusion—which form a cinematic equivalent to the Waterloo scenes in Stendhal's novel *La Chartreuse de Parme. Senso* is in a true (and non-derogatory) sense a melodrama, a modern story set in Nineteenth century dress, with visual compositions reminiscent of Nineteenth century painting and the music of Verdi and Bruckner. The film is a *tour de force* of heightened realism, flawlessly maintaining its mood, admirably acted and constituting a dazzling exposition of pure *mise en scène*.

Le notti bianche   Even further removed from neo-realism is *White Nights* (*Le notti bianche,* 1957), adapted by Visconti and his inseparable collaborator Suso Cecchi d'Amico from a story by Dostoievsky and set in a studio constructed *décor* of cold and snowy night-time streets. On three successive nights Mario (Marcello Mastroianni) meets the beautiful Natalia (Maria Schell) and learns from her the story of her life and her love for the enigmatic lodger (Jean Marais). In its maintenance of mood—in this case a dream world of ideal love—*Le notti bianche*

Alida Valli and Farley Granger in SENSO

is as remarkable an achievement as *Senso*. Mario lives in the real world of prostitutes and pop music, while Natalia herself is utterly cut off from time and history, living in a fairy tale universe. Yet in the end it is she who is proved right: the lodger reappears to claim her back at the very moment when she was about to yield to Mario. *Le notti bianche* is a most striking reminder of Visconti's cinematic origins. The reappearance as a prostitute of Clara Calamai calls to mind the guilty passion of *Ossessione,* in which she played the heroine. Above all the setting recalls the influence of the French poetic realism of the Thirties on Visconti. He did work briefly in 1936 with Jean Renoir, but *Le notti bianche* recalls far more the doom-laden streets of Marcel Carné's *Quai des Brumes* or *Le Jour se lève.*

Rocco and His Brothers (Rocco e i suoi fratelli, 1960) is a return to realism and in a sense a continuation of *La terra trema,* in that it traces the fate of a Southern family which has emigrated to the city of Milan. Like the earlier film it is a story of defeat and disintegration for the family, crushed by its environment and by social forces it cannot comprehend. Though similar in content, *Rocco e i suoi fratelli* could

Rocco e i suoi fratelli

hardly be more different in style from the neo-realist masterpiece. In inspiration it is a conscious mixture of the most diverse literary sources: Dostoievsky's *The Idiot* (for the figure of Rocco) and Thomas Mann (the family chronicle), the Sicilian Giovanni Verga and the Milanese writer Giovanni Testori. It also uses star actors drawn from several countries: Katina Paxinou, Alain Delon and Annie Girardot alongside Renato Salvatori and Claudia Cardinale. The Parondi family arrives in Milan from Lucania to attempt to build a new life and its story is told through the fates of the five sons who become successive focuses of attention. Vincenzo, who has preceded the family to the North, wants to break out of its close network of total loyalties to have a simple life. Simone becomes a boxer but his weaknesses of character and tragic passion for the prostitute Nadia lead to his downfall. Rocco is depicted as a saintly character who sacrifices his own life to make good his brother's debts and failings. By contrast, the two younger brothers are less complicated: Ciro, with his job at Alfa Romeo, is able to integrate himself fully into life in the North, while Luca contemplates a return to the South. *Rocco e i suoi fratelli* is an important but uneven film, an uneasy mixing of epic and melodrama, realism and symbol.

Il gattopardo

In 1962 Visconti contributed the episode *Il lavoro* to the collective film *Boccaccio 70,* but far more satisfying was *The Leopard* (*Il gattopardo,* 1963), a very faithful adaptation of the novel by Tomasi di Lampedusa. Visconti was obviously the ideal director to capture the novel's vision of a dying aristocracy struggling to maintain itself against a harsh Sicilian landscape. The novel's Nineteenth century narrative pattern fits perfectly with Visconti's own preoccupations and his film traces with a slow and deliberate rhythm the waning of the noble home of Salina and the corresponding rise to eminence of the enormously wealthy ex-peasant Don Calogero Sedara. The prince himself refuses to take active steps to halt the decline of his personal fortunes or to help build a new Sicily but his nephew Tancredi swims with the tide and assures his own position by marrying Don Calogero's beautiful daughter Angelica. Visconti combines an awareness of the subtle intricacies of political manoeuvring with an evident nostalgia for the aristocratic past (most evident in the long concluding ballroom scene) and extracts first-rate performances from the foreigners in his cast (Burt Lancaster as the Prince and Alain Delon as Tancredi), as well as the Italians (Romolo Valli as the Prince's confessor and Rina Morelli as his wife).

Vaghe stelle dell'Orsa

Sandra/Of a Thousand Delights (*Vaghe stelle dell'Orsa,* 1965) represents a fresh departure—a tragedy compressed into the story of one family, turned in on itself and nursing resentful memories of events of twenty years before. Sandra, the daughter, who returns with her American husband to the family mansion in the crumbling town

of Volterra, suspects her mother and stepfather of denouncing her Jewish father to the Gestapo. The mother, now an inmate in a mental clinic, madly pounding out the music of César Franck, counters with an accusation of incest between Sandra and her brother Gianni. The latter, all too aware now of the implications of his childhood relationship with his sister, has written a semi-autobiographical novel confessing his "guilt." He wants Sandra back and when she refuses he kills himself. The film has obvious overtones of (if not direct allusions to) the myth of Orestes and Electra, and the dimensions of social analysis which characterised *Rocco* and *Il gattopardo* are missing. In *Vaghe stelle dell'Orsa* the action is compressed into short scenes, abruptly cut together with the camera constantly zooming in to pin down the tormented characters.

As a stylistic exercise *Vaghe stelle dell'Orsa* was remarkable but *The Stranger* (*Lo straniero*, 1967) which followed, was an almost unmitigated disaster. This version of Albert Camus's novel *L'Etranger* is visually beautiful, making good use of the landscape and light of Algeria. But it failed totally to capture the sense of the absurd vital to Camus's vision and reduced Meursault's story to a pedestrian tale enlivened only by a few humorous character sketches. Many of Visconti's best films have been based on, or inspired by, novels, but all his sympathies go to the Nineteenth century concept of narrative and he finds himself totally out of sympathy with Camus's essentially mid-Twentieth century world.

After contributing an episode to *Le streghe* (1967), Visconti continued his investigation of Twentieth century life with the more

Lo straniero

promising material of *The Damned* (1969). The director's own preferred title is *Götterdämmerung,* a clear indication of the operatic
dimensions intended for this study of Nazism as a perverted and deca-
dent ideology. An ambitious production financed by Warner Brothers—
Seven Arts, it was shot in English with a cosmopolitan cast including
Dirk Bogarde and Ingrid Thulin. *ra*

FELLINI

Federico Fellini was born in 1921 at Rimini, a seaside town in
Northern Italy. The sea, and, by extension, water in all its forms, has
been a constant element in his work, and it may be that the regular
winter spectacle of bathing-tents, denuded of canvas and reduced to
mere scaffolding, lies at the root of that preoccupation with structures
which occur, as images of disquiet, in all his films up to and including *8½.*

To his Catholic upbringing he owes a sense of water as the element
of baptism and a means of regeneration, as well as a familiarity with
the church as essential to social life—it occurs in some way in all his
films. He takes on the whole a jovial attitude to it, though there are
times when he attacks it bitterly, but he has not yet gone so far as
to exclude it altogether. Another important element in his work is the
circus, which he has always loved, and which leads him to include
clown-like figures in many of his films, and to conclude his masterpiece,
8½, with the circular figure of a circus-ring, Guido himself (representing Fellini) being the ring-master.

As a young man Fellini went to Rome, where he worked as a
journalist, caricaturist, and gagman, and writing sketches and songs.
It was as a gagman that he entered the cinema (three films for Mario
Mattoli) but soon he was working on scripts, for a number of different
directors, finally, in 1945, working with Roberto Rossellini on *Roma,
città aperta,* both on the script and as assistant director, as he did
again on *Paisà* the following year. The experience with Rossellini was
decisive. It convinced him that the cinema was his natural medium,
and, in touring Italy for sites and episodes, he learned to see his own
country with new, and astonished eyes. In the next few years he
worked again with Rossellini (*Il Miracolo,* co-writer with Tullio
Pinelli; *Francesco, Giullare di Dio; Europa 51*), with Pietro Germi
(*In Nome della legge; Il Cammino della speranza; La Città si difende;
Il Brigante di Tacca del Lupo*), and with Alberto Lattuada (*Il Delitto
di Giovanni Episcopo; Senza pietà; Il Mulino del Po*). On *Variety
Lights* (*Luci del varietà,* 1950) Fellini was co-director, and worked
on the script with Lattuada himself, Pinelli, and Ennio Flaiano, the two
latter forming with Fellini an enduring association. Fellini has always,
as director, worked with a small group of friends, and clearly enjoys
with them a closeness that is reflected in the films as a unity of conception and approach. By 1950 he had his scriptwriters and one of
his cameramen, Otello Martelli, and, by 1952, in *The White Sheik*

(*Lo Sceicco bianco*) he was joined by Nino Rota, whose music has been an integral part of all his films to date, with the single exception of *Un 'Agenzia matrimoniale,* the Fellini episode of *Amore in città* (1953), the only time that Flaiano, too, was absent.

The White Sheik was the first film on which Fellini was sole director. It is his only farce, but already many of the later elements are present. His ability to see the follies of others and to love people the more for them is there in abundant measure. The city square as an image of loneliness, and the rubbish lying about in it as an image of disillusion and the mess that we make of our lives; the presence of the sea; the troupe of sleazy performers and their tents; and the picture of the church as an establishment offering a good deal of genial entertainment.

In the following year Fellini made *I vitelloni,* frankly autobiographical, in which his long experience as a scriptwriter enabled him to control a story (of a group of layabouts) which could easily have fallen out of balance, and to which his work in neo-realism contributed the quality of social observation that gave the film so much substance. It was not without some moral sternness, but the picture it presented is of a cheerful idleness and an attractive naturalness for which organised life as we know it has no place.

I vitelloni

I vitelloni attracted worldwide attention, and, as a result, Fellini was given the opportunity of having two American stars for his next film, *La strada* (1954), whose real star, however, was Fellini's wife, Giulietta Masina. *La strada* established her internationally as a unique performer, of the quality of the great clowns. This film is central to Fellini's work. It recognised that the opposite of love is not hate but indifference, and embodied the belief that, against all odds and all appearances, love would finally triumph. In this film Fellini made extensive and developed use of a system of images carrying a direct emotional charge (i.e. not symbols), and, with the paramount importance it gave to private feeling rather than social conscience, it marked an absolute break with neo-realism. For this it was strongly attacked by Zavattini. (The world prestige of neo-realism at first considerably damaged Fellini's international reputation; he was judged by standards irrelevant to his work and his true talents were for a time widely ignored.)

His next film, *The Swindlers* (*Il bidone,* 1955), offered an answer to Zavattini in Zavattini's own terms. It pointed, with a neo-realist truth of observation, to the degrading lives of the poor, and showed that degradation in· a very unappealing light. It also showed, and invited a degree of sympathy for, the callous and cheerful exploitation which poverty and ignorance inevitably engender. A dominant theme of the film was the onset of age and moral collapse, and it was a measure of Fellini's humanity and moral truthfulness that he excited

Il bidone

compassion, almost indeed an elegiac regret, for the death of a man who had finally cheated, not only his victims, but his companions as well. In subject matter the film was a possible sequel to *I vitelloni;* visually it was much more assured and showed a deliberate and selective use of a very personal imagery.

*Le notti di
Cabiria*

The Nights of Cabiria (*Le notti di Cabiria,* 1956), again starred Giulietta Masina, and was the second in a series of three films to centre on her, the third being *Giulietta degli spiriti.* Fellini has said that through his wife he has been able to explore mysteries of feeling and intuition that would be inaccessible to him without her, and there is a quietness of tone in the Masina films very different from Fellini's usual movement and vitality. Gelsomina, feeble-witted, was the key to an order of wisdom and truth; Cabiria, a prostitute, offered an image of purity and honour; Giulietta, a prosperous middle-class wife, was beset by religio-erotic visions and found peace and confidence only in emotional independence.

La dolce vita

Apart from the script of *Fortunella* (1958, *dir* Edouardo De Filippo), a starring vehicle for his wife, which he wrote with Flaiano and Pinelli, Fellini produced nothing more until 1960 when, after an unusually long period of gestation, there appeared *The Sweet Life* (*La dolce vita*). This was the second in a series of deeply autobiographical films (*I vitelloni* being the first and 8½ the last). Marcello (in *La dolce vita*) was what Moraldo (in *I vitelloni*) might have become. In this film Fellini broke away from a realistic environment, since, although each set could be justified on naturalistic grounds, the total impression was of a complex world of near-fantasy, so rooted in real appearances that it nonetheless had the force of actuality. Marcello pinned his hopes on the example of a friend, Steiner, whom he wrongly believed to have found a rich and satisfying way of life. The vanity of these hopes and the extent of his error were brought home to Marcello with uncompromising brutality when he discovered that Steiner had killed both his two children and himself. Marcello's immediate reaction was one of despair, but the film ended on a note of fragile, if authentic, hope.

For all that it encompassed tragedy, *La dolce vita* was a celebration of life and movement. There was a quality of special cohesion and elated liberation that Fellini plainly values, and since a good party offers these in concentrated form, parties abound in his films, and especially in this one. An atmosphere of scandal surrounded the film during shooting and on its release, and the phrase "la dolce vita" has become internationally current.

The making of *8½* (*Otto e mezzo,* 1963) was attended with even more mystery, although the enigmatic title was simple enough: it was Fellini's "8½th" film, the odd half being supplied by the episode of

Sandra Milo in Fellini's OTTO E MEZZO

Boccaccio '70—The Temptation of Dr. Antonio (La Tentazione del Dottor Antonio, 1962), his first film in colour, and the first in which he used a fabricated fantasy, as opposed to a fantastical interpretation of objective reality. *8½* opened with a piece of fabricated fantasy, implying a connection with *La dolce vita* and suggesting an identity between Guido and Marcello. (They were of course both played by Marcello Mastroianni.) Guido, a film director, was a deliberate representation of Fellini himself; his problem was that he could not get started on the film everyone was expecting him to make, and the subject of the film (i.e. *8½*) was the nature of inspiration and creativity in man. Guido was surrounded by people whose fortunes depended on his new film, and escaped from the pressures they were exerting through reminiscences of his childhood and flights of imagination. His scriptwriter, Daumier, argued for a synthetic approach, marshalling all the arguments that had been levelled at Fellini himself, and adding more, while a young and beautiful girl, The Ideal, tempted him to take refuge in a dream world. Guido rejected both of these and finally recognised that inspiration had failed him and that he could not make the film. His acceptance of defeat was embodied in suicide which, like the tragic deaths in *La dolce vita,* expressed the catastrophic nature of formative experience. He came to life again full of joy and strength renewed, and saw that he would have to accept his life as it was, not as he would wish it to be. In a final sequence (the rapturous tone of which supported the idea of resurrection), all the characters except The Ideal (who had been rejected) joined hands round a circus ring with Guido as ring-master. Guido had failed to make his film, but Fellini, whom Guido represented, had brought his to a triumphal conclusion. There was therefore suggested the concept that creativity in man is not separate from renunciation and defeat, but that these are woven into its very substance. That a theme so profound should be embodied in a work so richly entertaining was in itself a true expression of Fellini's complex nature.

In *8½* Fellini worked with an absolute freedom among his own imagery, and brought to a perfected form many of the inventions that he had developed over the years, and that, having perfected, he now discarded. *Juliet of the Spirits (Giulietta degli spiriti,* 1965), his first full-length colour film, marked a new beginning. The third of the Masina films, it needs to be seen in the context of the other two rather than with its immediate predecessor, *8½.* It was a static and descriptive film, concerned with Giulietta's state of mind, not with her activities, and the other characters, though substantially present in the narrative, nevertheless embodied different aspects of Giulietta's personality and problems.

With *Satyricon* (1969), again in colour, Fellini achieved a long-cherished ambition to reach back to pre-Christian times for a moral

Otto e mezzo

Giulietta degli spiriti

schema owing nothing to the traditional framework of Western behaviour. It also allowed him to plan the visual appearance of the film
on principles of pure fantasy, while keeping the characters aggressively
real. It was the first film for which neither Pinelli nor Flaiano had
worked on the script with the director himself. *sb*

The Fifties and the early Sixties witnessed a tremendous expansion
in the Italian film industry brought about by a systematic policy of co-
production with other European countries and with America. Between
1950 and 1963 Italy produced 872 co-productions, of which 656 were
with France, 114 with Spain and 30 with Germany. American producers increasingly found Italy a cheaper place than Hollywood for
mounting elaborate productions such as *Ben-Hur* (1959, *dir* William
Wyler) and *Cleopatra* (1963, *dir* Joseph Mankiewicz), and a number
of American actors took up residence in Italy.

With the Neo-realist movement, one of the particular strengths of
the Italian cinema has been its strong connections with a critical tradition. In general, the Fifties were characterised by a less committed, and
more commercial kind of cinema with such directors as Bolognini
and Germi, than were the Sixties. Directors such as Pasolini, Pontecorvo and Rosi who emerged in the early Sixties, showed themselves to be highly committed film-makers with a strong social consciousness; in addition their concern with the role of the film-maker in
Italian society, which is still to some extent an under-developed society, led them to question the whole Neo-realist tradition. **Pier Paolo
Pasolini** (*b* 1922), one of the cinema's major theoreticians as well as
a film-maker, was the most important director to emerge during this
period. A poet, philosopher, essayist and novelist, Pasolini had already
become an established cultural figure in Italy before turning to the
cinema. He began his film career by scripting a number of films for
Bolognini, Fellini and others. His first two films, *Accattone* (1961)
and *Mamma Roma* (1962) were documentary in their approach to
their subject matter, low-life in the Rome slums, and both showed
strong attachment to the peasantry which characterises all his later
work. Although Pasolini is a convinced Marxist, his attitude to the
peasantry is basically romantic, and often in conflict with Marxist
ideology; his concern with the spirituality of the peasantry and the
need to restore a sense of the supernatural to life indicate his strong
Catholic heritage, although he is a professed atheist. After making two
episode films, *La ricotta* (1962) and *La rabbia* (1963), and a film
Comizi d'amore in 1964 which has rarely been shown, he proceeded
to shoot his most ambitious film to date, *The Gospel according to St.
Matthew* (*Il Vangelo Secondo Matteo*, 1964), in which Pasolini examines the text of St. Matthew's Gospel in terms of myth. Set in Southern Italy, Pasolini's approach is almost documentary, making use of

non-professional actors and *cinéma-vérité*-type camera work. The result is not, as one would expect from a Marxist, a critique of Christianity, but a compelling account of the power of Christian myth. After making a comparatively minor film (*Uccellacci e uccellini*) in 1966 and two more episode films, *Le streghe* and *Capriccio all'Italiana*, he returned to the subject of myth with *Oedipus Rex* (*Edipo Re*) in 1967, a re-interpretation of Sophocles in terms of Freud. The film opens with memories of childhood, in which the mother is seen as the focal point of the child's existence; the film then moves into Sophocles's version of the myth which Pasolini sets in a kind of pre-historic location that suggests the wholly irrational world of the Unconscious. The theme of sex dominates *Teorema*, made in 1968, which is the first film Pasolini has made depicting bourgeois life. In it he traces the gradual disintegration of a bourgeois family which is brought about by the arrival of an outsider to whom they feel themselves drawn sexually. The father gives away his factory to his workers and strips off and wanders through a railway station, while the maid is levitated and later buried as a saint.

Rosi   **Francesco Rosi** (*b* 1922) is a director with a less equivocal approach to the cinema of commitment. Originally a stage producer, Rosi served his apprenticeship as an assistant director under Visconti. The legacy of Neo-realism is clearly visible in his films, particularly in his use of non-professional actors whenever possible. However, Rosi's approach to his subject differs radically from the Neo-realists; instead of applying a story to existing reality, Rosi attempts an analysis of society from which he then derives a story. In this way, the cinema becomes a

Mafia in the mountains. Rosi's SALVATORE GIULIANO

way of analysing social problems. The first feature films which Rosi controlled completely as a director were both gangster films: *La sfida* (1958) was concerned with Mafia activities in Naples, and *I magliari* (1959) was the story of a group of Italian gangsters who live by selling faulty goods to German housewives in Hamburg. It was with *Salvatore Giuliano* in 1962 that Rosi came to be recognised as a director of importance. The film focuses on the guerilla activities of the Sicilian folk hero and outlaw Salvatore Giuliano, his involvement with the Mafia and his eventful murder by the authorities who had no further use for him. Rosi approaches the narration obliquely, interleaving Giuliano's guerilla activities with his laying out and burial, using a series of flashbacks, and thus achieving a real sense of the complexity of events. The highly stylised use of figures in landscape, shot in high contrast black-and-white, achieves an epic quality. One of Rosi's outstanding achievements as a film-maker is that he succeeds in being polemical and at the same time objective, which is particularly striking in his next film *Le mani sulla città* (*Hands over the City*, 1963), a story of corruption in city administration, which describes the activities of a group of business men towards changing a town planning scheme for their own interests. The story is again set in the south, in Naples, and once more Rosi's commitment to the Left does not prevent him from being analytical and objective. In *Il momento della verità* (*The Moment of Truth*, 1965) Rosi takes bull-fighting as his subject, and makes as striking a use of colour as he had formerly with black-and-white. The film accompanies the rise of a *torero* from a poor farming district to the arena, and his eventual death there, and Rosi's main interest centres round the ritual of the arena itself and the part it plays in influencing collective behaviour. The commercial failure of the film undermined Rosi's freedom in the Italian cinema, and *C'era una volta* (*Cinderella-Italian Style*, 1967) a fairy tale set in mediaeval Spain starring Sophia Loren, was made largely out of commercial expediency. Meanwhile, a number of projects have failed to materialise, among them a film about Che Guevara.

Quite clearly both Pasolini and Rosi have extended and re-defined the Neo-realist tradition. **Gillo Pontecorvo** (*b* 1919) is another director seeking to achieve this, although his earlier films, especially *Kapo* (1965), a psychological study of life in a concentration camp, were fairly traditional in their approach to their subject matter. However, *La battaglia di Algeri* (*The Battle of Algiers*, 1966), a documentary reconstruction of the events leading up to the independence of Algeria, making use of non-professional actors from Algiers, is a most remarkable film, a triumphant but objective celebration of historical events by people actively involved in it. Among the more traditional film-makers, **Ermanno Olmi** (*b* 1931) is perhaps the most outstanding. Olmi began his career by making industrial shorts with a group of film-makers in Milan, and his first fictional film, a short, *Il tempo si e fermato* (*Time Stood Still*, 1959), the story of two men cut off in the snow in the Bergamo valleys, was remarkable for its minute observation of detail and its psychological insight. *Il posto* (*The Job*, 1961) was perhaps Olmi's most important film, the bitter-sweet account of a young man from the suburbs who goes to Milan to find a job in an industrial firm. *I fidanzati* (*The Fiancés*, 1962) studied adult life and the attempt to find some kind of lasting relationship. After making an uncharacteristic and rather pedestrian life of Pope John with *E venne un uomo* (*A Man Called John*, 1964) Olmi came into his own again with *Un certo giorno* (*One Fine Day*, 1969) in which he traces the efforts of a top executive to take over the main job in his firm. Olmi's observation of his characters is extremely complex and subtle, and his exploration of the machinations of office life possess a sense of the absurd that takes his work far beyond its surface realism. **Valerio Zurlini** (*b* 1926) is a traditionalist in the best sense of the word. He began his career in documentaries, and his three most outstanding films are *L'estate violente* (*Violent Summer*, 1959), *La ragazza con la valigia* (*Girl with a Suitcase*, 1960) and *Cronaca familiare* (*Family Diary*, 1962). Zurlini is a humanist with considerable psychological insight. *L'estate violente* is set at the time of the fall of Mussolini in 1943, and describes the relationship between the widow of an officer killed in action and the son of a Fascist official and their attempt to escape from the reality of the war. *La ragazza con la valigia* analyses a similarly incongruous relationship; that between a respectable bourgeois young man and a Milanese chorus girl. *Cronaca familiare*, based

The opening sequence of Olmi's I FIDANZATI

on a novel by Vasco Pratolini, is perhaps Zurlini's most accomplished work, and one of his most complex, in which he uncovers the history of a family by using the device of an elder brother recounting the story to a younger brother who has died. Zurlini's controlled use of the second person narrative achieves an atmosphere of great intimacy and intensity. **Elio Petri** (*b* 1929), formerly a critic and scriptwriter, is a director with diverse talents. His first feature *L'assassino* (1960) gained him instant critical recognition, and his next picture, *I giorni contali* (1962) conveyed a similar sense of moral disquiet in its study of a metal worker who becomes obsessed with death after witnessing an accident, and his attempt to imbue his life with some meaning. Petri's examination of the themes of loneliness and despair is a highly sensitive one, and the fact that he chooses a working class milieu marks it out from other films on this theme. *La decima vittima* (1965), perhaps Petri's finest film, is entirely different in tone; a social satire realised in terms of science fiction, it poses a battle of the sexes, which is organised by computer, making use of a vast arsenal of futuristic weaponry. **Marco Ferreri** (*b* 1928) is a director who also excels at this kind of highly stylised comedy. He began his career as the producer of *Amore in città* and worked for some years in Spain where he made the black comedy, *El Cochecito* (*The Wheelchair*, 1959). One of Ferreri's principal themes is the emasculation of men by women, which he explores in *L'ape regina* (*Queen Bee*, 1963) and in his recent film, *Dillinger ē morto* (*Dillinger Is Dead*, 1969), a remarkable film, which depicts a man totally imprisoned by consumer society to the

Italy

147

point that he murders his wife with the same finesse as he prepares his gourmet dinner. Ferreri is totally iconoclastic and is undoubtedly one of the masters of black humour. His *Seed of Man* (*Il seme dell'uomo,* 1969) has further proved his ability to use an isolated group of people to pass trenchant comment on the modern world.

Among the young directors who have emerged in the Sixties, **Marco Bellocchio** (*b* 1940) and **Bernardo Bertolucci** (*b* 1940) are outstanding. Bellocchio began his career in 1965 with *I pugni in tasca* (*Fists in the Pocket*), a story of a family of epileptics set in the bourgeois, provincial milieu. It is a powerful and deeply disturbing film, in which Bellocchio uses epilepsy as a metaphor for the frustration of the young when confronted with adult society. His next film, *La Cina e vicina* (*China Is Near,* 1967), continued this criticism of the bourgeois family, but this time in terms of satire. Bertolucci worked as Pasolini's assistant on *Accattone,* and his first film *La commare secca* (*The Grim Reaper,* 1962), based on Pasolini's script, was an extraordinarily accomplished first film, using non-professional actors, which described a murder investigation. His next film, *Prima della rivoluzione* (*Before the Revolution,* 1964) is set in a bourgeois milieu, and depicts the efforts of a young bourgeois, Fabrizio, to become a revolutionary, and his inability to do so. Bertolucci sees the rationality of the bourgeoisie as the main obstacle to be overcome. In his next film, *Partner* (1968), he explored the possibilities of luxurious colour, looking in great depth at the questions raised by *Prima della rivoluzione* (the possibility of revolution and the relationship between art and life) in his study of a drama teacher in Rome, who seeks to carry the Theatre of Cruelty to its ultimate conclusion. But if *Partner* was too submerged in admiration for Godard, *Il conformista* and *The Spider's Strategy* (*Strategia del ragno,* both 1970) brought Bertolucci to the forefront of world cinema and demonstrated his extraordinarily versatile command of film style. *The Spider's Strategy* recalled *Senso* with its sumptuous, summery visuals and a sense of high tragedy as a young man discovers that his father's anti-Fascist heroism was worthless, while *Il conformista* penetrated the complex and ambivalent mind of a hired assassin (Jean-Louis Trintignant), recapturing the dying Thirties in a series of masterly flashbacks.

The impact of television in the late Fifties led to a growing awareness on the part of producers of the need to counteract the trend in declining audiences by revitalising the spectacle film which had always been popular with audiences in the past, making full use of the potentialities of scope and colour. The peplum and costume film which had always been popular with audiences were joined by the Western and horror *genres* to form a thriving popular cinema attracting a great variety of talents. **Mario Bava** (*b* 1914), often working under the pseudonyms of "John M. Old" or "John Foam," is perhaps Italy's most

Jean-Louis Trintignant in Bertolucci's IL CON- FORMISTA

important horror master. Originally a lighting cameraman, Bava's films achieve a highly atmospheric, classic Gothicism. The finest examples of his work are *La maschera del demonio* (*Black Sunday*, 1960), a story of mediaeval witchcraft, *Sei donne per l'assassino* (*Blood and Black Lace*, 1964), a modern horror story, and *Terrore nello spazio* (*Planet of the Vampire*, 1965), a science fiction horror story. The Egyptian **Riccardo Freda** (*b* 1909) is distinguished both for his films in the horror *genre* and for his work in the peplum, having made a number of films in the "Maciste" cycle. *Lo Spettro* (1962) is perhaps his finest horror film. **Domenico Paolella** (*b* 1915) has made a notable contribution to the peplum *genre,* having made a number of films in the "Hercules" and "Maciste" cycles, together with a quite extraordinary film *Prigioniere dell'isola del diavolo* (1961), the story of a group of women imprisoned on an island. Perhaps the *genre* which has had more impact outside Italy is the Italian Western. The trilogy of **Sergio Leone** (*b* 1926) *Per un pugno di dollari* (*A Fistful of Dollars*, 1964), *Per qualche dollaro in piu* (*For a Few Dollars More*, 1965) and *Il buono, il brutto, il cattivo* (*The Good, the Bad and the Ugly*, 1966) are particularly notable, and representative of the *genre,* which is often highly critical of the American ideology, placing great emphasis on the brutality of the Wést and the importance money played in shaping its value system. Among directors of historical costume dramas, **Vittorio Cottafavi** (b 1914) reigns supreme. Cottafavi began his film career working as an assistant to Blasetti and De Sica. His most outstanding film is *I centro cavalieri* which he made in 1964, describing the wars between the Castilians and the invading Moors in 1000 A.D., making full and dramatic use of colour, and displaying a fine sense of low comedy. *cj*

5. Germany and Austria

GERMANY

A REVIVAL IN THE FORTUNES of the German film was out of the question in 1945. In fact certain tendencies from the Goebbels period continued, and right into the Fifties many German films were mere *apologia* for the behaviour of the German people under the Third Reich; they deplored the violation of the individual by an anonymous Destiny, and boasted heroes who had "kept their hands clean." Only in the work of **Wolfgang Staudte** (*b* 1906) was there any critical comment on the immediate past. Staudte, who had begun his career under Hitler with some innocuous comedies, shot the first German postwar film, *The Murderers Are among Us* (*Die Mörder sind unter uns,* 1946). A soldier returns from the Front intent on taking revenge on an officer responsible for war crimes; but (he is a doctor) he overcomes his hatred by saving the life of a small child. The style of the film, although shot on location among the bombed streets of Berlin, was still primarily expressionistic. But Staudte improved on this with one of the best postwar German films, *Rotation* (1949). The hero works in a printing factory; after the fall of Hitler, he is pushed into a party political decision, and turns against the Nazis. *Rotation* was very symbolic, and ended after 1945 with a hope that a better society would develop in Germany. Staudte's criticism of the behaviour of the lower middle classes under National Socialism was extremely valid here, and he managed to create a strong dramatic structure for his political themes. Also excellent was his adaptation of a novel by Heinrich Mann, *Der Untertan* (1951), in which he gave a savagely satirical picture of the German underdog mentality. Until the start of the Fifties, Staudte's films were produced by the East German company DEFA. In his later work, unfortunately, Staudte has opted for uncommitted entertainment films, in spite of a few efforts at political comment such as *Roses for the Prosecutor* (*Rosen für den Staatsanwalt,* 1959), and *Herrenpartie* (1964). Staudte's re-make of *The Threepenny Opera* (*Die Dreigroschenoper,* 1963) was a failure.

Helmut Käutner's (*b* 1908) first postwar picture, *In jenen Tagen* (1947) was in stark contrast to Staudte's work, for it was typical of

150

The first postwar German film: Staudte's THE MURDERERS ARE AMONG US

the trend towards self-apology that was to dominate German production. In six episodes, linked by the story of a car that ends on the scrapheap, Käutner describes the behaviour of different types of people under Hitler. But his characters are either suffering victims or apologists, caught up in a vast machine that they cannot understand and for which they are not responsible. As imaginative and lively as *In jenen Tag* was in terms of detail, it refused to reflect critically on the past, and in parts suffered from mawkishness.

Wolfgang Liebeneiner, one of the most prominent directors of the Nazi period, made a sentimental version of Wolfgang Borchert's homecoming drama *Draussen vor der Tür* under the title of *Liebe 47* (1947). Other films tried to express contemporary criticism in the form of satire or cabaret wit (e.g. Käutner in *Der Apfel ist ab,* 1948, and R. A. Stemmle in *Berliner Ballade,* 1948).

After the few hesitant and not very profound attempts to make worthwhile contemporary pictures immediately after 1945, the German cinema sank into a long period of mediocrity, commercialism, and political conformity. This low level extended until the mid-Sixties, and

151

Bruno Schmidt and Sabine Sinjen in ES

was due in the main to the fact that 1945 did not really mark a decisive break in German social and cultural history; no new generation came forward, and there was no new sense of political consciousness. It is not worth mentioning individual German films of the Fifties (except perhaps Peter Lorre's remarkable essay in expressionism, *Der Verlorene*, 1951). The principal *genres* were the so-called "local film," which usually took place among foresters and overflowed with sentimentality, and the "doctor film," which emphasised authoritarian personalities without any hint of criticism (a major example was Rolf Hansen's *Sauerbruch—das war mein Leben*, 1954). Other films related how the innocent "little man" became the victim of a cruel story, as did Kurt Hoffmann in his overrated satire *Aren't We Wonderful?* (*Wir Wunderkinder*, 1958), and Robert Siodmak in *Mein Schulfreund* (1960). Bernhard Wicki shot in 1960 a subjective and honest anti-war film, *The Bridge* (*Die Brücke*), which was flawed by its social analysis; Rolf Thiele's *The Girl Rosemarie* (*Das Mädchen Rosemarie*, 1958) tried to criticise wealthy society but never got beyond a series of superficial and rather banal gags.

Only during the latter half of the Sixties did a revival of West German film really begin. At last a coherent group of young directors brought about a breakthrough. The first encouraging sign in the established feature film world came with *Es*, directed by Ulrich Schamoni, and *Young Törless* (*Der junge Törless*), directed by Volker Schlöndorff, in 1966. Unfortunately, although in their different ways both Schamoni and Schlöndorff showed an individual approach, they soon

abandoned their pioneering course, Schamoni settling for uncompli-
cated entertainment films and Schlöndorff shooting expensive spectaculars like *Michael Kohlhaas* (1969) for American producers.

The most significant talents in the new German cinema are **Alexander Kluge** (*b* 1932), and **Jean-Marie Straub** (*b* 1933), who is
of French origin. Kluge, who was impressive as a novelist, has brought
to the cinema an intellectual, essay form, hovering on the borderline
between fiction and documentary. *Yesterday Girl* (*Abschied von
gestern*, 1966), and *Die Artisten in der Zirkuskuppel—ratlös* (1968)
do not have an enclosed shape; instead, they remind one of mosaics that
could be extended in different directions. Although they each have a
thread of storyline—in *Yesterday Girl* the failure of Anita G. to settle
down in Western Germany, in *Die Artisten* the efforts of Leni Peickert
to reform her family circus—the appeal of the films lies in Kluge's
own contribution, his reflections and associations. These often have a
coded, symbolic form and constitute a second level in the films.

The cinema of Jean-Marie Straub is distinguished by a peculiar
mixture of asceticism, commitment, and alienation. With *Unreconciled*
(*Nicht versöhnt,* 1965), Straub made a screen version of a novel by
the contemporary author Heinrich Böll, in which the action takes place
partly during the Nazi period and partly in the present. Straub used
amateurs and let them talk in a forced, amateurish way so that the
dialogue at certain points in the film is barely comprehensible. And yet
paradoxically Straub often manages to reveal the essential truth of the
lines that his actors speak. Similarly, in *The Chronicle of Anna Magdalena Bach* (*Die Chronik der Anna Magdalena Bach,* 1968), Straub attempted to make a film about music that was completely free of all
music-film conventions. The camera remains a static onlooker while
long passages of music and monologues are performed without inter-
ruption. Straub's films have polarised the opinions of the German
critics, dividing them sharply into conservative and progressive camps.

Other able directors of the "Young German Cinema" include Edgar
Reitz (*Mahlzeiten*, 1967, and *Cardillac*, 1969); Vlado Kristl (*Der
Damm*, 1964, and *Der Brief*, 1966); and Johannes Schaaf (*Tätowie-
rung*, 1967).

Since about 1968 a number of 16mm independent productions have
started to come out of Germany, along the lines of the American underground. This movement has gained momentum and has offered a
very real alternative means of film-making to the existing production
and distribution sectors. These independent films are released through
co-operatives, and during the past two years they have come to dominate the German programmes at the Oberhausen and Mannheim festivals. Three significant names in this movement are Helmuth Costard,
Werner Nekes, and Hannes Fuchs.

From October 7, 1949, when the German Democratic Republic

DDR was inaugurated, it is no longer correct to speak of a "German" cinema. The differences between East and West Germany have become too pronounced for their films to be grouped together. DEFA became the state-owned film company in the East, but after Staudte's *Der Untertan,* it abandoned "critical realism," and concentrated on the problems of social reconstruction and the establishment of a new society. But DEFA productions showed that the artistically important ones dealt with the past, while films set in the present day tended to suffer from dogmatism and stereotyped thinking. Among the films made by DEFA during the Fifties were *Stronger than the Night (Stärker als die Nacht,* 1954, *dir* Slatan Dudow), a resistance drama set during the Nazi period, and *Berlin—Ecke Schönhauser* (1957, *dir* Gerhard Klein), a commentary on the East Berlin teddy boys, made in the style of Italian neo-realism. Several other films tried to translate the political tenets of the *régime* into cinematic terms and were artistic failures.

The key talent at DEFA during the Fifties and Sixties proved to be **Konrad Wolf** (*b* 1925, son of the dramatist Friedrich Wolf, who emigrated to the U.S.S.R. during the Nazi period). In 1957 and 1959 Wolf shot two important films, *Lissy* and *Stars (Sterne).* Both took place during the Third Reich (discussion of the Hitler epoch was pursued intensively in the East German cinema, while it was practically neglected by the West Germans), and with their sensitive characterisation and critical perception they remain the most impressive products of the postwar period in either Germany.

Wolf's *Divided Sky (Der geteilte Himmel,* 1964) was significant

Konrad Wolf's DIVIDED SKY, with Renate Blume and Eberhard Esche

for it dealt with the division of Germany (a subject rarely touched by DEFA productions) and was entirely free of dogmatism. The style of the film was individualistic and up-to-date, its dramatic structure based on a brilliant montage of action scenes.

In 1965 several "self-critical" films at DEFA were suddenly banned, and a new period of rigidity set it. Even Wolf's *Ich war 19* (1968) seemed colourless compared to his earlier films. *ug*

AUSTRIA

At the end of the war and after the destruction of Nazi Germany, Austria was occupied and divided among the Allies. The partly damaged studios and companies were confiscated and looted. A paradox now emerged. Any new and independent Austrian film industry would have to start from scratch. The studios were in disarray, and the best talents had gone abroad. But political and economic factors were all in favour of an Austrian film renaissance, for there was no production whatsoever in Germany, and therefore no competition, while money was plentiful in a time of speculation and black marketeering.

Unfortunately the personality to use, unite, and organise these favourable factors, was missing. Numerous private companies shot up, produced a few cheap and meretricious quickies, and then sank into oblivion. The first postwar Austrian film, *The Long Road* (*Der weite Weg*), was completed in 1946, with the help of the occupying forces, followed a little later by *Believe in Me* (*Glaube an Mich*), with the help of the Americans, and from then onwards the number of features increased year by year (1946: 4, 1951: 28, 1956: 37 films). Not many

Helmut Käutner's THE LAST BRIDGE, with Tilla Durieux and Maria Schell

155

of these were very notable. Pabst's *The Trial* (*Der Prozess*, 1948) and *The Last Act* (*Der letzte Akt*, 1955), together with Helmut Käutner's *The Last Bridge* (*Die letzte Brücke*, 1954), were probably the last Austrian films of world significance. In the meanwhile West German production grew stronger thanks to the economic "miracle" and imposed its distribution laws and taste on the Austrian industry. With the appearance of television and the consequent loss to the cinema (1958: 16,324 TV sets—1968: over one million), the continual drift towards Socialism, and the rising cost of living, it was hardly surprising that a crisis arose. Cinemas were forced to close, and production in the late Sixties came almost to a standstill (only seven features in 1968). The continuing quarrels within the state department for film have frustrated various timid attempts to improve the situation, and to all intents and purposes the Austrian film no longer exists. *gd*

6. Scandinavia

ALTHOUGH SWEDEN was not directly involved in the Second World War, she was stirred by it morally and emotionally, and the year 1939 marked the renaissance of the Swedish film after nearly two decades of mediocrity. Alf Sjöberg returned to direction with *They Staked Their Lives* (*Med livet som insats*, 1939), while **Anders Henrikson** (1896–1965), who acted in this film, completed a bitter study of young love that ended with a suicide, entitled *A Crime* (*Ett brott*, 1940) and symbolised the new generation's disgust with its elders' flippancy.

So the ground was prepared for a series of pessimistic films that ran parallel in many respects to the disenchanted novels of Stig Dagerman and other members of that group of writers known as *fyrtitalisterna*, whose anguished despair still evokes the decade strongly. There were, of course, by contrast the bucolic comedies of **Edvard Persson** (1888–1957) and the rather less rumbustious and more Chaplinesque films of the clown **Nils Poppe** (*b* 1908), such as *Money* (*Pengar*, 1946), *The Balloon* (*Ballongen*, 1946), and *Private Bom* (*Soldat Bom*, 1948, *dir* Lars-Eric Kjellgren). But more characteristic of the period were the works of **Erik "Hampe" Faustman** (1919–1961), Sjöberg, and Ingmar Bergman.

Faustman's most significant film was *Foreign Harbour* (*Frammande hamn*, 1948), which showed how anti-Fascist feelings were deep-rooted in the working classes of Sweden, and concentrated its action in a Baltic port where munitions for General Franco's forces were being smuggled aboard a cargo ship without the crew's knowledge. For many

Swedish critics, Faustman was the only really committed film-maker of the Forties, although like all propagandist art his films have dated badly. Faustman's fear of Naziism was mirrored in other films, notably *Frenzy/Torment* (*Hets,* 1944), the famous study of school life scripted by Bergman and directed by Sjöberg.

Frenzy can now be seen as the seminal film of the Forties in Sweden. It not only launched Bergman on his career (he began directing a year later, with *Kris*), but it also established Alf Kjellin and Mai Zetterling as the major romantic stars of their generation. They were teamed again, most successfully, in Sjöberg's *Iris and the Lieutenant* (*Iris och löjtnantshjärta,* 1946) which dwelt with charm and nostalgia on the clash between youth and age in a large bourgeois family. Miss Zetterling soon emigrated to England where she worked under contract to the Rank Organisation, and Kjellin moved to Hollywood later in his career.

Apart from the comedies, there was one worthy attempt to escape from the drab naturalism of Forties cinema in Sweden. Alf Sjöberg's *The Road to Heaven* (*Himlaspelet,* 1942) was a brilliant re-creation of life in the country area of Dalarna during the Eighteenth century, and had the tone of a *Pilgrim's Progress* as it followed the pious and agreeably naïve Mats Ersson on his quest for God.

Beneath the theatrical finesse of his direction, Sjöberg was a reformer at heart, and in *Only a Mother* (*Bara en mor,* 1949) and *Miss Julie* (*Fröken Julie,* 1951) he laid stress on the social tensions still latent in Swedish life. The Social Democrats took a long time to

ALF SJÖBERG

Alf Kjellin and Mai Zetterling in Sjöberg's IRIS AND THE LIEUTENANT

157

change the conditions of many families in rural Sweden, and the gipsy-like labourers in *Only a Mother* were born, and died, in poverty during the Forties. Eva Dahlbeck's performance as Rya-Rya, the attractive young maid who is urged towards an early death by physical toil and child bearing, was one of the best of the decade.

In *Miss Julie,* Sjöberg for once avoided the theatrical antecedents of his subject, and this screen version of Strindberg's play flowed from start to finish with an urgency uninterrupted by clumsy exits and entrances, long monologues or verbal reminiscences. Sjöberg used flashbacks boldly and imaginatively, sometimes even showing two scenes in a single frame, when, for example, *Miss Julie* recalled her childhood in the arms of her lover (a device used similarly by Elia Kazan in *The Arrangement*). The film suggested that the frustrations of Miss Julie and her lover stemmed from the rigid social structure in which they lived, their tragedy being perhaps in Sjöberg's eyes more Marxist than Freudian in its overtones.

But Sjöberg had passed his peak. His films of the Fifties and Sixties were mostly unimpressive except on a purely formal level. There were moments of expertise and truth in *Barabbas* (1953), an elaboration of Pär Lagerkvist's novel about the fate of the thief released when Jesus was crucified, and in *Karin Månsdotter* (1954), the central inspiration of which was Strindberg's *Erik XIV.* But a certain heaviness in the atmosphere, and a stiff quality in the playing, tended to mar the total effect; and in *Wild Birds* (*Vildfåglar,* 1955), *The Judge* (*Domaren,* 1960), and *The Island* (*Ön,* 1966), Sjöberg's characterisation came close to caricature. In these later films, his technical assurance could not disguise the banality and the implausibility of the material. At his best, Sjöberg was the equal of Bergman and Stiller. But, as his 1969 version of Strindberg's *The Father* (*Fadern*), suggested, he was never happier and never more reliable than when re-creating a play on film.

INGMAR BERGMAN

Ingmar Bergman (*b* 1918), however, even in his early period, was rarely at ease when translating the work of others to the screen. He was eager to fashion his own world of the imagination, to use settings and plots that could accommodate his complexes and frustrations without being weighed down by the details of everyday urban life. Bergman began in the theatre, and still retains a lively affection for it (he was Head of the Royal Dramatic Theatre in Stockholm from 1963 to 1966), but his films have a dimension of fantasy denied to the stage. The most incisive weapon in his cinematic armoury, the close-up, is impossible in the theatre, and it is this recurrent use of close-ups that enables Bergman to communicate with his audience so intimately and so tangibly.

His early work, in the Forties, much encouraged by the enlightened head of Svensk Filmindustri, Carl Anders Dymling, continued in the same vein as *Frenzy*. His heroes were bitter young men, fiercely reluctant to come to terms with the adult world and to accept the illusions that sustained older figures like Captain Blom, the contemptuous bluffer in *A Ship Bound for India* (*Skepp till Indialand,* 1947), or the old actor Mikael Bro in *To Joy* (*Till glädje,* 1950). Reacting strongly against the stern upbringing of his parents, Bergman seemed forced to make films quickly and urgently. Between 1945 and 1950 he completed eight features, and scripted three films for other directors.

The tormented romanticism of these early years was tempered by Bergman's description of his lovers' predicament. The opening scene of *Thirst/Three Strange Loves* (1949), with Bertil and Rut in a hotel room in Basle, conveyed with tactile force the stale quality of a marriage once the first pleasure of love has gone. There was a sense of imprisonment, summarised in one of the closing pieces of dialogue, "Hell together is better than hell alone." Bergman's men and women have clung together in a hostile world because they cannot face solitude, that awful penalty to which Isak Borg is condemned in his nightmare in *Wild Strawberries*. "True aloneness is a juggling act, and behind it lurks a constant fear," says Greta Ellius to her maudlin sister-in-law in *So Close to Life,* and the search for companionship is the principal thread in all Bergman's films. Most of his early heroes quickly rejected the idea of God as a soulmate. In *Prison/The Devil's Wanton* (*Fängelse,* 1949), an old teacher suggests to a film director that he make a picture about Hell, Hell on earth. A journalist friend (played by Birger Malmsten, Bergman's *alter ego* of the period) thinks that he knows the ideal heroine for such a film, and *Prison* is largely concerned with the relationship between these two outsiders, the man cynical and world-weary, the girl frail and exploited. At the end, the director tells his teacher that the picture cannot be made, because it would have to assume a belief in God. "As one no longer believes, there is no point to it at all." But this epigrammatic conclusion (a familiar feature of Bergman's films) is less significant than the encounter between Tomas, the journalist, and Birgitta-Carolina, the girl. Only in each other's company could these two creatures of circumstance find a brief flash of happiness, a happiness all the more poignant for being so transitory.

The evanescent joy so keenly sought by the Bergman hero was most lyrically expressed in *Summer Interlude/Illicit Interlude* (*Sommarlek,* 1951), Bergman's first masterpiece. Summer for the Swedes is a time of pleasure, a relief from the long, dark winter months, and a season that can be identified—more so than in any other country—with life's brightest phase. It is only by re-living a distant summer of happiness with her dead lover, Henrik, that the ballerina, Marie, can banish her suffering and her depression. *Summer Interlude* may have been a film about disenchantment, but its joyful moments were registered by Bergman with complete spontaneity and a deeply-felt passion. Here too the close-up was used to searching effect, forcing the spectator to identify with Marie's anguish as, seated before the mirror in her dressing room, she removed her eye-lashes almost as if she were peeling away the grimy untruths that had dogged her since Henrik's death.

Summer with Monika (Sommaren med Monika, 1953) was another essay in this *genre,* but the tone was naturalistic rather than romantic. With its depiction of a relationship founded solely on sexual attraction, *Summer with Monika* was the first of Bergman's films to earn a reputation abroad for "frankness," and it established Harriet Andersson as an erotic symbol comparable to Brigitte Bardot later in the decade. Bergman was obviously convinced that the woman was the dominant partner in any union of the sexes. Harriet Andersson, Eva Dahlbeck, Bibi Andersson, Ingrid Thulin, Liv Ullmann—each of these actresses has played honest, uninhibited, basically stable women in Bergman's cinema, to whom their male counterparts have turned for maternal affection, sexual fulfilment, or intellectual stimulus. Several of Bergman's films have viewed life through female eyes: *Waiting Women/Secrets of Women (Kvinnors väntan,* 1952), *Journey into Autumn/Dreams (Kvinnodröm,* 1955), *So Close To Life/Brink of Life (Nära livet,* 1958), *The Silence (Tystnaden,* 1963), and *Persona* (1966).

Bergman certainly does not share the misogynistic outlook of Strindberg. He sympathises with his women in their encounters with men who are stupid and insufferably egotistical. In *The Silence,* the sisters

Harriet Andersson with Hasse Ekman in SAWDUST AND TINSEL

react in different ways to a world in which men seem necessary but incapable of rational thought: Anna takes a waiter to her bed while Ester masturbates, and is ministered to by an aged *maître d'hôtel*. In *So Close to Life,* the men seem to blame for the troubles of the three women in the maternity ward. One is cold and insensitive, another is overweening and complacent, and the third, unseen, speaks viciously to the girl he has made pregnant. In Bergman's eyes, a woman's behaviour is naturally instinctual; paradoxically, her life moves with a surer logic than her male counterpart's. In *Journey into Autumn,* a film rich in melancholy, both girls, Doris and Susanne, are elated and disillusioned by men during a day trip to Göteborg. Susanne finds that her lover cringes before the withering scorn of his wife; Doris, at first fascinated and touched by the attentions of the elderly Consul, slowly grows aware of his pitifully limited outlook. Such self-preoccupation is a common failing of the artist, and no film-maker is more self-contemptuous than Bergman. His artist-figures are unique in modern cinema, uncertain of their own calling, emotionally weak, spiritually terrified. They perform against their will; they are greeted with silence and dislike when they communicate an unpalatable truth, and they are ridiculed and humiliated when they fail. Bergman has often used circus or vaudeville metaphors to describe this experience (the artist walking a tightrope, etc.) and in *Sawdust and Tinsel/The Naked Night* (*Gycklarnas afton,* 1953), he brought to life a circus milieu. In a brief, twenty-four hour span, Albert Johansson perceives not only his miserable ineptitude as an entertainer, but also his need for companionship. It is a journey towards self-discovery, a process that may be discerned in nearly all Bergman's major works. The protagonist travels geographically, but more often than not he moves in a circle, returning whence he left—Albert's caravans trundling through the dawn, Anna and Johan in the train once more at the close of *The Silence,* Elisabet Vogler and Alma locked in the hospital yet again at the end of *Persona.* This outward and visible journey always hints at an inner, spiritual progression. Nowhere is this more deftly realised than in *Wild Strawberries* (*Smultronstället,* 1957), in which the distinguished old professor, Isak Borg, is forced to re-live elements of his past in dream form. Slowly his veneer of self-complacency slips away, until in the final scene he can return to his childhood and see his parents waving gently to him on an idyllic shore. It is only by casting aside all pretensions that the Bergman protagonist can achieve a degree of purity; if not quite the "grace" of a Bresson hero, at least a kind of reconciliation with life. That this is a profound need is suggested in the words of Frost, the clown, towards the end of *Sawdust and Tinsel,* as he tells Albert that in his dreams his wife had told him to crawl into her stomach, and there he shrank and shrank until he was only a small foetal seed. This image is evoked in the last moments of *Shame*

(*Skammen,* 1968), as Jan and Eva, marooned in the Baltic, drift away from civilisation until their boat is merely a speck in the vast sea.

These several themes, recurring in various forms in nearly all Bergman's films, have ensured his stature as an artist with a world-view very much his own. Oblivious to social change around him, he has persisted in studying the problems of the individual rather than the community; he has remained an outsider in a period when nearly all the world's leading directors have declared their left-wing sympathies. The salvation of one man's soul is infinitely more important to Bergman than the plight of a city or a nation, and it is perhaps on account of this that his work has a dignity and a respect for human complexes not often found in contemporary cinema.

During the Sixties, Bergman turned more and more towards the intimate drama, what he calls "chamber cinema," in which the characters are restricted in number to three or four. His style, which in *The Face/The Magician* (*Ansiktet,* 1958) had for many shown signs of becoming too precious and elaborate, was resolutely pruned of all decoration. The human face, not the *décor* or the setting, was the dominant feature of *Through a Glass Darkly* (*Såsom i en spegel,* 1961), *Winter Light* (*Nattvardsgästerna,* 1963), *The Silence, Persona, Hour of the Wolf* (*Vargtimmen,* 1968), and *Shame.* The face is a mask, but in even the most carefully composed mask there are points and expressions that betray the mind behind the features. Alma spends the entire time in *Persona* trying to penetrate the impassive gaze of Elisabet Vogler, the celebrated actress who has unaccountably ceased to talk. In *Through a Glass Darkly,* Gunnar Björnstrand's remarkably sensitive face seems almost perceptibly to collapse as he is confronted with the results of his selfish behaviour; an ambitious writer, he has subordinated his family to his art even to the point of using his daughter Karin's illness as a source of inspiration. The same actor, playing the minister in *Winter Light,* finds that he no longer believes in his faith, that he cannot save one of his own parishioners from committing suicide, and that his emotions are so congealed by self-deception that he cannot respond to the love of Märta Lundberg. In each of these personalities there is something of Bergman himself. "What have you done that will endure?" he has asked himself, "Is there a single metre in any one of your films that will mean anything for the future, one single line, one single situation that is completely and absolutely real?" Bergman has always posed questions; he has never preached resignation. Even in death there is some satisfaction if a man has truly come to know himself, his faults and his vagaries, his lusts and his potentialities.

Opposite: close-ups in Bergman's recent work. Bibi Andersson and Max von Sydow in A PASSION (above), and Bibi Andersson in PERSONA (below)

His most stirring film, if not his most sophisticated or pure in form, has been *The Seventh Seal (Det sjunde inseglet,* 1957), partly because its heroic Knight, Antonius Blok, is no defeatist. The events that he witnesses and the people he meets on his return from the Crusades give at last a pattern and a meaning to his wasted life. Each character in the film wears, like a pierrot or a harlequin, his sentiments on his sleeve, and offers a portion of human experience ranging from the tender to the farcical. In several unforgettable sequences, such as the procession of the flagellants and the burning of the witch, Bergman invests horror with an exquisite feeling of release, the Totentanz against a baleful sky dissolving to a sunlit shore and the Holy "Family" moving off in their wagon, sheltered from the Apocalypse by love. Behind it all one feels the presence of Bergman, who was brought up in a vicarage and was much fascinated by the medieval frescoes that lined the churches where his father preached. Like Fellini, Bergman has responded to a creative need to come to terms with this religious background, to seek—through the very act of film-making—an answer to the metaphysical questions that have haunted him. *The Seventh Seal* represented the final, magniloquent salute to a society that implicitly accepted God's existence without disputing His indifference.

Bergman's historical films are regarded with suspicion by many critics. They feel that he is dressing modern problems in medieval clothing. But the problems facing both the Knight in *The Seventh Seal* and Töre in *The Virgin Spring (Jungfrukällan,* 1960), were as severe and meaningful in the Middle Ages as they are today. Rather as an animator uses the cartoon form to express truths in terms so lucid that in a naturalistic form they would be ridiculed, so Bergman has resorted to a historical framework for some of his most probing works. Few affirmations of humanity are so directly exciting as the Knight's on leaving the confessional after talking to Death. "This is my hand. I can move it, feel the blood pulsing through it. The sun is still high in the sky and I, Antonius Blok, am playing chess with Death." But in a modern context the idiom would be unacceptable. In *The Virgin Spring,* guilt, rather than any metaphysical dilemma, was at the basis of the drama. Here was a film in which Bergman looked forward to the stark simplicity of his work in the Sixties—Fourteenth century ballad of rape and revenge rendered with a terrible beauty into cinematic form.

Bergman was involved with the cinema long before the debate over form and content arose. It is what his films say, or rather what they *imply,* that has engaged a worldwide audience, and he has almost always found a style to suit his subject-matter. There have been failures of course—*A Lesson in Love (En lektion i kärlek,* 1954) was simply not so funny as *Smiles of a Summer Night (Sommarnattens leende,* 1955) because its dialogue was robbed of pith by the uninspired set-

The dinner sequence from Bergman's SMILES OF A SUMMER NIGHT

tings and hazy characterisation. *Now about These Women* (*För att inte tala om alla dessa kvinnor,* 1964) was staged with a lavishness that would not have disgraced a Hollywood musical, but it failed because it lacked the dramatic strength and the verbal repartee to sustain its baroque imagery.

In *Smiles of a Summer Night,* however, Bergman did triumph with a delicious blend of wit and eroticism, manoeuvring his turn of the century characters like elegant puppets among the sun-dappled lawns and elaborate interiors. The familiar threats were translated into puns, the arguments into facile repartee. Bergman's women once again asserted their sophistication and their moral resilience. The hilarious finale, as Egerman, the pompous attorney, was fooled almost to death in a game of Russian roulette, suggested that Bergman was slyly aware of the illusion he had created. "I perform conjuring tricks with a conjuring apparatus so expensive and so wonderful that any performer in history would have given anything to own or to make use of it," he wrote shortly after *Smiles of a Summer Night* had won a major prize at Cannes. Both *The Seventh Seal* and *The Face* exploited to the full the illusions of the medium, with the mesmerist Albert Emanuel Vogler taking revenge on his tormentor, the sceptical Doctor Vergérus, at the end of *The Face* by means of sleight of hand and spectacular ruses.

During the Sixties, however, there were signs that Bergman came to realise the dangers of an audience's being bewitched by the medium itself, and in *Persona, Hour of the Wolf* and *A Passion* there were

Brechtian caesuras in the drama that brought the spectator up short, forcing him to confront the film both subjectively and objectively. Perhaps Bergman also sensed the arrival of a new film-going public and the departure of those who regarded the cinema as merely an entertainment.

Bergman's career has been a continual progression towards the communication of his personal views to the audience, and *Shame* was a film that avoided almost every cinematic convention. It was so lucid that Bergman's own fear of war and of his own cowardice became visible in every scene. Only in Sweden, possibly, could Bergman have achieved such chasteness of expression without compromising his work according to the dictates of the front office. He has always worked with as small a crew as possible, and his company of players appear regularly in his films (he usually writes his major roles with actors like Gunnar Björnstrand and Max von Sydow specifically in mind). Gunnar Fischer and Sven Nykvist have, between them, photographed nearly all his films. This team spirit is rarely found in the cinema industry of other countries. Bergman has always refused to work in Hollywood, to deprive himself of "that unique family feeling which is typical of film-making in Sweden." "To make films is for me a natural necessity," he has written, "a need similar to hunger and thirst. For certain people to express themselves implies writing books, climbing mountains, beating children, or dancing the samba. I express myself in making films." Discounting his extensive theatrical career, Bergman has directed over thirty films during the past twenty-five years.

During the Fifties a much more flashy director than Bergman made an impact on foreign audiences with *One Summer of Happiness* (*Hon dansade en sommar,* 1951). **Arne Mattsson** (*b* 1919) played on the summer emotions of the Swedes in this film, and, after winning a prize for the best music score (by Sven Sköld) at Cannes, *One Summer of Happiness* went on to become the biggest-grossing Swedish film ever released in North America. Full of remorseful sobbing and—for all its occasional nude scenes—a prudish attitude to sex, it dated quickly, and cannot be compared to Mattsson's three major works—*The Bread of Love* (*Kärlekens bröd,* 1953), *Salka Valka* (1954), and *The People of Hemsö* (*Hemsöborna,* 1955). In *The Bread of Love,* the evocation of a snowy corner of Finland during the Russo-Finnish war of 1941 was haunting and lastingly persuasive, with the soldiers trapped in a minefield and reacting irrationally under stress. *Salka Valka,* adapted from a major novel by Halldór Laxness, illustrated with bold, graphic ease the essential clash in the Nordic mind between religious discipline and uninhibited desire. *The People of Hemsö* was the third screen version of Strindberg's story of Mrs. Flod, the widow of Hemsö Island, whose assumed wealth provoked a jealous feud between her family and her second husband. Mattsson, using colour to emphasise the terracotta tones of the cottages and land in the archipelago, showed himself able to cope with a rollicking tale that would have resisted any heavy-handed treatment.

But Mattsson, although he has become a prolific director with over fifty features to his credit, has abandoned the very personal style he imposed on his material in the Fifties, and in the last ten years or so he has devoted himself to cheaply if cleverly made thrillers and horror films that are soon forgotten.

In 1963, with Swedish film production down to its lowest total (seventeen features) since 1930, a life-saving reform was introduced. The Swedish Film Institute was the idea of Harry Schein, and by establishing it the government in effect gave financial aid and encouragement to producers and creative directors. Under the awards system, a film considered by a jury to be of fine calibre could still recoup its costs despite a failure at the box-office. The Swedish industry could now afford to look outside its own domestic market, and a number of new directors made their *début*. In 1962–63, three figures attracted attention from critics who for nearly a decade had been used to Bergman's dominating the film scene. **Bo Widerberg** (*b* 1930), **Jörn Donner** (*b* 1933), and **Vilgot Sjöman** (*b* 1924) were all writers; each adopted a different approach to the cinema. For Widerberg, the most outspoken of the trio, it was vital to comment on Swedish society as it was at the time of filming. Bergman, with his metaphysical arguments and his allegedly Puritanical view of sex, had become a stifling influence. Widerberg set his first film *The Pram/The Baby Carriage* (*Barnvagnen,* 1963) in Malmö, where he himself had spent his youth. It was the story of a girl oscillating between two boys, the one a pop musician, the other a more complicated intellectual type. It communicated something of the feel of Sweden in the Sixties, the urban life, the ostensibly high standard of living concealing a dissatisfaction with established *moeurs,* and its style—effervescent, unrefined—was in marked contrast to the punctilious technique of Bergman and Sjöberg.

Donner's *A Sunday in September* (*En söndag i september,* 1963) also pinpointed this dissatisfaction in contemporary youth, but, probably because of its young director's background as a commentator on the political scene in Germany and elsewhere in Europe, it adopted more an international than a Swedish stance. The physical environment means little to Donner's characters. They are concerned with their emotions and their responses. There are no climaxes or glib endings in his films, but it is this deliberate rejection of conventional dramatic methods that weighs down many of them, and it was not until Donner returned to his native Finland that he was able to make a really successful box-office film (*Black on White,* 1968). He remains one of the most stimulating critics of his own and other people's work.

Vilgot Sjöman's *The Mistress* (*Älskarinnan,* 1962) looked the most

Lena Nyman with Vilgot Sjöman (also the director) in I AM CURIOUS—BLUE

ordinary of these three films, and it was hampered by a humourlessness that dogged Sjöman's films until *I Am Curious*. It was essentially a 'prentice film, banal in its subject matter (girl falling in love with married man and rejecting her regular boy friend), and only occasionally imaginative in its treatment. But the dialogue was good, and in his handling of Bibi Andersson as the girl, Sjöman showed that female characterisation was to be his *forte*. Ever eager to emphasise the taboos in Swedish society, Sjöman then made a screen version of Lars Görling's sensational book about juvenile delinquents, *491* (1964); a study of the clash between puberty and the menopause in a girl and her mother as they are attracted to the same man—*The Dress (Klänninger,* 1964); and *My Sister My Love (Syskonbädd 1782,* 1966), inspired by a fairly recent case of incest in northern Sweden where a girl gave birth to a child by her brother. This last film in particular was immaculately made, re-creating the Eighteenth century as surely as Bergman had re-created the middle ages in *The Seventh Seal.*

Sjöman had already had a sharp brush with the censorship Bureau over *491*. But it was nothing compared to the controversy arising from

I Am Curious (*Jag är nyfiken,* released in two parts, *Yellow* and *Blue,*
in 1967 and 1968), which represented something totally new in Swedish cinema. It was part *cinéma-vérité,* part comedy, and part erotica. Lena Nyman was the rebellious young blonde who questioned her fellow citizens in the street about their non-committal attitude to Vietnam, Spanish Fascism, and sexual habits. With Sjöman appearing in the picture himself, and with no attempt being made to give dramatic structure to the story, *I Am Curious* became a broadsheet, an anti-Establishment diatribe for some and a voyeuristic feast for others. It has taken its place in film history not only on account of its enormous grosses in the U.S.A. and elsewhere, but also because it virtually emasculated the role of the censor in Sweden.

The confusion in Widerberg's approach was illustrated in two films
of the Sixties: *Raven's End* (*Kvarteret Korpen,* 1963) and *Ådalen 31* (1969). Both attempted to pass comment on the social state of Sweden, and yet both sought their subject matter and their atmosphere in the Thirties, before the Social Democrats came to power. Widerberg has suggested that for all their professed determination to secure equality, the Social Democrats have not succeeded in eliminating class and monetary divisions. But the drab poverty of the working people in Malmö in 1936 (in *Raven's End*), though brilliantly evoked in filmic terms, failed to point any relevant comparison with the situation in 1963, while the oddly lyrical treatment of the strike and tragedy in the Ådalen valley in 1931 in Widerberg's film had the effect of a ballad recollected in tranquillity. It was an interesting but flawed effort to reconcile an aesthetic approach with a didactic one.

A far more harmonious film was *Elvira Madigan* (1967), in which Widerberg's talent for exquisite visual compositions was perfectly allied to his simple story of a tightrope artiste hopelessly in love with a Swedish army officer at the turn of the century. The fragile acting of Pia Degermark as Elvira made the poetry of this film unusually persuasive. It fell to pieces when sharply analysed by the critics; its beauty was something to be experienced, not aloofly observed.

Elvira Madigan might be considered the outstanding achievement of Widerberg's career, but his most underrated film is undoubtedly *Love 65* (*Kärlek 65,* 1965), in its modest and contemporary manner just as poignant as *Elvira Madigan.* Like Fellini's *8½,* it made an excellent attempt to pin down the film director's struggle to overcome his own weakness and create something firm and valuable in his art. *Love 65* was not all of a skein; it consisted of fragments of action and long stretches of improvised dialogue, some of it painfully accurate. The scenes between Keve (Keve Hjelm) and Evabritt (Evabritt Strandberg) came closer than almost any Swedish film of the Sixties to a convincing picture of infatuation.

Mai Zetterling (*b* 1925) has shown a similarly strong tendency towards social comment, but she lacks Widerberg's intuitive sense of film poetry. Her studies of female inferiority in an exclusively masculine society—such as *Loving Couples* (*Älskande par*, 1964) and *The Girls* (*Flickorna*, 1968)—were abrasive and unsympathetic despite their technical polish. An intelligent actress in her own right, Miss Zetterling has always been able to direct her female stars with aplomb. But she has not yet demonstrated that she can make a film free of false or pretentious scenes.

Troell

One of the most financially successful films of recent years in Sweden was *Here's Your Life* (*Här har du ditt liv*, 1966), which marked the feature film *début* of **Jan Troell** (*b* 1931). It ran for 167 minutes (the longest Swedish picture ever made), and was based on a four-part novel cycle by Eyvind Johnson. This extraordinarily exciting saga of a young man's coming to terms with life and human deficiencies between 1914 and 1918 had a humour and a richness that were particularly Swedish while at the same time being rare in the Swedish cinema. Troell's patient style and outlook allowed his characters to grow of their own accord as the film progressed, and the protagonist of his next work, *Who Saw Him Die?* (*Ole dole doff*, 1968), was also far from the stereotyped school master one is confronted with on the Hollywood screen. Both these pictures earned Troell several major festival awards, although they failed to yield large profits in foreign markets. With his gift for characterisation and the control of narrative pace, Troell is the most promising Swedish director since Bergman. His work is not embellished with a crusading zeal, as is Widerberg's or Zetterling's. Instead it celebrates tolerance and humour—qualities that make Swedish life less dour than it may at first appear to the foreign visitor.

Although ticket grosses and attendances began a downward drift at the end of the Sixties, the Swedish film industry remains full of talent and enthusiasm. The work of the Swedish Film Institute has brought several new directors to the fore, and has also encouraged the screening of quality films in remote areas of the country. Jan Halldoff, Kjell Grede, and Jonas Cornell have all made an auspicious start to their careers, and in Cornell's *Hugs and Kisses* (*Puss & kram*, 1967) there was a cool wit and domestic insight that recalled the comedies of Stiller. Like many another Swedish film, it stirred up censorship trouble in some countries, but during the past few years it has become clear that Sweden's frank depiction of sexual relationships on film is modest compared with the average product of the American underground cinema. It is undeniable, however, that the commercial bonanza reaped

Opposite: Swedish films of the Sixties. WHO SAW HIM DIE?, with Per Oscarsson (above left); DEAR JOHN, with Christina Schollin and Jarl Kulle (above right); and HUGS AND KISSES, with Sven Bertil Taube and Agneta Ekmanner (below)

by pictures like *Dear John* (*Käre John*, 1964, *dir* Lars-Magnus Lindgren) and *I Am Curious* has grown from their notoriety rather than from any critical acclaim. *pdc*

CARL DREYER

Between 1931 and 1964, Carl Dreyer completed only four features and a handful of documentaries and shorts. *Day of Wrath* (*Vredens dag*, 1943) was perhaps his masterpiece, the one film in which his brilliant visual sense allied surely with his interest in the human spirit. The fear of witchcraft is predominant. Anne (Lisbeth Movin) is a young girl driven inexorably to the stake by her mother-in-law's campaign in the village. From being a harmless creature, confused and then delighted by an illicit affair, Anne gradually comes to believe that she really may be a sorceress. She refuses to deny the charges against her, and the death sentence is as much a liberation—a summation—as it is a punishment.

The most successful aspect of *Day of Wrath* is its historical verisimilitude. Practically every composition has the clean, measured proportions of a Flemish painting: the white ruffs contrast sharply with the dark robes of the characters. It is a cruel film, and unashamedly so. Some of the outdoor scenes, when Anne meets her lover, are artificial and ponderous. The formal perfection seems to have produced a feeling of sterility. But these faults apart, *Day of Wrath* remains a milestone in religious cinema. The entire film is a criticism of bigotry in all its forms, showing how the spirit of persecution spread like a shadow over the lives of ordinary people during the Seventeenth century. Anne finds her simple wishes construed as evil and monstrous by her religious superiors; like Joan of Arc, she is a martyr to intolerance.

A year later Dreyer made *Two People* (*Två människor*, 1945) in Sweden, but it was a failure because, according to Ib Monty, "Dreyer was unable to get the actors he wanted. In many respects it caricatures his style." Then came a decade of shorts and documentaries, among which *They Caught the Ferry* (*De nåede faergen*, 1948) was outstanding. Ostensibly a road safety film, this short contained an atmosphere as chilling and sinister as *Vampyr*'s. A couple on a motor-bike rush across the narrow road of a Danish peninsula from one ferry to another and are involved in a crash with an old car. The *frissons* included a sudden glimpse of the clothed skeleton at the wheel of the car and the sight of the bodies floating insubstantially beneath the surface of the water as the ferry leaves without them.

In *The Word* (*Ordet*, 1955), winner of the Leone d'Oro at Venice, Dreyer brought to Kaj Munk's play a dimension of simplicity very much his own. There was, as always in Dreyer, a clash between goodness and evil, between the pharisaical "death-seeking" sect and the "life-affirming" sect of the little village in Jutland. Justification by faith produced the miracle at the close of the film when Inger, the wife who had died in childbirth, was brought back to life. Dreyer's single-mindedness prevented him from amending and developing his style through the years. The stolid dialogue sequences of *The Word* were no different to those of *Mikaël*, made some thirty years earlier, and it was this enclosed, theatrical quality that made it appear archaic.

Ten years later, *Gertrud* (1964) enraged a generation weaned on the footloose antics of Godard, and its world *première* in Paris represented a personal catastrophe for Dreyer. Gertrud was the last of the memorable feminine personalities in Dreyer's world, trying to revive a lost love affair and assert a hold over a man's life, and finally retiring into isolation.

Dreyer died before he could embark on the filming of his script on the life of Christ, and his project for a screen version of Medea also came to nothing. His small but very consistent body of work is pessimistic in the way that Pascal meant when he wrote, "We search for happiness, yet we find only misery and death." This capacity for encountering and accepting pain in his heroes and heroines is perhaps identifiable with the capacity for attaining salvation—the stake, like the Cross, is the place where love is victorious over evil. Dreyer's style has been compared to that of Bosch, Vermeer, Racine, and Uccello, and he will be remembered most of all for his tireless examination of the human face, and his revelation and grasp of the spirit that lies behind it.

Since the war, few Danish films have achieved an international reputation. The country produces about twenty features a year plus a considerable number of shorts and documentaries, but most of these are for domestic consumption, including a high proportion of bawdy

*Gunnel Lindblom
and Per
Oscarsson in
Henning
Carlsen's
HUNGER*

173

comedies starring local favourites like **Dirch Passer** (*b* 1926). **Lau Lauritzen, jr.** (*b* 1910) surprised critics at the first Cannes Festival with *The Red Earth* (*De røde enge,* 1945), a taut and intelligent story of the Resistance during the German occupation. **Bjarne** (*b* 1908) and **Astrid** (*b* 1914) **Henning-Jensen** made a notable contribution to the postwar industry in Denmark. Together they shot several documentaries, as well as features like *Man's Daughter* (*Ditte Menneskebarn,* 1946) and *Palle Alone in the World* (*Palle alene i verden,* 1949), which dealt sympathetically with the problems of childhood and adolescence. The Henning-Jensens have also made some films separately.

With the help of the Danish Film Foundation, established in 1965 to help finance worthwhile productions, some interesting new names have appeared. **Henning Carlsen** (*b* 1927) enjoyed his greatest success with *Hunger* (*Sult,* 1966), an immaculate, unflinching film of Knut Hamsen's book about a starving author in Nineteenth century Oslo. **Palle Kjaerulff-Schmidt** (*b* 1931) became an assistant director in 1954, and, working with the scriptwriter Klaus Rifbjerg, he made some valuable features during the Sixties. *Once There Was a War* (*Der var engang en krig,* 1966) was a thoroughly engaging and generous evocation of the life and fantasies of a fifteen-year-old boy during the Nazi occupation. In a tender but never sentimental way, this film emphasised Kjaerulff-Schmidt's gift for directing players in humdrum settings.

Sven Grønlykke's *The Windmills* (*Balladen om Carl-Henning,* 1969) was hailed as a breakthrough by many Danish critics, and symbolised the determination of a new generation of producers to cater for an international market.

Jorgen Roos (*b* 1922), whose ethnological films about Greenland and the Faro Islands are reminiscent of Flaherty in their warmth and directness, is the ablest of the Danish documentarists. He was Dreyer's cameraman on *They Caught the Ferry. pdc*

During the German occupation, Leif Sinding blotted his reputation by accepting the job of Director of the Norwegian Film Industry, and for a long period after the war he was unable to work in the cinema. In 1953 he returned with *Selkvinnen,* but this and his later films were spoilt by a bitterness and a vein of hypocrisy that had not been evident in his prewar work.

From 1940 onwards there were hopes of improving the Norwegian film situation. Directors like Toralf Sando, Walter Fyrst, Olav Dalgard, Edith Calmar, Titus Vibe-Müller, and Knut Andersen all offered works of interest, although it is true to say that no Norwegian film-maker since the war has sustained a high reputation for long. **Arne Skouen** (*b* 1913) began as a novelist and playwright in the Thirties and after the war his name as a writer grew in importance. His first film was

made in 1949, from a scenario based on his novel *Children of the*
Street (Gatpojkar). Since then he has done sixteen features and some
shorts. *Flames in the Night (Det brenner i natt, 1954)* was a striking
study of a pyromaniac, a timid newspaper proof-reader by day, by night
a man for whom arson is a lust and a necessity. This was the first Norwegian film to be shown at Cannes. *Nine Lives (Ni liv, 1957)* and
Surrounded (Omringet, 1960) were war stories that underlined
Skouen's talent for suspense and location filming. *An-Magritt (1969)*
starred Liv Ullmann and Per Oscarsson but fell short of its expensive
pretensions.

Since 1964 the Norwegian government has supported the film industry by granting 35% of the gross earnings at the box-office towards the
budget of each feature. This grant may be increased to 45% in the
case of colour films or black-and-white pictures with exceptionally high
production costs, and in 1968 some 2,740,000 Norwegian crowns were
given in this form. In 1967 Paul Lokkeberg's *Liv,* the story of a photographer's model, was screened at the Berlin Festival and with its enthusiasm and liveliness it seemed to herald a fresh approach to cinema in
Norway by a young generation. Energetic newcomers like R. Lasse
Henriksen, Arild Kristo, and Rolf Clemens are leading the way in their
determination to make contact with other countries and to set up co-
productions where feasible. *pdc*

When the Russo-Finnish war ended, there followed a number of
films concentrating on the struggle, but several new names quickly
emerged from the depression. **Matti Kassila** (*b* 1924) shot various
documentaries and soon demonstrated a certain talent for comedy, as
in *Maija Finds a Tune (Maija löylää sävelen, 1950)*. **Edvin Laine**
(*b* 1905) was responsible for the most famous Finnish film of the
postwar period, *The Unknown Soldier (Tuntematon sotilas, 1955)*,
which focused for nearly three hours on the plight of a group of men
involved in the war with Russia. **Erik Blomberg** (*b* 1918) earned
some festival appearances with his screen version of a Scandinavian
legend, *The White Reindeer (Valkoinen peura, 1952)*. **Maunu Kurk-
vaara** (*b* 1926) contributed the Finnish sketch to the Scandinavian
co-production *4 x 4,* and **Mikko Niskanen** (*b* 1929) was for a time
considered the most promising director of the Sixties, on account of
his studies of men acting under the stress of war. But his *Under Your
Skin/Skin Skin (Käpy selän alla, 1966)* was unfortunately typical of
the period in Finland, with its false lyricism and humourless concentration on sex.

Three men have contrived to fight against the discouraging state of
the film industry in Finland (where there is no "Film Institute" as there
is in Sweden and Denmark, and where an actors' strike disrupted production between 1963 and 1965): Jörn Donner, Risto Jarva, and Aito

Mäkinen. Donner had already made some shorts in Finland before he moved to Sweden to shoot his first feature. In 1967 he returned to Finland, and the next year his *Black on White* (*Mustaa valkoisella*) was released. A brisk film shot skilfully in colour, *Black on White* told a light story of infidelity but also subtly condemned a society drawing its sustenance from glamour and egocentricity.

Having established his own production company, Donner then proceeded to make *Sixtynine* (1969), and *Portraits of Women* (*Naistenkuvia,* 1970), in which, as in *Black on White,* he played a leading role himself. Mäkinen had founded the Finnish National Film Archive with Donner in 1957, and was a powerful force behind the network of film societies that spread across the country in the Sixties. His own feature, *Four Times Only* (*Vain nelja kertaa,* 1969) showed distinct promise and a healthy scepticism towards the Finnish way of life. Jarva's *Time of Roses* (*Ruusujen aika,* 1969) has been described as "a study of the meritocracy of tomorrow with a profound influence from the prophet Marcuse."

Annual production in Finland has reached a dozen features in recent years, and there is talk of a film reform that would help domestic film-makers. *pdc*

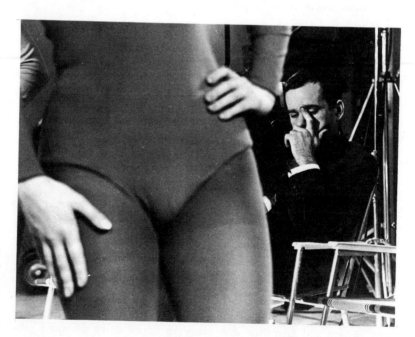

Jörn Donner and unidentified model in his own BLACK ON WHITE

7. Eastern Europe

D URING THE OCCUPATION the Nazis took over the growing
Barrandov studios in Prague and Czech production was sharply
reduced. *No* Czech film propounded Nazi ideology. Three important
directors overlapped into this period or began then. **Karol Steklý**
(*b* 1903) went into cinema from the stage, writing potboiler scripts
from 1933 to emerge as a director in 1945 and achieve prominence.
Elmar Klos (*b* 1910), a Czech documentarist, teamed up with Slovak
Ján Kadár (*b* 1918) who filmed the reconstruction of the Slovakian
railways after the Second World War. From 1952 this unique pair
made an impressive list of features with many prize-winners, chief
of which was *A Shop on the High Street* (*Obchod na korze*, 1964),
the first Czech film to take an Oscar.

In 1945 President Beneš signed the decree nationalising the film
industry—production, distribution and showing. In the same year the
Prague Film ("and Television" was added in 1960) Faculty of the
Academy of Dramatic Arts—known as FAMU—was founded. Cinematography was to be considered first as an art form and only second
as a commercial proposition. Several production groups were set up
with consultants and script-readers. A director whose work was rejected
by one group could approach others. At first the atmosphere was ex-
pansive. Old and tried talents were employed and new names appeared.
Late 1945 saw the completion of three films begun under the Occupation: one by Frič, *The Magic of the River* (*Řeka čaruje*) by **Václav
Krška** (*b* 1900), and a fine historical drama, *Rosina, the Foundling*
(*Rosina sebranec*) by Vávra—chief professor of directing at FAMU.
1946 saw ten features produced (most by veterans) and *Men without
Wings* (*Muži bez křídel*) by **František Cáp** (*b* 1913) took a prize
at Cannes. In this year **Karel Zeman** (*b* 1910) and **Jiří Trnka** (1912–
1969) began their work in puppet films and animation, both taking
prizes. 1947 was important on three counts. *The Strike* (*Siréna*) by
Steklý took the grand prize at Venice and not only remained his best
film (it dealt with a miners' strike in 1889) but established a trend.
Warriors of Faith (*Jan Roháč z dubé*) by **Vladimír Borský** (1904–
1962) was the first Czech film in colour—about a Fifteenth century
religious reformist-leader opposed to the Emperor. Most important was
the first feature of the new Slovak film industry, *Reiterate the Warning!*
(*Varuj!*), for which Frič had been invited to Slovakia. Bielik helped
the Czechs, Steklý and Frič with the screenplay based on a play by Ivan
Stodola, and he also played the male lead. The next year he directed

his own first feature, *Fox-holes* (*Vlčie diery*)—about a family in the Slovak national rising against the Magyars in 1848. **Jiří Krejčík** (*b* 1918), a student in Prague Technical University when it was closed by the Nazis, becoming an extra in the Barrandov studios, progressing through short films to become an important director, made his first feature now—*A Week in a Quiet House* (*Tyden v tichém domě,* 1947). Krška made *The Violin and the Dream* (*Housle a sen,* 1947), a lyrical biography of violinist Josef Slavík, and his treatment of cultural figures was to help him through the years of ideological restriction soon to begin. **Jiří Weiss** (*b* 1913) who made documentaries in Britain during the war, returned to Prague and shot *Stolen Frontier* (*Uloupená hranice,* 1948) dealing with the rape of Czech border regions in 1938. Production rose from three features in 1945 to eighteen in 1947.

From 1948 the expansiveness was stifled by Zhdanov-Stalinist restrictions. An Artistic Council was put in charge of the production groups; emphasis was put on ideology and propaganda; even critics conformed to Zhdanov dictates. From 1950 only the most adroit directors could produce really major works. **Josef Mach** (*b* 1909) made a fine comedy, *The Village Revolt* (*Vzbouření na vsi,* 1949) about men insisting on a new tractor while the women wanted an automatic laundry. By applying the *Lysistrata* stratagem they got their laundry. In serious fields, ideologically safe stories of war and resistance were permitted. **Jiří Sequens** (*b* 1922), trained in Prague, Moscow and at IDHEC in Paris, concentrated on well-finished, exciting stories. **Vladimír Slavinský** (1890–1949), **Miroslav Cikán** (*b* 1896) and **Václav Wasserman** (*b* 1898) completed works in this constricted period. Public and even critics chafed under the constricted productions. In 1951 the output dropped to seven Czech features and one Slovak.

FAMU   Pressures eased in 1955–56. The first graduates of FAMU entered the studios after 1950. Under Dr. Antonín Brousil the school turned out directors, dramaturgists, cameramen and technicians often so well-grounded that they moved interchangeably. The first great names included cameraman **Jaroslav Kučera** (*b* 1929) and **Zdeněk Podskalský** (*b* 1923) who also studied at VGIK in Moscow, emerging as a clever director of brilliant comedy and returning to teach at FAMU. There were **Karel Kachyňa** (*b* 1924) and **Vojtěch Jasný** (*b* 1925) who worked together on five films and then, though graduates in photography, became highly individual directors—Jasný at once lyrical and experimental, and Kachyňa adept at dramas enveloped in widely differing atmospheres, ultimately working with **Jan Procházka** (*b* 1929), a script-writer and prominent author, and cameraman **Josef Illík** (*b* 1919), as a distinctive team. The Slovak **Jozef Medved'** (*b* 1927) was in this group.

Selected highlights of the transition period after 1956 would include: *The Unvanquished* (*Neporazení,* 1956), by Sequens; *September Nights*

(*Zářijové noci*, 1957) by Jasný; and *Wolf Trap* (*Vlčí jáma*, 1957) by Weiss—a Venice prize-winner with a superb performance by Jiřina Šejbalová, a very experienced actress, as a wife older than her husband who is attracted to a young woman played by Jana Brejchová who appeared in 1952 at the age of thirteen and is now perhaps the most famous Czech actress. Bielik's *Forty-Four* (*Štyridsat'štyri*, 1957) about a mutiny by Slovak soldiers in the Austrian army during the First World War was a prize film. *A School for Fathers* (*Škola otců*, 1957) by **Ladislav Helge** (*b* 1927) was a fine study of a teacher concerned with child guidance. Jasný's *Desire* (*Touha*, 1958) linked four episodes to seasons of the year and this lyrical film was a Cannes prize-winner. *Out of Reach of the Devil* (*Kam čert nemůže*, 1959) by Podskalský was a comedy in colour about a hospital consultant as an updated Faust and a female temptress, Mephistophela, played by a fine actress, Jana Hlaváčová. Vávra's dramatic *First Rescue Party* (*Prnví parta*, 1959) about a mine disaster was another prize-winner. Krejčík's *Awakening* (*Probuzení*, 1959) dealt with delinquency. Weiss's *Romeo, Juliet and Darkness* (*Romeo, Julie a tma*, 1960) took many prizes, had a wide showing, and told a sensitive tragic love story of a young student and a Jewess during the Occupation, the leads being played by **Dana Smutná**, Weiss's wife, and the fine young Slovak actor, **Ivan Mistrík**. *Skid* (*Smyk*, 1960) by **Zbyněk Brynych** (*b* 1927) was an exciting story of an adventurer who undergoes plastic surgery to change his future—the story drafted by the talented male lead, **Jiří Vala**. Jasný's *I Survived Certain Death* (*Přežil jsem svou smrt*, 1960) was an extraordinary recreation of Mauthausen concentration camp. Helge's *Spring Breeze* (*Jarní povětří*, 1961) showed Prague University students in the events of 1948. *The White Dove* (*Holubice*, 1960) by **František Vlácil** (*b* 1924), a student of philosophy and history, and painter turned director, was an exquisite, prize-winning film of haunting appeal, superbly photographed by the versatile cameraman **Jan Čuřík** (*b* 1924).

Subjects expanded into social fields; plays, novels and classics were adapted by excellent scenario writers. Some of the most important were: **Ota Hofman** (*b* 1928), a FAMU graduate; **Ludvík Aškenazi** (*b* 1921); **Otakar Kirchner** (*b* 1923); **Lubomír Možny** (*b* 1923); **Jiří Muchta** (*b* 1915); **Josef Alois Novotný** (*b* 1918); and **Pavel Kohout** (*b* 1928) who became a director in the late Sixties. Important Slovaks were: **Ivan Bukovčan, Jun.** (*b* 1921), dramatist and critic, **Albert Marenčin** (*b* 1922) an author, journalist and translator; **Maximilián Nitra** (*b* 1922); **Jozef Alexander Tallo** (*b* 1924); and **Tibor Vichta** (*b* 1933), FAMU graduate.

By the Sixties production facilities included the large Barrandov studios in Prague, the Czech Army Units, the Short Film studios, the Koliba studios in Bratislava (Slovakia) and the Kudlov studios in

Some Scriptwriters

179

The Czech New Wave. Above, Nemec's DIAMONDS OF THE NIGHT. Below: Menzel's CAPRICIOUS SUMMER

Gottwaldov, with well-equipped laboratories especially in the first and last. Important puppet and cartoon films emanate from five or six studios in this field. Both Czech and Slovak documentary work is wide-ranging and significant. **Čeněk Duba** (*b* 1919 in Yugoslavia) is a feature director also important in reportage and documentaries: he covered the Olympiad in Helsinki in 1952. The Gottwaldov studios produce documentaries and are well-known for children's films, a field in which some directors work almost exclusively. **Jan Valášek** (*b* 1926) and **Milan Vošmik** (*b* 1919) make children's films in Prague. A typical progression is that of the Slovak **Jošef Pinkava** (*b* 1919), a leading Gottwaldov director, assistant to Jaroslav Novotný till 1949, then making instructional and sports films, and stories of young people. After 1963 his characters move into post-adolescence and he deals sympathetically with their problems.

By 1962 production had reached thirty-one Czech and six Slovak features—typical figures for the present day. And in 1962–63 works of another generation of FAMU graduates reached the screens, touching new responses and exploring new styles. In 1962 **Věra Chytilová** (*b* 1929) made her medium-length graduation film for FAMU, *The Ceiling (Strop)* about a fashion model, done with detached observation—the director had been a mannequin at one stage of her career. At the same time the Slovak **Stefan Uher** (*b* 1930), a FAMU graduate, made his second feature, *Catching the Sun in a Net (Slnko v sieti)* which took the Czech Critics' prize. These films began what was to be called the Czech New Wave: both cast non-professionals, were candid and very personal. Surprises came in quick succession. **Miloš Forman** (*b* 1932), a graduate in dramaturgy from FAMU, turned to directing, with his second film, *Peter and Pavla (Cerný Petr)* appearing in 1963 as well as Chytilová's full-length *Something Else (O něčem jiném)*— concurrent studies of a housewife and an Olympic gymnast, and *The Cry (Křik)* by **Jaromil Jireš** (*b* 1935) who studied direction and photography at FAMU and is a portrait-photographer and music critic too. **Alfred Radok** (*b* 1910), besides directing the successful comedy, *Old Man Motorcar (Dědeček, 1957)*, conceived The Magic Lantern (Laterna Magika) for the Brussels Exposition and its extension in 1960, and both Forman and Jireš worked on this stage-cum-cinema form. 1964 saw Uher's *The Organ (Organ)* about art, death and Slovak Gothic churches, *Diamonds of the Night (Démanty noci)* by **Jan Němec** (*b* 1936), *Everyday Courage (Každý den odvahu)* by **Evald Schorm** (*b* 1931), and *Josef Kilian (Postava k podpírání)* by **Pavel Juráček** (*b* 1935) and **Jan Schmidt** (*b* 1934). Exciting attention everywhere, these films ranged from the "objective reality" of Forman who went outside the studios, showing wizardry in selection of non-professionals and editing keen observations with ironic wit, to the

Kafkaesque-world of Juráček and Schmidt. *Pearls of the Deep* (*Perličky na dně*, 1965), a five-part episode film, became a symposium of new directors, photographed by Kučera (Chytilová's husband), and derived from stories by Bohumil Hrabal who professes an affinity with Kafka. Besides Jireš, Chytilová, Schorm and Němec, it included a brilliant, sardonic sketch by **Jiří Menzel** (*b* 1938) whose *Closely Observed Trains* (*Ostre sledované vlaky*, 1966) took an Oscar and was quickly followed by the successful *Capricious Summer* (*Rozmarné léto*, 1968) from the novel by the prominent Vladislav Venčura. **Antonín Maša** (*b*. 1935), a FAMU dramaturgist turned director, made another Kafkaesque film, *Hotel for Strangers* (*Hotel pro cizince*, 1966)—a period-piece of about 1912 with brief sequences harking back to silent techniques.

While this new group surged into prominence, development along freer lines went on in the main stream. Kachyňa made *Hope* (*Naděje* 1963) about an alcoholic, played by **Rudolf Hrušínsky** (*b* 1920) who holds the Czech State Prize and Artist of Merit award, and who made his screen *début* in 1936; and *The High Wall* (*Vysoká zed'*, 1964), about a young girl climbing a hospital wall to see a young man with an injured spine, played by **Vit Olmer** who has directed several short films. Krejčík's work expanded from *Midnight Mass* (*Polnocna omsa*, 1962) based on a successful play by Karvaš, to an excellent comedy, *The Unfortunate Bridegroom* (*Svatba jako remen*, 1967). Kachyňa in 1966 and 1967 showed the range of atmosphere he could achieve with Procházka and Illík in *Coach to Vienna* (*Kocár do Vídne*)—all shrouded in the enveloping gloom of a coniferous forest, and in *Night of the Bride* (*Noc novesty*), using the sharpest black-and-white for an intense drama of the dissolution of the convents and collectivisation of 1950. Jasný made *That Cat* (*Až přijde kocour*, 1963) which collected prizes everywhere with its elaborate mixed techniques, photographed by Kučera. **Oldřich Lipský** (*b* 1924), a prominent director of comedy, made the enormously successful *Lemonade Joe* (*Limonádový Joe*, 1964) —a parody of *bad* Westerns. Brynych's *The Fifth Rider Is Fear* (. . . *a pátý jezdec je strach*, 1964), was an intense drama with superb detail and locations in the oldest parts of Prague associated with the Golem legend. The Slovak **Peter Solan** (*b* 1929), from FAMU, made *The Boxer and Death* (*Boxer a' smrt*, 1962) with the fine Slovak actor, **Štefan Kvietik**, and this was awarded a special prize in San Francisco and was said by many to be most successful in capturing the special tensions of a concentration camp. Sequens made one of his most superbly finished films, *Assassination* (*Atentát*, 1965), about the murder of Heydrich, marvellously photographed by Milič, and for which Karel Lier reconstructed a large church to be bombarded and flooded. Podskalský made a slickly finished comedy in *Never Strike a Woman Even with a Flower* (*Ženu ani květinou neuhodíš*, 1966) with

Brejchová and her husband, the versatile and experienced Vlastimil Brodský.

But in 1966 the pressures came down again; scripts were rejected as being "not commercially viable"—an incomprehensible criticism as Czech films grew increasingly popular. Most pointed was an edict that Chytilová (for *Daisies*—*Sedmikrásky*, 1966) and Němec (for *A Report on the Party and the Guests*—*O slavnosti a hostech*, 1966) be given no further funds to realise their "nihilist vehicles." Export of *Party* was banned until the political relaxation in 1968 when it was promptly invited for showing at Cannes. Then newer names appeared, or young reputations grew. **Hynek Bocan** (*b* 1935), a FAMU graduate highly regarded by the school and savants, achieved immediate acclaim with *Nobody Gets the Last Laugh* (*Nikdo se ne bude smát,* 1965) from a novel by the controversial Milan Kundera whose socially daring book, *The Joke,* was filmed by Jireš in 1968. Bočan went on to make *Private Gale* (*Soukromá vichřice,* 1967) from the second volume of a tetralogy by Vladimír Paral, a chemist turning exclusively to writing in 1965— this was a fine comedy film intricately constructed, the rival male leads brilliantly played by Josef Somr and Pavel Lankowsky. Perhaps the most unusual director to emerge in the latest stages has been the Slovak **Juraj Jakubisko** (*b* 1938), from FAMU, with *The Crucial Years* (*Kristove roky,* 1967) claiming that the significant aspects of life are love, death and "craziness." Another Slovak, **Juraj Herz** (*b* 1934), trained as an actor, has made three films in quick succession, *The Lame Devil* (*Kulhavý dábel,* 1967), a burlesque of love set in several periods, the director playing the title role, and *The Cremator* (*Spalovač mrtvol,* 1968) showing an obsessional study of a German becoming fanatical about his life-role as a burner of corpses in a concentration camp.

Forman, Chytilová, Juráček, Kadár and Klos have begun to work abroad or under foreign finance but the results and pattern of these excursions have yet to be assessed. *ld*

When the Soviet Union was attacked by Germany in 1941, the whole of its film industry—like everything else in the country—was immediately geared to the war. Mosfilm and Lenfilm were evacuated to Tashkent, in Central Asia, but the newsreel departments remained in the areas of attack and in the first two years of the war, newsreel was the most important film-making *genre.* Soviet wartime cinema is renowned for its courageous front-line reporting, which provided material for many outstanding full-length documentaries. Among the film-makers involved were Yuli Raizman, already well known as a feature film director, and the distinguished documentary directors **Roman Karmen** (*b* 1906) and **Ilya Kopalin** (*b* 1900).

One of the most widely-shown documentaries was *A Day of War*

U.S.S.R.

(*Den voiny,* 1942, *dir* Mikhail Slutsky), a compilation of material shot by a hundred and sixty cameramen on a single day, depicting various aspects of the war. Dovzhenko made *The Battle for Our Soviet Ukraine* (*Bitva za nashy Sovetskuyu Ukrainu,* 1943) as a tribute to the partisan fighters.

In the later part of the war, many popular features about individual acts of heroism, especially in the partisan movement, were made at Tashkent. Some of them might appear naïve to modern eyes, but in the wartime atmosphere of intense patriotism and bitter hatred for Fascism, they had a profound and stirring effect. Among the most successful were *At Six O'Clock in the Evening after the War* (*B shest chasov vechera posle voiny,* 1944, *dir* Ivan Pyriev) and *She Defends Her Country* (*Ona zashchishchaet Rodinu,* 1943, *dir* Friedrich Ermler, *script* Alexei Kapler). Mark Donskoy achieved a very high level of realism in *The Rainbow* (*Raduga,* 1943), a stark tragedy of the struggle of village partisans against the Nazis.

Towards the end of the war, Eisenstein completed his celebrated

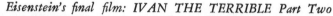

Eisenstein's final film: IVAN THE TERRIBLE Part Two

Ivan the Terrible (*Ivan Groznyi*, 1944), the second part of which was sharply criticised by the authorities and was not released until 1958.

Anti-Fascism remained the dominant theme after the war and found important expression in *The Young Guard* (*Moladaya gvardiya*, 1948), directed by Sergei Gerasimov, about youngsters who formed a resistance group in occupied territory, and *The Story of a Real Man* (*Povest nastoyashchem chelovek*, 1948, *dir* Alexei Stolper). Contemporary themes were tackled mainly through stories of individual endeavour, like Donskoy's *The Village Teacher* (*Selskaya uchitelnitsa*, 1947), Gerasimov's *The Country Doctor* (*Selskii vrach*, 1952) and Pudovkin's *The Return of Vassili Bortnikov* (*Vozvraschenie Vasiliya Bortnikova*, 1953). But this last film was a disappointing work from a great film-maker, and, in fact, official pressure and restrictions made it almost impossible to deal realistically with the contemporary scene. For a time even the best directors were forced to fall back on simple, uncontentious biographical material for romanticised films about the lives of the great.

By 1953, the disastrous Stalin policy of "quality, not quantity" had stultified creativity and feature production had fallen from over a hundred annually to under ten. Scripts, however, were still being written and young film-makers continued to emerge from the Film School (V.G.I.K.) so that, in the regenerative period that followed the death of Stalin, the wheels were able to start turning again quite quickly. The mid-Fifties can be seen as a kind of transitional period. Problems of everyday life were presented in lively and provocative ways in films like *The Big Family* (*Bolshaya semya*, 1954, *dir* Yosif Heifitz), *The Heights* (*Vysota*, 1957, *dir* Alexander Zarkhi), *Spring in Zarechnaya Street* (*Vesna na Zarechnoi ulitse*, 1956, *dir* Felix Mironer and Marlen Khutsiev) and in satirical comedies by Mikhail Kalatozov and Eldar Riazanov (*b* 1927). They paved the way for a fresh burst of creativity at the end of the Fifties, with **Grigori Chukhrai** (*b* 1921) and **Sergei Bondarchuk** (*b* 1920) emerging as dominant new forces in the cinema.

Transitional Period

New Directors

The Soviet Union had suffered more grievously in the war than any other country and the tragedy of the war and its aftermath continued to be the major pre-occupation of film-makers until well into the Sixties. But now the simple heroics of the past began to be replaced by a more mature and personalised approach. Chukhrai's *The Forty-first* (*Sorok pervyi*, 1956) although set in the Civil War period, was an important breakaway from the good and evil conception of the typical war film. (It was, in fact, a re-make of a 1926 film about the love between a Red Army girl and a White Guard officer). His *Ballad of a Soldier* (*Ballad o soldate*, 1960), a charming and very touching episodic account of a young soldier's attempts to reach his home during a short leave from the front, played a big part in restoring the image of Soviet

U.S.S.R. cinema abroad, as did Kalatozov's wartime romance *The Cranes Are Flying* (*Letyat zhuravli*, 1957), which introduced the attractive and talented actress **Tatiana Samoilova** (*b* 1934) to world audiences, and Bondarchuk's *Destiny of a Man* (*Sudbo cheloveka*, 1959). *Peace to the Newcomer* (*Mir vkhodyaschemu*, 1961) released in Britain as *All Quiet on the Eastern Front*, made by the very popular film-making team **Alexander Alov** (*b* 1923) and **Vladimir Naumov** (*b* 1927), was one of the first successful attempts to make a mature retrospective evaluation of individuals in the Nazi army.

A whole number of new young directors made their *début* at that time and continued to flourish through the following decade. Among them were **Yuli Karasik** (*b* 1923), **Moisei Kalik** (*b* 1927), **Vadim Derbenev** (*b* 1934), working at the Moldavian studios, **Igor Talankin** (*b* 1927) and **Georgi Danelyia** (*b* 1930). *Seryosha* (*Serezha*, 1960), a child's-eye view of life directed by Talankin and Danelyia, was widely shown abroad, as was Danelyia's *I Walk around Moscow* (*Ya shagayu po Moskve*, 1965), a free-ranging, contemporary-style study of young people. His comedy *Cheer Up!* (*Ne boruyi*), featuring many prominent actors in cameo roles, was one of the big successes of 1969.

One of the most interesting and talented directors to emerge in this period was **Andrei Tarkovsky** (*b* 1932), whose *Ivan's Childhood* (*Ivanovo detstvo*, 1962) was an early indication of the harsh-eyed lyricism that was one of the keynotes of the late Sixties. His *Andrei Roublov,* made in 1965 and released in 1969, was hailed as a masterpiece by many critics.

At the same time, a strongly critical approach to the "cult of the personality" period began to be expressed on the screen, and films revealing some of the hitherto concealed social conditions and personal tragedies under Stalin played a part in the "de-Stalinisation" process. Among the first were *Battle on the Road* (*Bitva v puti*, 1961 *dir* Vladimir Basov) and Chukhrai's *Clear Skies* (*Chistoe nebo*, 1961), both more notable for their influence on subsequent screen developments than for their own intrinsic qualities. A major landmark was *The Chairman* (*Predsedatel*, 1965), made by the talented young director **Alexei Saltikov** (*b* 1934). This intensely dramatic revelation of the appalling conditions and the struggle for survival on a collective farm just after the war, broke fresh ground and paved the way for further exploration into the sore spots of recent history. It was distinguished, too, by a dynamic performance from **Mikhail Ulyanov** (*b* 1927) in the leading role. Among the even sharper films that followed it were several dealing with political conflict in the newer Union Republics, notably *Nobody Wanted to Die* (*Nikto ne khotel umirat*, 1965), made by the leading Lithuanian director **Vitautus Žalakevičius** (*b* 1930) and *Bitter Grain* (*Gorki zerna*) made in the Moldavian studios by the young film-making team Lysenko and Gazhui.

Although there continued to be a large number of routine, naturalistic films about the Revolution and the war, the mid-Sixties saw a big turn towards films with contemporary themes. Among the older generation directors who exerted a strong influence in this development were Mikhail Romm and Yuli Raizman. Romm's *Nine Days of One Year* (*Devyat dnei odnogo goda*, 1961), featuring the popular actors **Alexei Batalov** (*b* 1928) and **Innokenti Smoktunovsky** (*b* 1925), is concerned with the personal and moral decisions facing young atomic scientists. Raizman's *Your Contemporary* (*Tvoi sovremennik*, 1967) which deals with a whole complex of controversial and social problems, especially the generation gap, was one of the most popular films of 1968. The middle-generation, Georgian-born director **Marlen Khutsiev** (*b* 1925) emerged as a highly significant and very gifted director of contemporary-style films dealing in complex and sensitive ways with problems of alienation. His *I Am Twenty* (*Mne dvadtsat let*, 1961–63) and *Rain in July* (*Yulskii dozhd*, 1967) aroused considerable controversy.

By the mid-Sixties, a new generation of highly talented directors and writers was beginning to challenge old attitudes still further by representing past and present on the screen in a mood of cool, analytical re-appraisal. Among the foremost were Tarkovsky and **Andrei Konchalovsky-Mikhailov** (*b* 1937). Tarkovsky followed *Ivan's Childhood* with *The Passion of Andrew* (*Strasti po Andreyu*, 1966), a study of the Fourteenth century icon-painter, which aroused a storm of controversy because of its savage depiction of early Russian history, and was held back from release until 1969. Konchalovsky's *The First Teacher* (*Pervyi uchitel*, 1965) looked at an old situation—the bringing of education to a backward Kirghizian village in the early years of Soviet power—with fresh eyes. His following film, *Asya's Happiness* (*Istoriya Asi Klyachinoi, kotoraya lyubila, da ne vyshla zamukh*, 1966) is about modern peasant life in Kirgizia. Several young directors from the various Union Republics made notable first films in the free-ranging, youthful "new cinema" style.

Multi-nationalism has been a characteristic of Soviet cinema since its inception and production in the Union Republics took on a fresh vitality in the Sixties. Two-thirds of the feature films produced in the U.S.S.R. come from the Republics, each of which has its own studio centre.

The Dovzhenko studios at Kiev, in the Ukraine, produce twelve or thirteen feature films annually. It was here that **Sergei Paradjanov** (*b* 1924) made his fascinating film reconstruction of a pre-Revolution peasant community, *Shadows of Our Forgotten Ancestors* (*Teni zabytykh predkov*, 1964) before returning to his native Armenia to make a biographical study of a national poet *Sayat Novar* (*Sayat Novar*, 1969). Lithuania produces only two or three feature films a year, but a remarkable high standard is achieved by a small but gifted group of film-makers headed by Žalakevičius and cameraman **Ionus Gričius** (*b* 1928).

Georgia   Georgia has a strong reputation for lively down-to-earth comedies. Among the best-known directors are **Tengiz Abuladze** (*b* 1924), who made the high-spirited domestic comedy *Grandma, Iliko, Illarion and Me* (*Ya, babushka, Iliko i Illarion,* 1963), **Eldar Shengalaya** (*b* 1933), who often blends legend with real life, and **Rezo Chkeidze** (*b* 1926), who made the wartime heroic-comedy *A Soldier's Father* (*Otets soldata,* 1965), featuring the distinguished Georgian actor **Sergei Zakariadze** (*b* 1909). Several new directors made lively, youthful first films in the late Sixties.

Among the middle-Asian republics, Kirghizia and Uzbekistan have made particularly rapid strides in film-making in the Sixties and in these studios, too, a number of young directors made very promising first films towards the end of the decade.

A consistent feature of Soviet cinema, throughout its history, has been its high-level production of screen versions of the classics—novels, plays, opera and ballet. Outstanding postwar examples are: Gerasimov's *And Quiet Flows the Don* (*Tikhii Don,* 1958), Heifitz's *Lady with a Little Dog* (*Dama s sobachkoi,* 1960), *Don Quixote* (*Don Kikhot,* 1957) and *Hamlet* (*Gamlet,* 1964) both directed by the distinguished Shakespeare expert and film veteran **Grigori Kozintsev** (*b* 1905), Bondarchuk's four-part epic *War and Peace* (*Voina i mir,* 1964–67) and *Anna Karenina* (*Anna Karenina,* 1967, *dir* Alexander Zarkhi), with Samoilova in the title role.

There is a steady flow of films for children, most of them made at the Maxim Gorky studios in Moscow. *nh*

Vladimir Ivashov and Evgeni Urbanski in
BALLAD OF A SOLDIER

The START group, and its successor SAF (Co-operative of Film Authors, founded 1937) formed the theoretical basis for modern Polish cinema. The practical basis was laid during the war, when Poland was occupied and its cinema virtually destroyed, by underground newsreel directors who managed to shoot footage of the Warsaw uprising of 1944, and by the film units that were organised in Polish military detachments in Britain, France, the Near East and the Soviet Union.

The special wartime experiences of the Polish people—the hardship of occupation, the agony of the concentration camps, the horrors of the Warsaw ghetto, the Warsaw uprising—provided the most important themes for films in the early postwar cinema, and indeed, for many years to come. The first films of the nationalised industry were documentaries, many of which used material shot during the war. The first postwar feature film, Buczkowski's *Forbidden Songs* (*Zakzane piosenki,* 1947), a chronicle of everyday life under Nazi occupation built around resistance songs sung in the Warsaw streets, has no personalised hero. In the following three years only seven films were made, but of these, three have proved to be of lasting value. Jakubowska's *The Last Stage* (*Ostatni etap,* 1948), is an immensely moving re-creation of life in a concentration camp, based on the director's own experiences at Auschwitz. Buczkowski's *The Treasure* (*Skarb,* 1948), about the housing problem, is notable as the first postwar comedy. Ford's *Border Street* (*Ulica Granicza,* 1949), depicts the last days of the Warsaw Ghetto, when the Jews seized arms and fought the Nazis until the entire ghetto was annihilated.

Production increased in the Fifties, and Ford emerged as the dominant director of the period with *Youth of Chopin* (*Mlodość Chopina,* 1952) and *Five Boys from Barska Street* (*Piatka z ulicy Barkiej,* 1954), about five lads who are regenerated after a period of demoralisation during the war, which won a prize at Cannes. Zarzycki's *Unvanquished City* (*Miasto Nieujarzmione,* 1950), concerned with the Warsaw uprising, was another notable film of that time and **Jan Rybkowski** (*b* 1912) made several worthwhile contributions to cinema development. But, in general, despite the increase in production, standards were low. The atmosphere of dogmatism, which affected film-making in all Socialist countries at the beginning of the Fifties, stultified creativity, and many films that had been conceived in interesting and imaginative ways were distorted by official requirements for a narrowly defined "Socialist realism." *Early Postwar Films*

The first big breakaway from dogmatism—the inauguration of a new and exciting period in Polish cinema—came in the late Fifties, with the emergence of three outstanding directors, **Jerzy Kawalerowicz** (*b* 1922), **Andrzej Wajda** (*b* 1926) and, a little later, **Andrzej Munk** (1921–1961). The establishment of self-supporting, decentralised production groups in 1955 resulted in a burst of creative *Three Outstanding Directors* initiative, and the term "Polish film school" began to be applied to the directors and scriptwriters who emerged. The key-note was personalisation, the accent was on youth, and, in a wide variety of styles and approaches, the directors sought to break away from generalised heroics, to re-examine the myths of the past, and to delve more deeply into individual psychology. At first, the war and its complicated and confused aftermath continued to provide the main themes, but later the films dealt with contemporary subjects.

Kawalerowicz's first films were *A Night of Remembrance* (*Celuloza,* 1953) and *Under the Phrygian Star* (*Pod gwiazda frygijska,* 1954) which together constituted a two-part epic of the developing class struggle between the wars. His strong feeling for narrative and suspense is apparent in some of his later films like *Shadow* (*Cien,* 1956) and *Baltic Express* (*Pociag,* 1959), while *Mother Joan of the Angels* (*Matka Joanna od Aniolów,* 1961) a strange and mystic Seventeenth century tale of nuns possessed by devils, demonstrates his flair for sustaining psychological tension. His actress wife Lucyna Wynnicka features in many of his films.

Wajda, whose films have been widely shown in the West, began his film career as a documentary director. His first feature films, constituting his celebrated "trilogy," trace with increasing complexity the experience and attitudes of young people during and just after the war. *A Generation* (*Pokolenie,* 1954) depicts a style of living adopted by youngsters growing up in a devastated and occupied country, for whom resistance is a natural part of everyday life. *Kanal* (*Kanal,* 1956) tells of the harrowing experience of a group of resistance fighters in the sewers beneath the streets during the Warsaw Uprising. *Ashes and Diamonds* (*Popiól i diament,* 1958) deals with the gradual disillusionment of a young man whose best feelings have been exploited by political adventurers in the early postwar years. The central character is played by **Zbigniew Cybulski** (1927–1967) the gifted young actor in dark glasses who became a symbol of the dilemma of the contemporary hero at odds with life. Wajda's *Innocent Sorcerers* (*Niewinni czarodzieje,* 1960) was the most distinguished of a number of films dealing with the problems of a younger generation and its search for a place in life.

Munk was very closely associated with the young documentary movement, which had begun to develop dynamic new approaches to the social problems of the times, and visually, his feature films are deeply influenced by his documentary experience. They are concerned with destruction of heroic myths, and with examining in psychological depth the anatomy of heroism and self-sacrifice. They are imbued with the bitter irony which is characteristic of Polish literary traditions. His first feature film, *Man on the Track* (*Czlowiek na torze,* 1957) was scripted by **Jerzy Stefan Stawiński** (*b* 1921) who became one of the

most important scriptwriters of the "Polish film school." Munk's next film *Eroica* (*Eroica*, 1958) aroused a storm of controversy. The leading character in the first part is a black marketeer and swindler who finally decides to sacrifice himself despite his own bad intentions. The second part, set among Polish officers in a prisoner-of-war camp, examines the way a legend takes shape. Munk's sharply satirical *Bad Luck* (*Zezowate szczeście*, 1960), also scripted by Stawinski, proved to be his last completed film. His death in a car crash in 1961, while working on *Passenger* (*Pasazerka*, 1963) was a sad loss to Polish cinema, as was the death of Cybulski in a railway accident in 1967. Wajda, who continued to make films of widely differing *genres* throughout the Sixties, obliquely commemorated Cybulski in *Everything for Sale* (*Wszystko na sprzedaz*, 1968) about an actor who is killed in an accident.

Among other directors associated with the "Polish film school" are **Wojciech Jerzy Has** (*b* 1925), **Kazimierz Kutz** (*b* 1929), **Stanislaw Rozewicz** (*b* 1924), **Jerzy Passendorfer** (*b* 1923) and **Tadeusz Chmielewski** (*b* 1927). Outstanding historical films of the period include Ford's *Knights of the Teutonic Order* (*Krzyzacy*, 1960) and Kawalerowicz's *Pharaoh* (*Faraon*, 1965).

The vitality of the "Polish film school" abated in the early Sixties and production in general was less interesting. But the two outstanding new directors—**Roman Polanski** (*b* 1933) and **Jerzy** (Yurek) **Skolimowski** (*b* 1938) emerged in this period. Polanski attracted international attention with his graduation film at Lódź Film School, the delightful comedy short *Two Men and a Wardrobe* (*Dwaj ludzie z szafa*, 1958). His first feature, *Knife in the Water* (*Nóz w wodzie*, 1961), a highly sophisticated study of the shifting relationships between

191

Polish spectacular: Aleksander Ford's KNIGHTS OF THE TEUTONIC ORDER

two men and a woman, established him as a front-rank director. Since *Knife in the Water* he has been working in Western Europe and America.

Skolimowski, who was co-author of the screenplays for *Innocent Sorcerers* and *Knife in the Water,* also drew acclaim with his graduation film, *Identification Marks—None (Rysopsis,* 1964). Like Polanski, he is a gifted actor. He played the lead role in his graduation film and in his first major work, *Walkover (Walkower,* 1965) which he scripted as well as directed. He is very much preoccupied by problems of identity and frustration. His following film, *Barrier (Bariera,* 1966), is a highly complex investigation into the attitude of the younger generation, rich in symbolism and intricate metaphor. The central character is a medical student who decides to give up his studies and gain instant prosperity by marriage. Skolimowski worked abroad in the late

Sixties. He made the charming and high-spirited comedy of youth *Le*
Départ (1967) in Belgium and an episode for the three-part film
Dialogue (*Dialog*, 1968) in Czechoslovakia, before returning to Poland
to make *Hands Up!* (*Rece do góry*, 1968).

Towards the end of the decade, a further group of directors
emerged, among whom **Witold Leszczyński** (*b* 1933) and **Henryk
Kluba** (*b* 1931) showed considerable promise. Both had worked
closely with the "Polish film school." Leszczyński's graduation film *The
Life of Matthew* (*Zywot Mateusza*, 1967), shot by the talented young
cameraman **Andrzej Kostenko** (*b* 1936) is a study of a lonely,
alienated man who reacts over-sensitively to his surroundings.

During the political turbulence of 1968 the production groups were
disbanded and re-organised on a new and more centralised basis.

While Polish feature films have been considerably influenced by
documentaries, documentary production has developed its own distinctive approach with emphasis on feelings and emotions rather than on
straight-forward reportage. Among directors of outstanding documentary films in the Sixties are **Kazimierz Karabasz** (*b* 1930), **Jan
Lomnicki** (*b* 1930) and **Wladyslaw Slesicki** (*b* 1927). Poland also
has an unusually high output of educational and scientific films.

Animation is the youngest branch of the industry, but it has advanced
very rapidly. Animated productions fall into two main categories—
simple puppet and cartoon films for children, and satirical or sophisticated cartoons for adults. Sophisticated techniques have been developed
to a very high standard. Leading directors include **Daniel Szczechura**
(*b* 1930), **Witold Giersz** (*b* 1927), **Walerian Borowczyk** (*b*
1923) and **Jan Lenica** (*b* 1928), (the last two of whom spent several
years working in Paris). *nh*

The Second World War, by cutting off foreign supplies, saved the **HUNGARY**
Hungarian industry, though the quality of the films produced was not
high. *People on the Alps* (*Emberek a Havason*, 1941, *dir* **István Szots**
b 1912) was an exception, but it was with *Somewhere in Europe*
(*Valahol Európában*, 1947, *dir* **Géza Radványi** *b* 1907) that postwar
cinema began visibly to move forward. In March 1948 the industry
was again nationalised; the first film it produced was *The Soil under*
Your Feet (*Talpalatnyi Föld*, 1948, *dir* **Frigyes Bán**, 1902–1969), a
story of peasant endeavour and defeat, epitomising the national experience, and commanding to this day a devoted admiration. 1949 saw
the first colour film, *Mattie the Goose Boy* (*Ludás Matyi*, *dir* **Kálmán
Nádasdy** *b* 1904 and **Laszló Ránody** *b* 1919), but for the next two or
three years the main aim was propaganda.

In 1954 *The Birth of Menyhert Simon* (*Simon Menyhért Születése*,
dir **Zoltán Várkonyi** *b* 1912) marked another step forward with a
story this time of peasant fulfilment, while *Merry-Go-Round* (1955)

and *Professor Hannibal* (1956) confirmed the growing reputation of **Zoltán Fábri** (*b* 1917) who, with *Twenty Hours* (*Húsz Óra,* 1964) and *Late Season* (*Utószezon,* 1967) has continued into the modern movement. *A Glass of Beer* (*Egy Pikoló Világos,* 1955, **Félix Máriássy** *b* 1919) caused a sensation with its neo-realistic picture of everyday life, and *A Sunday Romance* (*Bakaruhában,* 1956–57, *dir* **Imre Fehér** *b* 1926) depicted a corrupt bourgeois society with a humane objectivity far removed from the propagandist tone of the early Fifties.

A renewed period of stagnation in the late Fifties led to a reform of the Film Academy and the founding of the Béla Balázs Studio, which offered opportunities to young film-makers, and in the early Sixties three films led the way to a new kind of cinema. *The Fanatics* (Megszállottak, 1961, **Károly Makk** *b* 1925), a triumphant version, as it were, of *The Soil under Your Feet, Cantata* (*Oldás és Kötés,* 1962, *dir* **Miklós Jancsó** *b* 1921), and *Dialogue* (*Párbeszéd,* 1963, *dir* **János Herskó** *b* 1926), all, in different ways, dealt with the problems of conscience and authority. These films were made by men of experience, not by young rebels, and this foundation of experience has given to

The sharp blacks and whites of Miklós Jancsó's world: THE ROUND-UP

the contemporary cinema a solid, rational confidence, marked technically by an absence of cheap effects and intellectually by an awareness of the problems of moral survival, in their full political context.

In 1964 **András Kovács** (*b* 1925), after two years in Paris, made *Difficult People* (*Nehéz Emberek*), which probed questions of authority and opened up discussion throughout the country. In 1966 he followed it with *Cold Days* (*Hideg Napok*), a visually enthralling account of private conscience versus military authority. In *Walls* (*Falak*, 1968) Kovacs examined the less obvious, but no less vital, problems of the generation who had survived initial readjustments and were now settled and prosperous within the *régime*. Kovács's work has contributed greatly to the moral scale and stature of this new cinema.

In 1966 the world was made aware of Hungarian films by the irruption on its screens of The *Round-Up* (*Segénylegények*) directed by Miklós Jancsó, who combines intellectual drive with great visual power. His concern is national self-knowledge and, in his studies of recent and not so recent history, he destroys the traditional romantic image with a combination of passionate intensity and blood-curdling coldness. More than anyone he reflects, visually, the spaciousness of Hungary itself, and the concept, which he de-romanticises, of Hungary as a nation on horseback. Jancsó's unique gifts for manipulating figures in a landscape have distinguished his subsequent films such as *The Red and the White* (*Csillagosok, Katonak,* 1967) and *Silence and Cry* (*Csend és Kiáltás,* 1968). *Miklós Jancsó*

Equally intelligent and penetrating, though less thrusting, is László Ránody, whose *Skylark* (*Pacsirta,* 1964), a delicate, feeling, exploration of the social nature of man, combines an exact sense of time and place with a timeless truthfulness and compassion.

Perhaps the most personal note of all has been struck by **György Révész** (*b* 1927) whose *Land of Angels* (*Angyalok Földje,* 1962) and *Three Nights of One Love* (*Egy Szerelem Három Ejsakaja,* 1967) both use a formal structure to embody a deeply lyrical intention. His work has been uneven, but at its best it has a free-wheeling ease, as in *Well, Young Man?* (*Hogy Állunk, Fiatalember?* 1963), and an effortless unity of image, sound, and feeling, in which form and content are truly one.

Among the younger directors, **István Szabó** (*b* 1938) has been widely acclaimed for *Father* (*Apa,* 1967), a fluid, lyrical film, remarkable for a contrapuntal use of image and music, and for its assured, illuminating, use of fantasy. **István Gaál's** (*b* 1933) first feature, *Current* (*Sodrásban,* 1964), a delicately balanced picture of young people just entering adult life, was notable for its great visual beauty. Among the newer directors to watch are **Pál Sándor** (*b* 1939) and **Ferenc Kósa** (*b* 1937), whose *Ten Thousand Suns* (*Tizezer Nap,* 1968), makes impressive use of the wide screen. Sándor Sára, who photo- *Younger Directors*

195

graphed both *Current* and *Ten Thousand Suns,* has now turned to direction himself. *sb*

YUGOSLAVIA

In the summer of 1945 a national cinema was established in Yugoslavia under a five year plan to help unite the country. All of the six films in the first three years (the first was Vjekoslav Afric's *Slavia* in 1946) dealt with the war years, and it is important to note that a contemporary theme was never attempted until 1957. Compared with developments in Poland, Hungary, and Czechoslovakia, the Yugoslav film took a long time to find its way. It developed piecemeal in each of the republics, geographically starting with the Northern-most film centres and working its way across the country. The germinal years were 1960–61.

Nationalisation

The first signs of a humanly alive cinema appeared in the films of **France Štiglic:** *Valley of Peace* (*Dolina Mira,* 1956) and *The Ninth Circle* (*Deveti Krug,* 1960), treating respectively the lives of a Negro and a Jew. Stiglic was seeking a more satisfying lyrical and esthetic form of expression, but the real breakthrough was to come from Bostjan Hladnik (together with Aleksandar Petrović in Serbia). Hladnik's experiments in form in his short film, *Fantastic Ballad* (1957), plus a turn of studies at IDHEC in Paris, resulted in *Dance in the Rain* (*Ples Na Kisi,* 1961), a film about youth obviously influenced by the French school. He followed with *The Sand Castle* (*Pescani Grad,* 1963), reviewing the war in a highly personal style through the hallucinations of a young woman. But his experiments proved too

The final struggle between the lovers in Makavejev's THE SWITCH-BOARD OPERATOR/ LOVE DOSSIER

daring for the Slovenian film standard of strict literary adaptation, and Hladnik found himself without work. Only one other Slovenian director has been able to make innovations since: Matjaz Klopčič, whose *A Non-Existent Story* (*Zgodba Ki Je Ni, 1966*), *Paper Planes* (*Na Papirnatih, 1967*), and *Funeral Feast* (*Pozdravi Mariju, 1969*), show a sensibility toward moral dilemmas.

It was inevitable that Yugoslavia should nurture a specialist in war films, and **Veljko Bulajić** (*b* 1928) has refined it to a style of epic realism. His first film, *Train without a Schedule* (*Vlak Bez Voznog Reda, 1959*), dealt with a current problem of people migrating from Dalmatia, devastated by war, to Slavonia. In *The War* (*Rat, 1960*) he used a script by Zavattini, and then returned briefly to a social theme in *Smouldering City* (*Uzavreli Grad, 1961*). He added to the war film realistic dimensions in the popular *Kozara* (1962), and psychological depth in *A Look into the Eye of the Sun* (*Pogled u Zjenicu Sunca, 1966*), before tackling the "national monument" that is *The Battle of Neretva* (1969).

Croatia

Croatian cinema is noted for interest in current problems, and the first real social film bordering on political criticism was Branko Bauer's *Face to Face* (*Licem u Lice, 1963*); it dealt with the economic mismanagement of a high official. Fadil Hadzic followed with *Privileged Position* (*Sluzbeni Polozaj, 1964*) chronicling bureaucratic abuses, and *Protest* (1967) using social reportage to investigate a young worker's suicide. But the film with the most political impact was Vatroslav Mimica's *Prometheus from the Island of Visevica* (*Prometej Sa Otoka Visevice, 1965*), which used a purified cinematic language in piercing the thoughts of a revolutionary-turned-bureaucrat. Mimica then drifted away into a personal style, exploring thoughts and memories in *Sunday or Monday* (*Ponedeljak Ili Utorak, 1966*), the use of colour in *Kaja, I'll Kill You!* (*Kaja, Ubit Cu Te!, 1967*), and psychological tensions in Chekhov's *An Event* (*Dogadaj, 1969*).

The new directors have taken the social film along completely separate paths: the refined psychology of Zvonimir Berković's *Rondo* (1966), the honest frankness of Ante Babaja's *The Birch Tree* (*Breza, 1967*), the moral indifference of the young in Branko Ivanda's *Gravitation* (*Gravitacija, 1968*), and the identity problem of the middle generation in Ante Peterlic's *An Accidental Life* (*Slucajni Zivot, 1969*).

Serbia

If Croatian film centres in general on "social" themes, Serbia can be singled out for its liking for "political" commentary. And whereas Croatia has only one "author" worthy of the name (Mimica), Serbia has four; Petrović (*b* 1929), Djordjević (*b* 1924), Makavejev, and Pavlović. The pivotal year for them all was 1965: Mimica's *Prometheus from the Island of Visevica*, Petrović's *Three*, Djordjević's *Girl*, Makavejev's *A Man Is Not a Bird*, and Pavlović's *The Enemy*.

Aleksandar Petrović's *When Love Is Gone* (*Dvoje*, 1961) appeared at the same time as Bostjan Hladnik's *Dance in the Rain,* and together they mark the beginning of modern Yugoslav film. In *The Days* (*Dani,* 1963) Petrović continued his search into the personality via poetic metaphors, and then revolutionised the war film in *Three* (*Tri,* 1965) by underlining it as a tragic and senseless dilemma. His *I Even Met Happy Gypsies* (*Skupljaci Perja,* 1967) combined cruelty with beauty, intellect with emotion, to form a poetic document; and his recent film, *It Rains in My Village* (*Bice Skoro Propast Sveta,* 1969) was a parable in the same vein on the constant evil in man.

Purisa Djordjević, like Petrović, worked in documentaries before developing into a lyrical poet. He formed the Kino-Klub in Belgrade in union with Makavejev, Pavlović, and others, who collectively make up the nucleus of Yugoslav directors. His central theme is the phenomenon of the revolution: *Girl* (*Devojka,* 1965), *Dream* (*San,* 1966), *Morning* (*Jutro,* 1967), *Noon* (*Podne,* 1968), treating it in the form of a collage and mixing dream with reality. His recent film, *Cross Country* (*Kros Kontri,* 1969), was a parody on authoritarianism.

Dusan Makavejev (*b* 1932) also presents a fascinating mixture of new and old, humour and irony, science and eroticism, love and crime, in a cinema of free associations. He is given to emphasising an idea, such as the collective hypnosis of workers in *A Man Is Not a Bird* (*Covek Nije Tica,* 1965), the similarities between humans and rats in *The Switchboard Operator/Love Dossier* (*Ljubavni Slucaj,* 1967), and the acrobat Aleksić as the symbol of the eternal national spirit against oppression in *Innocence Unprotected* (*Nevinost Bez Zastite,* 1968) (a re-examination of the 1942 original which Aleksić starred in and directed).

Zivojin Pavlović (*b* 1933), the "Poet of the Ugly" and a well-known writer, confronts the viewer with a series of selections from real life tied together to present a harsh view of the world. His heroes are doomed because they cannot invent or adapt to the cruelty around them, and are victims of a political brutality riddled with contradictions. His first film, *Enemy* (*Neprijatelj,* 1965), emphasised the co-existence of good and evil in man; he then stretched this view to include the whole emotionally impoverished world in *The Rats Wake Up* (*Budenje Pacova,* 1967), *When I Am Dead and White* (*Kad Budem Mrtav i Beo,* 1968), and *Ambush* (*Zaseda,* 1969).

Political frankness is even more evident in the works of lesser known directors: Vladan Slijepcević's bitter attack on the corruption of power in *The Protégé* (*Sticenik,* 1966), Djordje Kadijevic's two-part examination of war-time violence in *Holiday* (*Praznik,* 1967) and *Expedition* (*Pohod,* 1968), Jovan Zivanović's black metaphor on war and oppression in *Do Not Mention the Cause of Death* (*Uzrok Smrti Ne Pominjati,* 1968), pathological killing in Mica Popović's *The Tough*

Ones (*Delije,* 1968), and political theatre in Zelimir Zelnik's *Early Works* (*Rani Radovi,* 1969).

Two young directors have recently caused the first stir in Bosnia-Hercegovina, pointing some direction for an industry that is beginning to bud. Bato Cengić used an orphanage in *Playing at Soldiers* (*Mali Vojnici,* 1968) to make an honest search into postwar times through a concrete realistic style. Boro Drasković, on the other hand, framed the problems of lost youth in a highly personal film style brilliant in conception: *Horoscope* (*Horoskop,* 1969). *Bosnia-Hercegovina*

The film company in Montenegro went bankrupt in 1966 and only co-productions are presently fostered, the most successful of which is Fedor Skubonja's *Downstream from the Sun* (*Nizvodno od Sunca,* 1969) (with Dunav Film in Belgrade), a human but sentimental document about a school teacher. *Montenegro*

Nothing has happened in Macedonia with the sole exception of the work of a visiting director, Vladan Slijepcević's *Where to Go after the Rain* (1967), attacking conformism and corruption in politics. The usual fare means historical patriotism describing the fate of a small nation disputed for centuries, including the recent expensive spectacle entitled *Samuel.* *Macedonia*

Judging from the cycles of film "authors" dating from 1967 in general, a few common characteristics are evident: the demythologising of reality, identification with individual heroes, political questioning, examination of good and evil, artistic searching, and a marked degree of fatalism. *rh*

When the Romanian film industry was established as an integral part of the nation's cultural life in 1945, it had little experience or tradition behind it. The first films—a programme of Romanian country scenes—had been shown as early as 1896, but film pioneers were handicapped by lack of resources and although features were produced from 1911 onwards, the general level was low. Organised production began on a limited scale when the National Tourist Office set up a Cinematography Department in 1935. It produced regular newsreels and documentaries, some of which were acclaimed abroad. *The Country of the Motzi* (*Tara Motilor,* 1938) gained an international award. It was made by **Paul Calinescu** (*b* 1902), who played a major part in establishing postwar cinema, and who made the first postwar feature film, *The Valley Resounds* (*Rasuna valea,* 1949), about young volunteers at a building site. **ROMANIA**

The film industry was nationalised in 1948. It suffered from a shortage of facilities and trained personnel, and for a time, feature production was limited in range, technique and quality. Feature output grew slowly but steadily and the newly-built Bucuresti studios achieved more-or-less full working capacity in 1957.

199

Films in the early Fifties were mainly screen adaptations of popular novels depicting the social changes that were taking place in national life, especially in the countryside. The most significant productions of the period were *Mitrea Cocor* (*Mitrea Cocor,* 1952, *dir* Victor Iliu) and Calinescu's *In a Village* (*De sfasurarea,* 1954), both dealing with revolutionary change in the countryside. Until the emergence of a new generation of players accustomed to the screen, acting tended to be over-theatrical. There was something of a breakthrough for screen acting technique in the satirical comedy *Our Manager* (*Directorul nostru,* 1955, *dir* Jean Georgescu).

The second half of the Fifties saw some interesting all-round developments. A turning-point was *The Mill of Luck and Plenty* (*Moara cu noroc,* 1956), also directed by **Victor Iliu** (1912–1968), a psychological drama of considerable maturity set in a Transylvanian village in the 1870s. The gifted theatre director **Liviu Ciulei** (*b* 1923) made his film *début* with *Eruption* (*Eruptia,* 1959), a promising but not altogether successful drama about oil-workers. His following film, *The Danube Waves* (*Valurile Danarii,* 1963), about a barge carrying German weapons along the Danube in 1944, established him as a first-class director. For his prize-winning *The Forest of the Hanged* (*Padurea spinzuratiler,* 1965), he used striking visual imagery to convey the inner conflict of an officer in the Austro-Hungarian army whose convictions collapse when he has to participate in the court martial of a deserter. It is one of the finest films in Romanian cinema.

Other significant productions of the late Fifties were *When the Mist Is Lifting* (*Viata nu iarta,* 1958), a personal drama of the First World War directed by **Iulian Mihu** (*b* 1926) and **Manole Marcus** (*b* 1928), and *The Secret Code* (*Secretul cifrului,* 1959), a wartime adventure film made by **Lucian Bratu** (*b* 1924).

Developments in the Sixties showed feature production to fall roughly into two categories. On the one hand, there were the big, epic spectacles based on historical themes, like Bratu's *Tudor* (*Tudor,* 1964), *The Dacians* (*Dacii,* 1966) and *Michael the Brave* (*Mihai Viteazul,* 1969), both directed by the versatile film-maker **Sergei Nicolaescu** (*b* 1930), and *The Outlaws* (*Haiducii,* 1965), directed by **Dinu Cocea** (*b* 1929), who began work on an ambitious sequel in 1969. **Mircea Dragan** (*b* 1932) used the epic style to deal with a more modern theme in *Lupeni '29* (*Lupeni '29,* 1961), depicting aspects of working-class struggle in the Twenties. His *The Column* (*Columna,* 1968) was a sequel to *The Dacians.*

The other category consists of personal and introspective dramas which broke away from the classical approach and consciously sought to develop more individualism and psychological depth. Among the directors who helped to break new ground are **Mircea Muresan** (*b* 1930), whose award-winning *Blazing Winter* (*Rascoala,* 1965) deals

in fresh terms with the peasant uprising of 1907, **Lucian Pintilie** (*b*
1933), whose first film *Sunday at Six O'Clock* (*Duminica la ora 6,*
1965), a youthful story of love, loyalty and betrayal in the wartime
resistance movement, won many international awards, and **George
Saizescu** (*b* 1932), whose *The Saturday Night Dance* (*Balul de
simbata seara,* 1968) is a very successful contemporary comedy about a
lorry-driver too shy to get himself a girl friend. **Andrei Blaier** (*b*
1933) shows a special flair for dealing with the problems of young
people in *The Mornings of a Sensible Youth* (*Diminetile unui baiat
cuminte,* 1968), as does **Savel Stiopul** (*b* 1926) in *The Last Night of
Childhood* (*Ultima noapte a copilariei,* 1966). Stiopul's earlier film
The Seasons (*Anotimpuri,* 1963), consisting of four episodes taking
place in a single day, representing childhood, adolescence, maturity
and old age, had already demonstrated his sensitivity and grasp of
technique.

Romanian work in the field of cartoons has been largely pioneered
by the brilliant animator **Ion Popescu-Gopo** (*b* 1923), who has also
directed a number of full-length live-action films based on fantasy or
legend.

Documentary production, as in many of the newer film-making
countries, was at first the spearhead of production and developed more
rapidly than feature production. Among the outstanding documentarists
are **Titus Mesaros** (*b* 1925), **Georghe Vitandis** (*b* 1929) and **Ion
Bostan** (*b* 1914). **Elisabeta Bostan** (*b* 1931) specialises in shorts
for children. *nh*

Although Bulgaria was the first Balkan country to produce films, **BULGARIA**
its pioneers, like those of Romania, were frustrated by lack of support.
Some fifty features were made before the Second World War, but only
a handful of them have any lasting value.

The industry was nationalised and put on a firm financial footing *Bulgarian State*
in 1950 and plans for the building of a new, well-equipped studio *Cinematography*
centre just outside Sofia were gradually put into operation. The first
postwar feature film was *Kalin the Eagle* (*Kalin orelat,* 1950, *dir* Boris
Borosanov), about a popular national hero.

Like Romania, Bulgaria had little experience or tradition to draw on,
and its early postwar films showed similar weaknesses. Most of the
feature films were based on strong anti-Fascist themes and although
often forceful and moving, they were inclined to simple heroics and
the black-and-white approach. Among the best were *Dawn over the
Homeland* (*Utro nad Rodinata,* 1951, *dir* Anton Marinovich), *Under
the Yoke* (*Pod igoto,* 1952, *dir* Dako Dakovski) and *People of Dimi-
trovgrad* (*Dimitrovgradtsi,* 1956, *dir* Nicolai Korabov and Dutcho
Mundrov).

A turn towards a more personal and complex approach was indicated by the Bulgarian-East German co-production *Stars* (*Sterne, dir* Konrad Wolf), a moving drama about a romance between a Jewish girl in a transit camp, at which people were selected for the death chamber, and a young German guard. It was made in 1959, at a time when, in any case, a new generation of directors was returning from the Moscow Film School and injecting fresh ideas into Bulgarian cinema. Well to the fore in breaking away from dogmatism and over-generalisation were **Rangel Vulchanov** (*b* 1928) and **Vulo Radev** (*b* 1923). Vulchanov's first feature film, *On a Small Island* (*Na malkia ostrov,* 1958), a highly individualised anti-Fascist drama scripted by the outstanding writer and poet **Valeri Petrov** (*b* 1920) was an important turning point. His experimental *Sun and Shadow* (*Slantseto i syankata,* 1962), also scripted by Petrov, a kind of screen essay in which ideas about war and peace flow from the visual imagery associated with the relationship between a boy and girl on a deserted beach, gained several international prizes. *The She-Wolf* (*Valchitsata,* 1965) is an imaginative but not wholly successful attempt at presenting a conflict between two people with basically opposite views on life, against a background of a school for juvenile delinquents. In 1968, Vulchanov embarked on a Bulgarian-Czechoslovak co-production *Aesop* (*Esop*).

Radev's films explore, with considerable psychological depth, the problems of conflicting loyalties, especially in wartime, and the inner motivations for heroism and treachery. His style is richly human and poetic, whether dealing with romantic tragedy, as in *The Peach Thief* (*Kradetsat na praskovi,* 1964), or with a highly dramatic conflict of wills, as in *The King and the General* (*Tsar i general,* 1966).

Among the outstanding films dealing with contemporary themes in the mid-Sixties are *Knight without Armour* (*Ritsar bez bronya,* 1966, *dir* Borislav Shariliev), a lyrical study of childhood scripted by Petrov, and *The Attached Balloon* (*Privarzaniat balon,* 1967, *dir* Binka Zheljazkova), an allegorical fantasy in which the balloon represents freedom of spirit.

In 1967, a crisp, new contemporary note was struck by *Sidetrack* (*Otklonenie*), a first film by **Todor Stoyanov** (*b* 1930) and **Grisha Ostrovski,** who use a highly complex construction to explore, through a chance meeting between a man and woman who were once in love, the change in social, political and moral attitudes over a twenty-year period. The role of the woman is played by **Nevena Kokanova** (*b* 1938), Bulgaria's most popular screen actress, who also had the lead role in *The Peach Thief.*

The most notable Bulgarian film of recent years: Radev's THE PEACH THIEF

Albania is the youngest film-making country in the Balkans. Before the war it had no film production at all.

The first film was a newsreel made in 1947. Until 1957, production was confined to documentaries and newsreels with the single exception of the feature film *The Great Warrior Skanderbeg* (*Velikii vion Albanii Skanderbeg*), made in Albania by the Soviet director Sergei Yutkevitch in 1954.

Regular feature production, at the rate of one a year, began in 1957, four years after the opening of the modern studios *Shqipëria e re*. By the end of the Sixties production had increased to about four feature films a year. Most of the films are based on war, wartime resistance and historical themes. Many of the early ones were heavily dogmatic and over-theatrical, but *Echoes on the Shore* (*Oshëtimë në bregdet*, 1966, *dir* Hysen Hakani*), an anti-Fascist drama set among fishermen during the war, represented a turning point by achieving a more fluid style and a maturer approach.

The first film to tackle contemporary day-to-day life was *Tana* (*Tana*, 1958) a village drama made by the talented young director Kristaq Dhamo. The first to deal with modern industrial life was *Broad Horizons* (*Horizonte te hapura*, 1968, *dir* Viktor Gjika), which dramatises a conflict of principle among the workers at a dockyard.

Outstanding among the documentaries of the Sixties was the colour film *Vangjush Mio—People's Painter* (*dir* Gësim Erebara; *cameraman* Piro Milkani) made in 1966 to commemorate the artist's seventy-fifth anniversary. *nh*

8. Japan and Elsewhere

A BRIEF SPATE OF FILMS about children came at the end of the Thirties in Japan while war films grew in number. At first a few directors avoided doing war films by adroitly choosing other types of story, but this was not allowed to last. **Kimisaburo Yoshimura** (*b* 1911) began with literary films, and in 1940 made *The Story of the Tank Commander Nishizumi* (*Nishizumi Senshacho-den*), retaining a modicum of idealism. It was extremely successful, and ranked with Tasaka's *Five Scouts*. Overall, his range of subjects and shifts of style make him a chameleon-like director. *The Fellows Who Ate the Elephant* (*Zo o Kutta Renchu*, 1947), about five hungry men, a zoo elephant that dies, and a tangle of bureaucracy, was a critical, satirical comedy—a *genre* developed in the early Fifties by others. In the same year he made *A Ball at the Anjo House* (*Anjo-ke no Butokai*) examining postwar conditions affecting a high-born family. It took the Japanese Critics' prize. For scriptwriter he used **Kaneto Shindo** (*b* 1912) who came from a farm to work in cinema, progressing to scripts and finally, in 1951, to direction. He wrote most of Yoshimura's scenarios from 1947 onwards, and the films of both men featured

Poetic composition in Mizoguchi's UGETSU MONOGATARI

Nobuko Otowa (*b* 1924), who married Shindo. She came from the Takarazuka Girls' Opera School. In *A Ball at the Anjo House* the leads were played by two famous people: **Setsuko Hara** (*b* 1920), with a *début* in 1935, who was to play several notable parts—some for Ozu and Naruse; and **Masayuki Mori** (*b* 1911), son of a novelist, leaving university to play *shingeki* parts on stage and making his screen *début* in 1942. He was to play the potter in *Ugetsu*, the husband in Kurosawa's *Rashomon,* and the Prince Myshkin role in Kurosawa's adaptation of *The Idiot.*

In 1942, the distribution circuits were unified, and in 1943 the Japan Motion Picture School (Nihon Eiga Gakko) was established. When the war ended in 1945 the Occupation administration proposed democratisation of the industry, abolishing all government control. At the same time they banned feudal stories and frowned on anything that smacked of tradition. The export of Japanese films was resumed in 1947. In the final years of the war no Japanese Critics' awards were given, and production for 1945 amounted to only thirty-five features.

The Fifties were marked by Japan's first colour films, the arrival of television, and the first Film Festival in Japan (held in Tokyo in 1954). Japanese feature production climbed back to 400 in 1955. The

The Fifties

205

first wide-screen film in 1957 completed the general improvement in techniques. Colour television was launched in 1960. From 1951 to 1968 more than 400 Japanese films won prizes at foreign festivals. Thus huge production figures were achieved between 1950 and 1968, with all modern methods to hand. The content of this flood was very uneven: "eroductions" (sensational or erotic films aimed at a special market); spy films; adaptations from commercial, classic, and important contemporary literature, foreign and Japanese, bringing out the idiosyncrasies and personal styles of directors; studies of everyday life with differing interpretations—personal, family, or social criticism (through comedy or realism); alienation; costume or period stories ranging from feudal conflicts between duty and conscience (also seen in modern Japanese gangster movies) to fantasies and ghost stories from the past.

The first colour film was *Carmen Comes Home* (*Carumen Kokyo ni Kaeru*, 1951) by **Keisuke Kinoshita** (*b* 1912), a director since 1943. His work covered a wide range: comedies showing human foibles, engaging and yet lacking in sentimentality; and serious, even tragic stories. His films include *Broken Drum* (*Yabure Daiko*, 1949), *She Was like a Wild Chrysanthemum* (*Nogiku no gotoku Kimi Nariki*, 1955), *Twenty-Four Eyes* (*Nijushi no Hitomi*, 1954), and *The Song of Narayama* (*Narayamabushi-ko*, 1958), drawing on *kabuki* style for its story of exposure of the aged on a mountain top.

Akira Kurosawa

After a protracted period as scenario writer and assistant to Kajiro Yamamoto, **Akira Kurosawa** (*b* 1910) began directing in 1943 with *Sanshiro Sugata*, a Meiji-period film about a judo expert. Now a world-famous director, his *Rashomon* (1950) took the Leone d'Oro at Venice in 1951, stimulating interest in costume drama and marking the start of a vogue for Japanese films in the West. An uncompromising, painstaking craftsman, he uses strong story lines in both period and contemporary settings. He is an *auteur* in the best sense of the word. He has handled all his own editing (which is in fact customary in Japan), and he has written most of his scripts. His period films present a microcosm of the modern world, divided into warring camps, and, at their best, they show the triumph of fortitude and magnanimity. The samurai is a soldier of fortune, a Japanese Robin Hood or a Japanese Shane. One senses that Kurosawa admires him more than anyone else, and that the lively, fearless spirit of his work stems from this ideal. *Living* (*Ikiru*, 1952), a study of an old man doomed by cancer, *Seven Samurai* (*Shichinin no Samurai*, 1954), *Throne of Blood* (*Kumonosu-jo*, 1957), and *Sanjuro* (1962) are among his best films. Toshiro Mifune starred in the last three of these, and has achieved international fame through his portrait of the swashbuckling samurai.

Kon Ichikawa (*b* 1915) began with a musical revue film. He married scriptwriter Natto Wada. Like Kinoshita, he brings humour

206

Wide-screen action in Kurosawa's THE HIDDEN FORTRESS

into his wide-ranging work, but he has also made serious films featuring outsiders like the young hero of *Alone on the Pacific/My Enemy the Sea* (*Taiheiyo Hitoribotchi,* 1963). With Kurosawa, Shindo, Kobayashi and others he tended to make black comedies in the early Fifties, satirically underlining social ills. *Punishment Room* (*Shokei no Heya,* 1955) was a study of delinquency—one of several at this time. *Crazed Fruit* (*Kuruttu Kajitsu,* 1956) by Ko Nakahira, dealing with 'teenage sex, aroused public protest. A series of films on prostitution culminating in Mizoguchi's last film, *Street of Shame* (*Akasen Chitai,* 1956) actually prompted the introduction of anti-prostitution laws. *Kon Ichikawa*

Ichikawa, using literary sources, and visualising all his work in advance, drew superb performances from Raizo Ichikawa, the extremely popular actress Ayako Wakao, and Keiko Kishi, as well as from older and younger players. Apart from his bravura, beautiful colour film, *An Actor's Revenge* (*Yukinojo Henge,* 1963), he also made the magnificent *Tokyo Olympiad* (1965).

Shindo, after a number of realistic dramas, made *The Island* (*Hadaka no Shima,* 1961), a contemporary melodrama with considerable beauty and obtrusive symbols; *Lost Sex* (*Honno,* 1966), about impotence brought on by radiation, with scenes of shimmering quality; and *Kuroneko* (*Yabu no Naka no Kuroneko,* 1968), a ghost legend. These all contained great visual elegance and exciting melodramatics, but tended to suffer from sentimentality.

Masaki Kobayashi (*b* 1916) an assistant director since 1941, contributed several films of social criticism during the Fifties, as well as the three-part epic *The Human Condition* (*Ningen no Joken,* 1959–61) about the Japanese in Manchuria during the Sino-Japanese war. *Masaki Kobayashi*

207

This featured a remarkable actor, Tatsuya Nakadai, who also performed superbly for Ichikawa and Teshigahara. *Harakiri* (*Seppuku*, 1962) and *Rebellion* (*Joi-uchi*, 1967) were tragedies set in feudal times. *Kwaidan* (1964) was an omnibus film of four ghost tales from Lafcadio Hearn (who became Yakumo Koizumi). Kobayashi said that with *Harakiri* he realised (at the Venice festival) the barriers between occidental and oriental audiences and thereafter tried to penetrate these. *Rebellion* and *Kwaidan* both exhibited an extraordinary control of movement within the frame and of cinematic pace in general.

Hiroshi
Teshigahara

Hiroshi Teshigahara (*b* 1927) is considered very advanced in Japan. The son of wealthy parents, he made *Woman of the Dunes* (*Suna no Onna*, 1963) on a small, privately-arranged budget. This unusual parable, brilliantly developed and strikingly photographed, established him internationally. *The Face of Another* (*Tanin no Kao*, 1966), a study in changing identity, was beautifully finished. Both films won many prizes, and Teshigahara used the experienced actor Eiji Okada as well as the versatile Kyoko Kishida.

Other young directors now prominent include **Shohei Imamura** (*b* 1926), whose *Insect Woman* (*Nippon Konchuki*, 1963) was well received, and whose *The Pornographer* (*Jinruigaku Nyumon*, 1966) asserted that the maker or purveyor of pornography satisfied a real function. There is also the quasi-documentarist **Susumu Hani** (*b* 1928), who, with his actress wife Sachiko Hidari has made studies of individual Japanese in foreign settings, as well as *She and He* (*Kanojo to Kare*, 1963) about a society drop-out; **Yasuzo Masumura** (*b* 1924), who worked under Mizoguchi and Ichikawa and studied in Rome after graduating from Tokyo University, responsible for some impressive melodramas—*Manji* (1964) and *Two Wives* (*Tsuma Futari*, 1967), both scripted by Shindo; and **Noboru Nakamura** (*b* 1913), an assistant to Shimazu and since 1941 a versatile director, notably of *The Twin Sisters of Koto* (*Koto*, 1963), *The Kii River* (*Ki no Kawa*, 1966), and *Portrait of Chieko* (*Chieko-sho*, 1967), starring the exquisite Shima Iwashita.

Yoshishige Yoshida (*b* 1933) began as an assistant to Kinoshita, and joined Shochiku in 1955. His *Forbidden Love* (*Mizu de Kakareta Monogatari*, 1965) and *The Affair* (*Joen*, 1967) featured his actress wife Mariko Okada, who played an important role in Masumura's *Two Wives.* ld

Nagisa Oshima

Nagisa Oshima (*b* 1932) has created something of a sensation in Western film circles with *Death by Hanging* (*Koshikei*, 1968) and *Diary of a Shinjuku Thief* (*Shinjuku Dorobo Nikki*, 1968), for while he may not be the most ably equipped representative of the new generation, he knows no fear and brooks no compromise in his assault on convention and his championship of the student movement in Japan. His films are full of barely repressed violence and protest. He sees eroticism as a means of escape from formalism. *Japanese Summer: Double Suicide (Murishinju Nihon no Natsu*, 1967) and *Boy (Shonen*, 1969) have emphasised his stature and his versatility, and he has shot fifteen features during the past decade. *pdc*

Bengali cinema showed early inclinations towards relatively modern socially-conscious drama especially in the work of actor-director "Prince" P. C. Barua of Assam whose *Debdas* (1935—Bengali and Hindi) created an archetypal "hero" and set new standards in realism. Between Barua and Debaki Bose (*Chandidas*, 1932) and generally in the films of New Theatres, Bengali cinema acquired a reputation for depth of subject and cinematic treatment which was enhanced manifold with the arrival of **Satyajit Ray** (*b* 1922) on the scene in 1954. Ray's *Pather Panchali* was an immediate success on its home ground before acquiring world fame, consolidated by its sequel *Aparajito* (1956) which won the highest award at Venice, and was followed by *World of Apu (Apur Sansar*, 1958) completing possibly the most famous trilogy in world cinema. Ray maintained a very high level with *The Music Room (Jalsaghar*, 1958), *The Goddess (Devi*, 1960), *Kanchanjungha* (1962) his only colour film, *Two Daughters (Teen Kanya*, 1961), and with *The Big City (Mahanagar*, 1963) and particularly *Charulata* (1964) broke fresh ground in theme and style. These two films and the first story of *The Coward and the Saint (Kapurush-O-Mahapurush)* constitute a sort of second trilogy, this time on the emerging woman in India. His films since then seemed to have groped around without much success and *The Hero (Nayak*, 1965) and particularly *The Zoo (Chidiakhana*, 1967) tended towards the commonplace in many respects.

The rise of a truly Indian and cinematic trend with Ray followed by **Ritwik Ghatak**—(*Ajantrik*, 1958; *Meghe Dhaka Tara*, 1960; *Subarnarekha*, 1965); **Mrinal Sen**—(*Baishe Sravan*, 1960; *Akash-Kusum*, 1964; *Matira Manisha*, 1966) in the Bengali cinema marked a polarisation in which the all-India film in Hindi made in Madras and Bombay gave up most of its social earnestness and serious cinematic efforts and inclined more and more towards lavish productions, in which the story is little more than a "vehicle" for the stars, the song-writer and the musical director. But not before, the films of Guru Dutt (*Pyaasa*, 1957; *Kagaz-ka-Phool*, 1959) had showed a sentimental charm in the treatment of love. **Bimal Roy** had made a series of films of a superior moral content (*Bandini*, 1963, *Sujata*, 1959, and the famous "neo-realistic" forerunner of *Pather Panchali* in *Two Acres of Land* or *Do Bigha Zamin*, 1953, strongly influenced by Italian films at India's first International Film Festival in 1952); **Raj Kapoor**, in spite of an innate flamboyance, expressed some social concerns in *The Vagabond (Awara*, 1951) which made him the best-known Indian after Nehru in the U.S.S.R. and *Keep Awake* (*Jagte Raho*, 1957) which won the grand prize at Karlovy Vary but threw them to the winds in the bland search for spectacle in *Union* (*Sangam*, 1965); **Khwaja Ahmed Abbas,** who writes many of Raj Kapoor's films, distinguished himself in a series of films beginning with *Children of the Earth* (*Dharti-ka-Lal*, 1949) shown in Moscow, Paris and London and followed by *The Lost Child* (*Munna*, 1954), *The City and the Dream* (*Shehr-Aur-Sapna*, 1966) which won the President of India's gold medal and shares, like its predecessors, the socialist leanings of its remarkably honest film director. In general, however, the all-India film has, in recent years, given up its previous social-reformist zeal and glorified the conventions of a traditional society and condemned modern points of view as evil. In this formula it has found the most comfortable solution to the problems of pleasing a predominantly tradition-bound society urged to change its outlook by a small minority on the one hand and faced by manifestations of science on the other.

The government of India took a hand in the re-organisation of the cinema by appointing a high-powered committee in 1951 and on its recommendation, made a central censorship uniformly applicable in all the states, established a set of prizes, a training school (Film Institute of India) in Poona, a Children's Film Society, a film archive, an occasional international film festival, and gave encouragement to the Federation of Film Societies of India which, starting with seven member societies in 1960 now has nearly one hundred ties in its fold. *cdg*

Soumitra Chatterjee in Ray's THE WORLD OF APU

Catch-words have a tendency to stick, in films as well as in politics. Some ten years ago film magazines were raving about the French *Nouvelle Vague;* a few years later they concentrated on the Brazilian *Cinema Nôvo.* A new type of film? In what respects was *Cinema Nôvo* new?

The traditional Brazilian film leant heavily on melodrama of an escapist nature. Brutality and eroticism, often with a streak of sadism, were standard ingredients. Besides there existed popular music films with carnival gaiety and carefree people on the Copacabana beach. In 1949 Alberto Cavalcanti returned to his native country to liberate the Brazilian cinema from the Hollywood influence. He failed but he directed *Song of the Sea* (*O canto do mar,* 1953) and produced Lima Barreto's *The Outlaw* (*O cangaçeiro,* 1953). Together with the Italian neo-realism these two films inspired young film-makers.

The first sign of something new was **Nelson Pereira dos Santos's** *Rio 40 degrees* (*Rio 40 graus,* 1955). It was a semi-documentary attempt to contrast the misery of the *favela* (the rapidly growing slum district) with prosperous politicians and Copacabana life. Its structure was somewhat contrived, but dos Santos was brave enough to stand up for the poor. Here one encountered the social criticism which characterises the best works of *Cinema Nôvo.*

Dos Santos is the precursor of *Cinema Nôvo,* but he is also the director behind one of its most mature films, *Barren Lives* (*Vidas secas,* 1963). This time he turned to the barren, famine-stricken *sertão* in the north-eastern provinces of Brazil. The *favela* and the *sertão,* these were the two main settings for the social protest of *Cinema Nôvo.* With uncompromising realism dos Santos describes the drought in this province where animals die and men toil to survive while vultures wait patiently in the trees.

The poor Fabiano settles with his family in a deserted house, but when the rain period comes, the owner returns and Fabiano has to work for him. The drought forces the family to move once more, and a new, hopeless desert walk begins. The film ends with a dazzlingly white dissolve and the year, 1942, just as it began with 1940. Nothing really changes. "We can't always live like animals," exclaims Fabiano's wife, but there is nothing in this fatalistic film to prove that they will not have to. *Vidas secas* is a film of resignation rather than rebellion. Fabiano accepts his poverty and the owner's comparative wealth. The film has a compelling authenticity that would have been inconceivable in the traditional Brazilian cinema. Description dominates over analysis, here as in most *Cinema Nôvo* films.

The illiterate people of the *sertão* easily fall prey to religious superstition in the form of itinerant "prophets." **Ruy Guerra's** *The Rifles* (*Os fuzis,* 1963) opens with a doomsday sermon, delivered by a hoarse voice against a background of brilliant light and sterile branches. A

BRAZIL white ox shall bring the life-giving rain. Soldiers are called in to a village to protect the grocer, who exploits the hunger of the villagers. The soldiers are seen in their traditional Latin American roles as protectors of the privileged. Finally the tension explodes in a short outburst of violence. A driver and ex-soldier breaks down and fires on the army trucks. He is brutally shot at close range. One detail shows how far Guerra stands from the ordinary adventure film. When the killer sees his victim, he vomits from excitement.

Os fuzis is very dynamic. Travelling shots are frequent, for instance when the soldiers are introduced through close-ups of rifle-butts and marching feet, attributes of power and violence. The hunted driver is followed by means of a telephoto lens which brings us into the middle of the bloody climax. If dos Santos may seem resigned, Guerra preaches rebellion. It is an isolated act here, but there is no doubt where Guerra's sympathies are. He works with an ageless theme of revolt: the starving against the wealthy, the oppressed against the oppressors. Religion is denounced in the epilogue when the holy ox is sacrificed by a disappointed crowd.

Glauber Rocha

The third great talent—but a very undisciplined one—of *Cinema Nôvo* is **Glauber Rocha** (*b* 1938). He made his first feature, *Barravento*, in 1961. It is a strange mixture of ethnographical and melodramatic components. The setting is a primitive fishing village where the poor fishermen are exploited by those who rent nets to them. Furthermore their own superstition serves as an obstacle to progress. The visual style has a certain force, for instance the recurring waves in the beach scenes, but Rocha hardly manages to integrate the disparate elements.

In his next film, *The Black God and the White Devil* (*Deus e o diabo na terra do sol*, 1963), the visionary streak in Rocha is even more evident. The waste land of the *sertão* is introduced under the credit titles by a slowly panning camera. The sequence ends with close-ups of the unseeing eyes of dead cows, probably starved to death. Manuel and his wife Rosa are attracted by the holy preacher Sebastião. But when Manuel even allows their child to be sacrificed, Rosa takes revenge by stabbing Sebastião. Rosa and Manuel escape from the ensuing tumult, only to be forced into a band of outlaws, the cruel *cangaçeiros*. A world of violence—torture, rape, castration, and mutilation—opens up in front of their horrified eyes. Only when the leader of the band is killed can they escape. Rocha tells this story in a ballad style. His feeling for the exploited seems to be acute and his thesis is: "The earth belongs neither to Gods nor to demons but to people." The poor must get better conditions here and now.

From the ballad Rocha turned to the opera for inspiration in *Land in Trance* (*Terra em transe*, 1966). It is a story about Eldorado, a fictitious state in South America or the third world. As a political

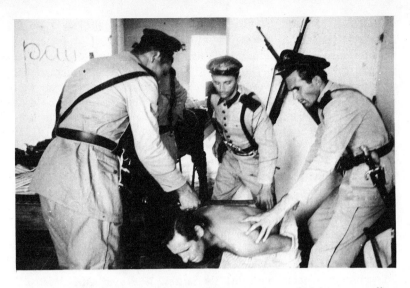

Brazil's "cinema nôvo." Still from VIDAS SECAS

allegory it denounces the egotism of right wing politicians as well as the confusion and the impotence of the left. "I am not politically organised," said Rocha during the Cannes festival in 1969, when his latest film *Antonio das Mortes* (1969) was shown. Here Rocha has chosen a Western theme about a tyrant, who hires a killer against peasants, and elaborated it with elements of opera and mythology.

Of course there are other directors worth mentioning. On the evidence of *The Assault on the Post Train* (*O assalto ao trem pagador,* 1962) Roberto Farias seems to be important. A train robbery gives some people a chance of breaking away from the crippling poverty of the *favela,* but they fail. It is a well handled, unpretentious film with a depressingly realistic picture of the *favela.*

Without being a homogeneous school, *Cinema Nôvo* has renewed the Brazilian cinema. The young directors have discovered the reality around them. It has become imperative for them to protest against inhuman conditions. In a country where survival is often a struggle for life and death against nature, aesthetics may seem irrelevant, but in the best of these films the indigenous tradition and a modern cinematic technique have worked together in a cinema of poerty and cruelty. *asv*

SPAIN

The nationalist movement soon dug into the past for its themes and the Forties were filled with titles that pointed to better days. Directors like the prolific **Juan de Orduña** (*b* 1907), a former actor, filled the screens with such monarchistic motifs as *Holy Queen* (*Reina Santa,* 1947) and *Mad with Love* (*Locura de amor,* 1948). Even before the period film began to decline, the pseudo-religious film was in the ascendant, and Orduña and company were being replaced by director

Rafael Gil (*b* 1913), whose talent yielded works like *Our Lady of Fatima* (*La Señora de Fatima,* 1951).

But though all these film-makers had taken their profession seriously enough, the pictures they made were simply not of an international stature, and it was not until 1951 that the Spanish industry showed any signs of enlarging its horizons. The first film that might be considered of particular interest was that year's *Furrows* (*Surcos*), a late-born piece of neo-realism by **José Antonio Nieves Conde** (*b* 1915). It was also the year in which two of the best-known contemporary directors, **Juan Antonio Bardem** (*b* 1922) and **Luis G. Berlanga** (*b* 1921), made a tandem *début* with the comedy *That Happy Couple* (*Esa pareja feliz*). Bardem had his biggest success soon afterwards with the slightly melodramatic *Death of a Cyclist* (*Muerte de un ciclista,* 1955), but showed a decline in later works, which included *Calle Mayor* (an adaptation of Sinclair Lewis's *Main Street,* 1956), and *The Player Pianos* (*Los Pianos mecanicos,* 1965). Berlanga proved the more flexible talent and went on to make an important contribution to the country's cinema with his sly satires. *Welcome, Mr. Marshall!* (*Bienvenida, Mr. Marshall,* 1953) was the first of these, followed at regular intervals by such titles as *Miracle Each Thursday* (*Los jueves, milagro,* 1957), *Plácido* (1961) and the classic black comedy *The Executioner/Not on Your Life* (*El verdugo,* 1963).

Young Spanish Cinema

The Sixties saw two new phenomena: a drastic increase in co-productions and the rise of a Young Spanish Cinema worthy of consideration. The first, though it was eventually to degenerate into a cheap and tired practice, played an important role in the integration of Spain into the world market (still a far from complete process). The foreign partners, predominantly Italy, were moved by purely economic motives, for Spain offered them many benefits, from landscapes to technicians, all at much cheaper prices. And from a plodding eighteen co-productions a year at the beginning of the decade, the practice surged to a peak of ninety-two in 1966.

Along with the expanding market, the Spanish cinema was shaped by an administrative change and the creation of a new set of laws finally designed to stress quality. The changes began to take place at the end of 1962, and the results started to appear in the spring of the following year. The first two works on the scene were *The Good Love* (*El buen amor,* 1963), **Francisco Regueiro's** (*b* 1934) atmospheric study of youth, and a comedy, *From Rose to Yellow* (*Del rosa al amarillo,* 1963), in which **Manuel Summers** (*b* 1935) set the pace of independence by acting as his own producer.

The first really important picture to come out of the Young Spanish Cinema and Spain was *Aunt Tula* (*La tia Tula,* 1964), an exceptional adaptation of the Unamuno novel in which **Miguel Picazo** (*b* 1927) held the Spanish female up for examination. The next came from

Geraldine Chaplin and Per Oscarsson in Saura's weird study of marriage, THE HONEYCOMB

Carlos Saura (*b* 1932), whose career dated back to 1959, but who had encountered endless difficulties in making serious films. With the dramatic *The Hunt* (*La caza,* 1965), however, his reputation was secured, and he quickly became the best-known of the young directors, with a series of excellent pictures that include the black comedy *Peppermint Frappé* (1967), and the psychological drama *The Honeycomb* (*La madriguera,* 1969).

Three other important young directors emerged during this same period: **Antonio Eceiza** (*b* 1935), with the fantasy *Dead but not Buried* (*De cuerpo presente,* 1965); **Basilio M. Patino** (*b* 1936), with a story of student life, *Nine Letters to Berta* (*Nueva cartas a Berta,* 1965); and **Angelino Fons** (*b* 1935), with the quasi-surrealist period piece *The Search* (*La busca,* 1966).

All this activity took place in Madrid, which, by tradition and bureaucratic basis, had always been the home of Spain's film industry.

But in Barcelona, the country's second city and a zealous keeper of a different tradition, the young had ideas of their own. The *escuela de Barcelona* ("School of Barcelona") meant both a specific group of co-operating directors and technicians and, on a larger scale, a sort of *avant-garde* fantasy that was directly opposed to the expressionistic realism of the directors of the *mesata*. Behind this movement was a natural bent for surrealism (as the home of such types as Gaudi, Miró, and Dali), and the specific model of novelist **Gonzalo Suárez** (*b* 1934). The first of the series of School films had been based on a script of his, *Fata morgana* (1966), that was directed by **Vicente Aranda** (*b* 1926). This was soon followed by several anti-storyline films that grew out of a single group project, the best of which was the feature-length *Dante Is Not Only Severe* (*Dante no es unicamente severo,* 1967), by **Jacinto Esteva** (*b* 1936) and **Joaquin Jordá** (*b* 1935). The best films of the movement, however, came from Suárez himself: *Ditirambo* (1967) and *The Strange Case of Dr. Faustus* (*El extraño caso del Dr. Fausto,* 1969). *wd*

LUIS BUÑUEL

After *Las Hurdes* Buñuel apparently disappeared from view. For completely different reasons, by different governments, both *L'Age d'Or* and *Las Hurdes* had been banned. Buñuel seemed in exile, working for a while as a producer in Spain then supervising war documentaries in New York for the Museum of Modern Art. After the war, he drifted south to Mexico where he directed two reputed pot-boilers for Oscar Dancigers who then let him make *Los Olvidados* (1950). By winning the Palme d'Or at Cannes the following year, *Los Olvidados* brought Buñuel's name for the first time before the public at large.

The Mexican Period

On the surface a film about delinquent youth in Mexico City, *Los Olvidados* is yet another presentation of the anarchic and destructive forces within the individual, forces that society has been unable to contain. The characters are all disturbingly interdependent, good and evil distributed in varying proportions throughout them all. From the gentle Ochitos to the raging blind man, Buñuel provides us with a crescendo of violence which is directly related to the world in which they live. Throughout this film, the feeling grows that in a world where political Fascism is just round the corner, one has to be violent in order to survive. Thus the title—*The Lost Ones*—refers to them all.

After this, his first major critical success, Buñuel once again worked in comparative obscurity in Mexico and France, directing films of uneven quality but of immense interest nevertheless. In fact, the better one knows these films, the more the unevenness seems an aspect of the production conditions while the interest remains the result of Buñuel's probing mind. Looked at thematically, the most memorable seem to go in pairs. Both *Susana* (1951) and *El Bruto* (1952) explored the disruptive effect that sexual passion can have upon a controlled community, while *El* (1952) and *Ensayo de un Crimen* (1955) both dealt with the inner plight of men locked within themselves, imprisoned in their own fantasies. His two films in English, *The Adventures of Robinson Crusoe* (1952) and *The Young One* (1960) were both set on islands and were in many ways the most affirmative films that Buñuel has ever made. Only when away from organised society, these films seem to say, can man begin to re-organise his world along more humane lines. Yet even here, *Robinson Crusoe* ends with Crusoe going back to the structured civilisation that he has known before, and there is a hint in *The Young One* that the island is to become a hunting reserve!

His films made in France about this time—*Cela s'appelle l'aurore* (1955), *La Mort en ce jardin* (1956), and *Republic of Sin* (*La Fièvre monte à El Pao,* 1959)—while more concerned with the more public world of political corruption than his Mexican films, are less immediately physical in the impact they have upon us and thus seem less characteristically Buñuelian. Certainly, it was from Mexico that he brought forth his next unquestionable masterpiece, *Nazarin* (1958), and from Spain his next great film after that, *Viridiana* (1961).

France

Ostensibly so different, these two films are thematically very close. They are both studies of spiritual pride and of the fecklessness of the "pure" man in a brutal and anarchic world. But it is not just the world that is wrong. One of the great qualities about Buñuel as an artist is his immense capacity for realism, his unshirking ability to see things as they are, no matter how desperate, no matter how disagreeable. In *Viridiana,* the beggars; in *Nazarin,* Hugo, the dwarf, and Andara, the whore: these characters are all meticulously observed. Along with the many animals that litter these films, they form part of the relentlessly physical world that Buñuel creates for us. It is the essential failing of both Viridiana and Nazarin that in their search for personal purity they refuse to acknowlege this physical world. They don't even see it. Hence, not only are they ultimately unable to be of any use to it, they actually make it worse. They unleash passions wherever they go, as if to compensate for their own repressions. So Nazarin walks with violence in his wake, and Viridiana's uncle, Don Jaime, humiliated by her unforgiving rejection of him, kills himself.

Nazarin and Viridiana

Nevertheless, there is a measure of tentative regeneration in both these films on the personal level: after her rape and her failure with the beggars, Viridiana burns her crown of thorns, lets down her hair, looks at herself in the mirror for the first time in the film, and goes to her cousin's rooms, prepared now to accept certain aspects of the world she had rejected before; while Nazarin, after his defeat and humiliation, allows himself to be blessed by a simple woman on the road and to accept some fruit from her. The ending of both these films gives us the sense that the central characters have learned something about themselves and the world they inhabit in the course of the film,

Silvia Pinal and Fernando Rey in Buñuel's VIRIDIANA

but what role they will be able to play is far from clear. Their salvation, if that is what it is, relates to themselves alone. The world outside, like Andara in *Nazarin,* remains totally unredeemed, apparently unchangeable.

Buñuel in the Sixties

Since *Viridiana,* Buñuel, in his sixties, seems to have come into his own. He has found it much easier to set up productions and now appears able to command greater sums of money to make more lavish-looking films. Unfortunately, this kind of acceptance seems to have had a somewhat trivialising effect upon his work. Whatever the comic/satirical delights of *The Exterminating Angel* (*El Angel Exterminador,* 1962), *Simon of the Desert* (*Simon del Desierto,* 1965), *Belle de Jour* (1967) and *La Voie Lactée* (1969), they are comparatively static works, operating almost exclusively on the level of *le gag.* They seem back in the Dali ethos of *Un Chien Andalou*—inviting us to laugh at other people's absurdities instead of creating a Swiftian world that implicates us all. From this point of view, in many ways the most arresting of all his films is *Le Journal d'une Femme de Chambre* (1964), with Jeanne Moreau. Transplanting Mirbeau's tale into the France of just before the war, a France where both church and state were about to give in to the forces of Vichy, a world where Fascism was on the march, it is the most political film that Buñuel has ever made. At the same time, it possesses a variety of human characters only rivalled by *Viridiana* and *Los Olvidados.* Within this historical setting, the film quite unambiguously celebrates the trumph of evil over good intentions, yet with a respect for all the characters that is disturbing in the extreme—another slash across our eyeballs!

If *Le Journal* offers us a desperate view of the world, this view also seems realistic. Characters and events are presented with compelling particularity, creating a strong sense of an actual place and time, of a precise moment in history. And if Buñuel's world seems pessimistic—indeed, very much a world without hope—it is simultaneously full of compassion, even for the characters that we might wish to despise. It is this compassionate realism, the depth of his perception, that finally makes Buñuel one of the great masters of the cinema. *ph*

CANADA

The pattern in Canadian cinema after 1945 was the same as before the war: great plans and small results. What was new, though, was a limited number of features made in Quebec in the French language. These came to an end with the introduction of television. The only notable production was the film version of Gratien Gelinas's play, *Tit Coq*. In English-speaking Canada, it was mainly a matter of British and American films being filmed on location.

Canada's problems were similar to those of British film-makers during the Thirties, when audiences preferred American films and American companies dominated distribution and exhibition. It has always been like this in Canada, where no government measures to encourage and protect domestic production were introduced. It is still this way, except for the fact that a growing spirit of awareness of Canadian identity and character has produced a strong movement for more Canadian films in home cinemas. This tide began in Quebec, where new, young directors, working with little money and equipment but with a great deal of artistry and enthusiasm have produced over thirty features during the past ten years, among them Gilles Groulx (*Le Chat dans le Sac*), Gilles Carle (*Le Viol d'une Jeune Fille Douce*), Michel Brault (*Entre la Mer et l'Eau Douce*), Raymond Garceau (*Le Grand Rock*), Jean-Pierre Lefèbvre (*Il ne faut pas mourir pour ça* and others), and Claude Jutra (*A Tout Prendre*). In Toronto and Vancouver, outstanding films have come from Larry Kent (*Sweet Substitute*), Allan King (*Warrendale*), Paul Almond (*Isabel*), Eric Till (*A Great Big Thing*), Don Owen (*The Ernie Game*) and others.

The National Film Board (founded 1939) has moved away from its concept of short-subject documentaries to make such interesting features as *Prologue* (Robin Spry), *Christopher's Movie Matinee* (Mort Ransen), *Don't Let the Angels Fall* (George Kaczender), *Drylanders* (Donald Haldane), and several others. During these years, however, Canada lost to the American and British cinemas such directors and actors as Sidney Furie, Norman Jewison, Arthur Hiller, Ted Kotcheff, and Susan Clark, Michael Sarrazin, Donald Sutherland, Alex Kanner, Joanna Shimkus, and Alexandra Stewart.

With the formation of the Canadian Film Development Corporation in 1968, more film-makers are finding it easier to finance their projects. The theatres (which once actually opposed the showing of Canadian films) realise that they have a responsibility to project Canada on the screen, and this, together with the growing influence of the NFB and CBC, is bringing about the creation of a national cinema in keeping with Canada's growth as a nation. *gp*

Australia   Since the Second World War, feature production has been made virtually impossible by overseas control of distribution (although location shooting of foreign films has kept a small industry in work. Among independent local films, Cecil Holmes's *Three in One* (1956) showed virtuosity and perception, but most have been disappointing. Today, a boom in co-production with American and British firms has increased the number and skill of Australian technicians available to make films, but guarantees of distribution for local features and, perhaps more important, a local directorial talent of genuine ability are still absent. *jb*

CUBA   The Cuban Revolution laid the foundations of a national film style. To be sure, feature films had been made long before, but they were often financed from abroad, and, conforming to entertainment formulas, they seem to have been rather stereotyped. In one of its first laws (March 24, 1959) the revolutionary government stated, "Cinema is an art." A programme to develop the cinema and further revolutionary spirit was drafted. ICAIC (Instituto Cubano del Arte e Industria Cinematográficos) became the central body of Cuban cinema. New cinemas were built, mobile units were organised, a *cinémathèque* was established, and foreign artists were invited. No less than forty-four feature films were produced during the years 1960–68.

From the very beginning the cinema was seen as an instrument of education, and this is most evident in the shorts. One of the primary aims of the documentary was to demonstrate the new Cuba, to inspire national feelings and maintain revolutionary enthusiasm. "The cinema is a weapon of the Revolution," says **Santiago Alvarez** (*b* 1919), the leading name in the Cuban short film field. Head of the shorts and newsreel department of ICAIC, he edits their weekly newsreel, which may contain propaganda for the sugar campaign as well as attacks on American aggression in South East Asia or exploitation in Latin America. Dynamic editing and instructive texts are common in these newsreels.

Considering the political development of the area, it is quite natural that the Cuban documentary should have a militant and didactic character. In *Historia de una batalla* (1962) **Manuel Octavio Gomez** (*b* 1934) drew a direct parallel between the fight against illiteracy and

the struggle with the invading mercenaries at Playa Girón (Bay of
Pigs). Exposing violence in the U.S.A. and attacking "Yankee imperialism," Alvarez scorned objectivity and worked with polemic contrasts and a dialectic technique. "Agit-prop" texts and excerpts from newspapers and newsreels are elements of this technique. *Muerte al invasor* (1961), dealing with the Playa Girón incident, saw the U.S.A. as the chief enemy of the Revolution. *Ciclon* (1963) is a more conventional documentary about Hurricane Flora playing havoc in October 1963, but *Now* (1965) depicted riots and police brutality in the U.S.A. to the accompaniment of Lena Horne's song. *Hasta la victoria siemple* (1967), which paid homage to Che Guevara, cited the Cuban example as a danger to imperialism. *Hanoi martes 13* (1967) was built on abrupt changes between peaceful work and attacking jet planes, between melodious singing and the sound of exploding bombs. Ironic contrasts were abundant. A picture of a burnt-out church was followed by a rapid still of Cardinal Spellman, a weeping Vietnamese girl by a smiling Lady Bird Johnson with her cine camera. In *LBJ*, (1968), another *exposé* of violence in the U.S.A., Alvarez cut from idyllic blue-tinted pictures of LBJ kissing a child to a red-tinted picture of a burning Vietnamese. *79 Springs* (1969) was a brilliantly edited portrait of Ho Chi Minh, poet, guerilla leader and statesman.

In the feature films as well, the Revolution, the liberation, has been a main theme. **Tomás Gutiérrez Alea** (*b* 1928, and graduated from the Centro Sperimentale in Rome) made the first feature: *Historias de la revolucion* (1960). Three episodes from the fight against Batista stressed the importance of solidarity, but Alea's style was still rather impersonal. *Las doce sillas* (1962) was a satirical farce about a bourgeois egotist who had learnt nothing from the Revolution. *Cumbite* (1964) demonstrated how nothing can be achieved without co-operation, and certainly not in the face of crippling superstition. Here Alea's style was based on his earlier documentaries and Italian Neo-realism. *La muerte de un burocrata* (1966) was a wild, farcical display of references to film history. Bureaucracy is always a worthwhile—and mostly safe—target for satire in a Socialist state, but Alea's film was somewhat mechanical in its effects. In 1969 Alea made his most mature film: *Memories of Underdevelopment.* Edmundo Desnoes's novel is an analysis of an outsider's problems in a revolutionary society. The novel has a certain diary character, and Alea shows us the surroundings through the eyes of Sergio, a twenty-eight-year-old man of bourgeois origin. He lives in a vacuum, in a mixture of past and present, since his wife and friends have emigrated. When others prepare the defence of their country during the missile crisis of 1962, Sergio just watches with binoculars from his flat. Alea's ambivalent and critical attitude is a promising sign in Cuban cinema.

The films about the guerilla movement have not romanticised it.

Cuba   Discipline is the key word rather than revolutionary ecstasy, sacrifice rather than easy victories. Julio Garcia Espinosa's *El joven rebelde* (1961, scripted by Zavattini) described how a brave young boy learns the necessity of responsibility and solidarity by joining the guerillas. Espinosa's style is functional, and pictorial values are never allowed to supplant the message. His later *Las aventuras de Juan Quinquin* (1967) about a popular hero's development from choirboy to rebel was a very personal and funny film in the picaresque tradition. It was often chaotic with its many surprise effects and rapid contrasts, but it offered a refreshing and vital portrait of the invulnerable Juan. In a dark and sometimes bitter film, *El desertor* (1968), Manuel Perez described the rigorous demands of the rebel movement, using oblique angles and close-ups with a shaky, hand-held camera. Pastor Vega's *De la guerra Americana* (1968) suggested two paths by which a Latin American peasant could escape his misery: become a guerillero or a mercenary.

Humberto Solas (*b* 1942) has concentrated on the situation of Cuban women. His *Manuela* (1966) was about a young peasant girl who joins the rebels for revenge but learns discipline and matures into a true revolutionary. His dynamic style was further refined in the imposing *Lucia* (1968), pictorially the richest Cuban film. The three episodes (1895, 1932, the Sixties) described three stages in the Cuban woman's political awakening. The difference in style between the fascinating frescoes of the first episode and the earthy humour of the last was evidence enough of Solás's talent. Gómez also chose a historical subject, the rebellion of 1868 against the Spaniards, for his *La primera carga al machete* (1967). It was a brave attempt to describe a historical event with the technique of *cinéma-vérité* or a television interview: a documentary approach, intense close-ups, a nervously roaming camera. *asv*

SWITZER-   During the Second World War Switzerland had the vital task of
LAND   preserving a Swiss film culture (also a theatrical tradition, because of the large number of German stage *émigrés*). It was considered necessary to project, filmically, the creative forces of democracy in Switzerland, and as a result the documentary grew in importance, even if the obvious successes were in the feature field: *Marie-Louise,* and especially *The Last Chance* (*Die letzte Chance*), both directed by **Leopold Lindtberg** (*b* 1902) and written by Richard Schweitzer.

By the end of the war, the situation in the Swiss cinema had begun to change. Gradually the internal restraints and the obligations to cut down on production began (this was also noticeable a little later in the theatre, cf. demise of the Schauspielhaus, Zürich). Yet Max Haufler was still able to shoot *People Passing By* (*Menschen, die vorüberziehn*), based on a play by Carl Zuckmayer; Lindtberg managed *Four in the Jeep* (*Die Vier im Jeep*); and Jacques Feyder shot the underrated *Une femme disparaît* in 1941—but the spirit of the committed Swiss cinema had evaporated, and around 1950 the rather flat, dialect comedy made its triumphant entry into the Swiss film world.

Franz Schnyder (*b* 1910), who was successful at the box office with his inadequate film versions of the key novels by Jeremias Gotthelf, continued as late as 1957 to focus on the Swiss man involved in the war (*Der 10 Mai*). **Kurt Früh** (*b* 1915) made quite an impact with *The Zürrer Bakery* (*Bäckerei Zürrer*), thanks to his convincing use both of local colour and of the often miscast actor Emil Hegetschwiler. And Kurt Hoffmann, after meeting Dürrenmatt, directed the latter's *Marriage of Mr. Mississippi* (*Ehe des Herrn Mississippi*) in a co-production with Wechsler.

First signs of a revival came in the documentary field—but it was clear that thoroughly trained directors and scriptwriters were lacking, and the rise of such qualified talents only occurred at the close of the Sixties, and even then only on an experimental basis.

In the Suisse romande, directors like **Alain Tanner** (*b* 1929), with *Charles mort ou vif* (1969), **Henry Brandt**(*b* 1921), with *Quand nous étions petits enfants,* Yves Yersin, and others were active.

German Switzerland slowly followed this example, through Kurt Gloor, Alexander J. Seiler, Fredi M. Murer and others. The main problem was money; the older production companies, tailored only to the Swiss market, had almost completely lost credit with the banks, and only in 1970 did the government agree to help the industry in a small way. But television (at first in the romande, and later in German Switzerland) entered the field, and began to co-finance feature films—in fact, to make them possible. The attempts by the National Film Centre to give films monetary subsidies were rejected but also approved. Money was becoming available from the various industries, local authorities and organisations, but the government refused the Centre's offers, taking officialdom to the limit.

Unfortunately Switzerland has never really established a healthy and at the same time artistically satisfactory film industry. Hope alone keeps the young directors pressing forward. *fb*

GREECE

In 1947, following the German occupation and in spite of the Civil War, a new start was made in the Greek cinema. Film studios were constructed, big production companies were founded, and, at least on a technical level, considerable progress was achieved. Several films attracted large audiences, among them sentimental comedies like Dimitri Ioannopoulos's *Voice of the Heart* (*Foni tis Kardias,* 1943), George Zervos's *Four Steps* (*Tessera Skalopatia,* 1947), and popular melodramas like George Tzavella's *The Drunkard* (*O Methistakas,* 1949), about the decay of an old man in the vulgar society of the postwar *nouveaux riches.*

223

These films, together with more ambitious efforts, social satires from stage originals like Alekos Sakellarios's *Marry a Girl from Your Own Village* (*Papoutsi apo to topo sou,* 1946), *Nazis Strike Again* (*I Yermani xanarhonde,* 1947), a wildly hilarious black comedy on the consequences of a supposed new German occupation, or Tzavellas's *Marinos Kontaras* (1947), an heroic story set in the islands of Paros and Santorini, showed the tendencies of the newly-born industry and formed a new generation of film-makers who were to dominate the Fifties.

Postwar Recovery

Portraying situations, events, feelings and behaviour very similar to those experienced by the Greek people during the German occupation and the liberation, Italian neo-realism had a considerable impact on the Greek cinema, and its influence can be traced to this day.

Grigori Grigoriou's *Bitter Bread* (*Pikro Psomi,* 1951) was a subtle, austere, and authentic study of the poor folk of Greece, relying on location work and non-professional players. Stelios Tatasopoulos's *Black Earth* (*Mavri Yi,* 1952), shot on location in the emery mines of the island of Naxos, contained some revealing and arresting performances from the village population and especially from George Foundas, a young actor (one of the very few who did not come from the theatre), and the finest male performer the Greek cinema has produced.

In *Barefooted Battalion* (*Xipolito Tagma,* 1953), presented at the Edinburgh Festival, Greg Talas, who worked as a film editor in Hollywood, exposed the audience to the despair, the deprivation, and the horror of the Nazi occupation, through the story of a group of

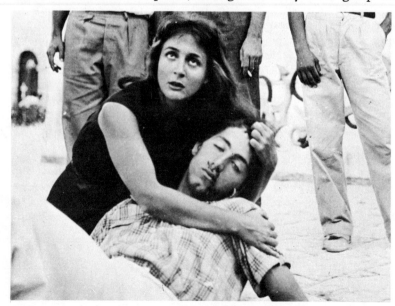

Elli Lambetti and Anestis Vlahos in Cacoyannis's GIRL IN BLACK

abandoned, starving young boys, who survive by stealing their food from the Germans and the black market.

In the ruins of the Byzantine city of Mystras, near Sparti, Frixos Idianis, a journalist, with Filopimin Finos, the head of Finos Film (still the most important production company in Greece), acting as his assistant, made *Dead City* (*Nekri Politia,* 1951), the story of a vendetta and a film that represented a shift towards a greater concern with human relationships.

The Magic City (*Mayiki Polis,* 1955) and *The Ogre of Athens* (*Drakos,* 1956) established **Nikos Koundouros** (*b* 1929) as one of the best directors of his generation. They were two essentially neo-realist films, revealing Koundouros's obsession with the American B-picture. His strong individual style was characterised by a lyrical quality, a violence expressed in satire, and a sense of rebellion against society.

Michael Cacoyannis (*b* 1922), a Greek Cypriot, came to Athens
after a brief career as producer, director and actor on the London stage, and introduced a new form of realism, a fresh approach to both subject and technique with his first picture, *Windfall in Athens* (*Kyriakatiko Xipnima,* 1953), a sentimental comedy suggesting the influence of the French comedies of the period and introducing a new leading couple, Elli Lambetti and Dimitris Horn, who were also to appear in two more highly successful films: the celebrated *Girl in Black* (*Koritsi me ta mavra,* 1956), by the same director, a drama founded on the centuries-old code of the Greek provinces regarding blemished family honour, with Walter Lassally's camera capturing the mysterious beauty of the island of Hydra; and a big box-office attraction, George Tzavellas's *False Pound Sterling* (*Kalpiki Lira,* 1954), a charming, slightly ironic comedy in four parts.

Cacoyannis's second feature, *Stella* (1955), based on an original story by the scriptwriter Iakovos Kambanellis, portrayed an emancipated young woman, a *bouzouki* singer who insisted on eluding the ties of society, family—and, above all, love. Although *Stella,* played by Melina Mercouri in her most vivid and truthful performance, did not exactly reflect (as did *Girl in Black*) the typical Greek woman's attitudes, the film enjoyed great popularity at home and also at the Cannes Festival.

American director Jules Dassin, who had already filmed Nikos Kazantzakis's novel *Christ Recrucified* as *He Who Must Die* in 1957, found in *Stella* a source of inspiration and in *Never on Sunday* (1960) he focused on a similar woman. Melina Mercouri won the acting award at Cannes for her role as the gay prostitute who revels in the peculiar conditions of her life and profession, while Manos Hadjidakis, who had also composed the music for *Stella* and many of the best Greek films, received an Academy Award for his score.

Greece *Stella, Girl in Black, A Matter of Dignity* (*To telefteo Psema,* 1958), and *Zorba the Greek* (1964, a co-production based on a novel by Kazantzakis) all had a dramatic climax that was strongly reminiscent of classical tragedy. It was hardly surprising that Cacoyannis's most ambitious work was *Electra* (1962), a screen version of the play by Euripides, as seen against the background of a contemporary Greek village. (It should be noted, however, that George Tzavellas's *Antigone* in 1961 was the first serious effort in the field.)

In 1955, some twenty features were produced. By 1966, this number had climbed to more than one hundred, with seven hundred more features being imported from other countries. Cinema had clearly become the most popular and least expensive form of entertainment in a country where the population barely exceeded eight millions. During this period of great economic growth, however, the creative talents of the Fifties were ignored. Due primarily to the distribution system, many films that had gained international recognition were not supported by adequate audiences in Greece itself, while the few exceptions (*Stella, Never on Sunday*) led to a whole series of melodramas, set in the notorious night clubs of Piraeus.

Several competent directors with more ambitious projects (among them Vassilis Georgiadis with the Greek Westerns *Mother's Curse,* 1961, and *Blood and Earth,* 1965; Grigoriou's charming, elegant comedies *Good Morning Athens* and *201 Canaries;* and Panos Glycofridis's resistance drama *Price of Glory*) have deliberately modelled their work on proven formulae, to ensure box-office success.

During the past three years, a crisis has struck the Greek cinema, with attendances falling and a rise in the number of colour musicals and spectacular war films, sponsored by the government. *mg*

Torre Nilsson Apart from the Brazilians discussed above, South America has failed to produce exceptional schools of film-making. Solanas's *La Hora de los hornos* (1968) has impressed festival audiences recently, but the sole figure of international stature to emerge from Argentina has been Leopoldo Torre Nilsson (*b* 1924). A brilliant, if somewhat oppressive stylist, he is well acquainted with world cinema. The harsh fear of evil in his work betrays an admiration for Bergman; the perennially perverse children (notably in *La Caida,* 1959) confirm a knowledge of Buñuel; and the subjective, furtive camera movements (especially in *The Eavesdropper,* 1964) are strongly reminiscent of Welles and Hitchcock. Yet this eclectic approach has succeeded well when applied to the distasteful, equivocal type of story in which Beatriz Guido (the director's wife) excels—the blighted life of young Anna in *The House of the Angel* (*La Casa del Angel,* 1957), and the corrupt aristocracy of *The Hand in the Trap* (*La Mano en la Trampa*) and *Summer Skin* (*Piel de Verano,* both 1961). *pdc*

9. Documentary and Animation

THE SECOND WORLD WAR brought new subject matter of danger, drama and death. The period saw the production in Britain and America of feature-length documentaries and also documentary style feature films. In Britain the characteristically calm approach of documentary, with its emphasis on thought rather than emotion, with the visuals presenting the drama, proved well suited to the turmoil of war. Documentary came into its own. The GPO Film Unit became the Crown Film Unit, in the charge successively of Cavalcanti, Dalrymple, J. B. Holmes and Wright. Based from 1941 at Pinewood studios, the Unit produced Watt and Jennings's *London Can Take It* (1940), Holmes's *Merchant Seamen* (1941) and *Coastal Command* (1942), Watt's *Target for Tonight* (1941), Pat Jackson's *Western Approaches* (1944), as well as the distinguished films of **Humphrey Jennings** (1907–1950), a Cambridge graduate, poet and art critic who had joined Grierson in 1934 and who with fine visual perception made *Words for Battle* (1941), *Listen to Britain* (1941), *Fires Were Started* (1943), *The Silent Village* (1943) and *Diary for Timothy* (1945). Working with Crown were the Royal Air Force Photographic Unit and the Army Film and Photographic Unit, responsible for the popular feature-length *Desert Victory* (1943) about the Eighth Army which was edited by Roy Boulting from material shot by service cameramen.

Short propaganda films for cinema showing were made by Crown and by units such as Realist. At ICI Max Anderson made the notable *The Harvest Shall Come* (1942). **Paul Rotha** (*b* 1907) established his own unit, produced the *Worker and Warfront* magazine series (under Duncan Ross), made his own social documentary *World of Plenty* (1943) and produced Budge Cooper's film on delinquency, *Children of the City* (1944). Rotha since the late Twenties had been a prolific writer on documentary with a seminal book on the subject (*Documentary Film,* 1936) and was to make many films distinguished by masterly handling of disparate source material, as well as to assay feature film-making, and to hold important film posts, and to continue to write widely about film.

In Russia epic feature-length documentaries about the great battles were made such as Karmen's *The Siege of Leningrad* (1942), *The Defeat of the Germans near Moscow* (1942), Dovzhenko's *The Fight for Our Soviet Ukraine* (1943) and *Stalingrad* (1943).

In America feature directors left the studios to make such films as Huston's *San Pietro* (1944), Wyler's *Memphis Belle* (1944) and

Ford's *Battle of Midway* (1942). Frank Capra made masterly use of newsreels and other material in the *Why We Fight* series (1943–45), with notable films like *The Nazis Strike* and *War Comes to America*. Documentary film-makers like Willard van Dyke, Irving Jacoby, Sidney Meyers, Jules Butcher and Irving Lerner worked for the Overseas Branch of the Office of War Information to make films like *Tuesday in November* (1945), *A Better Tomorrow* (1945) and *The Cummington Story* (1945) explaining American democracy to a Europe used to Fascist propaganda, and these films were circulated to schools after the war.

Grierson creates the NFBC   In 1938–40 Grierson had toured the Commonwealth and in Canada had created the National Film Board of which he became First Commissioner. Norman McLaren, Stuart Legg, Raymond Spottiswoode and Stanley Hawes joined him from Britain and among their achievements was *The World in Action* series (1940–46) produced by Legg, and *Canada Carries On* produced by Hawes. Grierson had also visited Australia and the Commonwealth Film Unit was established there with Harry Watt and Joris Ivens among the first of its film-makers. Stanley Hawes came later to head the Unit and among the Australian directors **John Heyer** was the most eminent with *The Valley Is Ours* (1949) and *Back of Beyond* (1952).

In Britain the impetus to make social documentaries continued into the early Fifties with such films as Jennings's *Cumberland Story* (1947) and *Family Portrait* (1950), Jill Craigie's *The Way We Live* (1946), Jack Lee's *Children on Trial* (1946), Ralph Keene's *Cyprus Is an Island* (1945), John Eldridge's *Three Dawns to Sydney* (1948), Terry Bishop's *Daybreak in Udi* (1949), Philip Leacock's *Life in Her Hands* (1950) and *Out of True* (1950), Paul Dickson's *The Undefeated* (1950) and *David* (1951), and Rotha's *Land of Promise* (1946), *A City Speaks* (1946), *The World Is Rich* (1947) and *World Without End* (1952), but the social mood changed, documentary's wartime place on the cinema screen was lost and in 1952 Crown was closed, hire charges put on government films and mobile government shows cancelled.

Only with the growth of television has the making of social documentaries re-emerged, this time with a vast new audience and with directors such as Denis Mitchell, Peter Morley, Richard Cawston, Philip Donellan, Ken Russell, Peter Watkins, Robert Vas and Kevin Billington.

Industrial Sponsorship   The vast use of film for training developed during the war by the armed services helped lead to an increased industrial sponsorship and to a continuing expansion in the use of 16mm projectors in education and industry. Leading industrial units in Britain included Shell, British Transport, the National Coal Board and films sponsored by Ford. Shell under Arthur Elton produced a wide range of films from the didactic

A famous Shell documentary: John Heyer's BACK OF BEYOND

to the socially aware and distinguished directors have included **Peter de Normanville** with such films as *Schlieren* (1959) and *Forming of Metals* (1959), and Bert Haanstra (see below), brought over from Holland by Elton in 1954 to make oil exploration films and *The Rival World* (shot in 1955 with Stuart Legg), a notable film about insects and their effect upon man. The British Transport Film Unit was established in 1949 under Edgar Anstey and has produced fine films allied to the travelogue *genre,* nature films such as Ralph Keene's *Journey into Spring* (1957) and *Between the Tides* (1958) and others such as John Schlesinger's *Terminus* (1961). The National Coal Board Film Unit was established in 1952 by **Donald Alexander** (*b* 1913) who after leaving Cambridge made a film about South Wales miners, had worked for Rotha, set up Data Film Unit after the war, and had produced *Mining Review,* a monthly cinema newsreel which began to go widely into cinemas in 1947 (and which, under Francis Gysin, is still running twenty-two years later). Alexander directed the energies of the National Coal Board Film Unit into the unrivalled production of a wide range of internal communications films.

The Ford Motor Company helped to sustain the Free Cinema movement of the Fifties which began with film-makers helped by the British Film Institute Experimental Film Fund and largely centred around **Lindsay Anderson** whose *O Dreamland* and *Thursday's Children* (the latter made with Guy Brenton) were released in 1954. Later, with Ford sponsorship, Anderson directed *Every Day Except Christmas* (1957), about Covent Garden market workers. Karel Reisz was financed by Ford for *We Are the Lambeth Boys* (1958) but when John Fletcher made *The Saturday Men* (1962) about footballers for the same series the Free Cinema movement had passed on. Tony Richardson also began his film-making career with the movement with *Momma Don't Allow* (1955) made with Karel Reisz.

Other notable British sponsored films include Basil Wright's *Waters of Time* (1951), Napier Bell and Legg's *Forward a Century* (1951), Simmons's *Bow Bells* (1952), the feature-length *Conquest of Everest* (1954), numerous films by James Hill such as *Giuseppina* (1959), Stobart's *Hazard* (1964), Carey's *Yeats Country* (1964), Jack Howell's Oscar winning *Dylan Thomas* (1963), Krish's *I Think They Call Him John* (1964), Ronald Riley's *Tribute to Fangio* (1963), Don Levy's *Time Is* (1964), many fine documentaries produced or directed by Derrick Knight, and distinguished films by Robert Vas.

The finest documentary of the postwar period was undoubtedly Flaherty's last film, *The Louisiana Story* (1948), a feature for Standard Oil of New Jersey which looks at a landscape and oil drillers through a boy's eyes. Also from America have come Irving Lerner and Joseph Strick's *Muscle Beach* (1949), Denis Sanders's *Time Out of War* (1954), and Lionel Rogosin's *On the Bowery* (1955).

Recent distinguished feature-length documentaries include Jean Aurel's *14–18* (1963), Erwin Leiser's *Mein Kampf* (1961), Paul Rotha's *The Life of Adolf Hitler* (1962) ably edited by Robert Kruger, Stoumen's *The Black Fox* (1964), Frédéric Rossif's *Mourir à Madrid* (1966) and Ichikawa's *Tokyo Olympiad* (1965). *kg*

Since 1945, Joris Ivens has worked principally in Communist territories, much to the chagrin of Dutch film circles, although some shorts, like the lyrical vision, *La Seine a rencontré Paris* (1957), and the dignified picture of Chile, *À Valparaiso* (1963, with a commentary by Chris Marker), have risen above the stridency of propagandist cinema. But then film has always been a means to an end for Ivens; a means of presenting the truth in a controversial situation, whether it be in Canada or Vietnam, Belgium or China.

Bert Haanstra Between them, **Bert Haanstra** (*b* 1916) and **Herman van der Horst** (*b* 1911) have won more than a hundred awards at international festivals since the war. Haanstra, while obviously a documentarist at heart, and a skilful exponent of the "hidden camera" technique, has brought to his films a distinctive blend of warmth, candour, and amusement. He has a profound and vigorous respect for man's capacity for sadness, gaiety, individuality, and self-sufficiency. Early successes like *Mirror of Holland* (*Spiegel van Holland,* 1950) and *Panta Rhei* (1951) revealed a natural rhythm in his style. His innate curiosity served him well in a series of shorts he made for Shell, the liveliest of which was *The Rival World* (1955), a classic description of the fight to control locusts.

Haanstra's technique is as immaculate as that of any contemporary film-maker. The succession of self-portraits blending into each other in *Rembrandt, Painter of Man* (*Rembrandt, Schilder van de mens,* 1956), and the symphony of processes described in *Glass* (*Glas,* 1958) are among the purest sequences in all documentary. *Glass* won an Academy Award for Haanstra. During the Sixties he completed two full-length studies of life in the Netherlands: *The Human Dutch* (*Alleman,* 1964), and *The Voice of the Water* (*De stem van het water,* 1966), both composed of variegated impressions and sentiments by no means limited to the Netherlands.

Herman van der Horst

Van der Horst lacks the smiling approach to life that makes Haanstra's work so appealing, but his best films—*Steady!* (*Houen Zo,* 1952), *Lekko* (1954), and *Amsterdam* (1965)—have adroitly integrated people into a landscape and a way of life and, especially in the North Sea fishing documentaries, into a dynamic communion with the water that recalls Grierson's *Drifters.* Almost Calvinistic in his single-mindedness, van der Horst watches over every stage of his films' production. The soundtrack in each of his shorts is composed with vigilant care, always endorsing, but never duplicating the image. Both *Symphony of the Tropics* (*Faja Lobbi,* 1960) and *Toccata* (1968) have won prizes for technical excellence.

Other Dutch Talents

Other Dutch documentarists of note include John Fernhout (Ferno), whose *Sky over Holland* won the Palme d'Or at Cannes in 1967; Hattum Hoving, Charles Huguenot van der Linden, Frans Dupont, George Sluizer, and Gerard Raucamp.

Many of the younger Dutch directors have turned to the fictional feature film as a means of communicating their ideas. **Frans Weisz** (*b* 1938), with *Illusion Is a Gangstergirl* (*Het Gangstermeisje,* 1967) and *Made in Paradise* (1969), has blown a breath of almost Italian air into the rather staid Dutch cinema. His imagination is rich and unsophisticated. He is totally involved in his subject, but he is still sufficiently intuitive a director to give his own preoccupations universal currency. Pim de la Parra and Wim Verstappen have been responsible for a high output of films between them, and have taught their colleagues to survive commercially by paring budgets to a minimum. Fons Rademakers, Adriaan Ditvoorst and Nikolai van der Heyde have also made features of above average promise. But although the Dutch Ministry of Culture and the Nederlandse Bioscoop Bond remain well disposed towards features, subsidies are largely divided among the numerous shorts and documentaries produced in the Netherlands each year. *pdc*

In Sweden, notable contributions to the development of the documentary and short film were made in the Forties by **Arne Sucksdorff** (*b* 1917) and **Gösta Werner.** Sucksdorff followed the Flaherty tradition to some extent, observing the natural precincts of his native mid west Sweden with warmth and also detachment, so that shorts like *A Summer Tale* (*En sommarsaga,* 1941), *The Gull* (*Trut!,* 1944), *Shadows over the Snow* (*Skuggor över snön,* 1945), and *A Divided World* (*En kluven värld,* 1948) revealed the rigorous laws of nature—the fight for sustenance among foxes, hares, and birds. In Sucksdorff's vision, man and beast are both hunter and hunted; it is only by recognising this unalterable fact that each can survive in an atmosphere of mutual respect.

Sucksdorff's training as a biologist and his spell as an art student in Berlin give the clue to his distinctive film-making. He is fascinated by innocence in the animal world, by the primitive, unspoilt community of *Indian Village* (*Indisk by,* 1951). But he is also eager to impose on his films a rhythm, a pattern, and a grace that are their glory and, on occasion, their flaw. *The Flute and the Arrow* (*En djungelsaga,* 1957), for example, was too schematic in its treatment of fear and sacrifice among the Murians of northern India. By comparison, *The Great Adventure* (*Det stora äventyret,* 1953) was a high point in Sucksdorff's career, a masterly blend of documentary and fiction, a film that evoked childhood happiness and the passing of the seasons with unerring taste and spontaneity.

Gösta Werner (*b* 1908) has used the principle of documentary—what Grierson called "the creative treatment of actuality"—as the springboard for his short films. In *The Train* (*Tåget,* 1948) and *Midwinter Sacrifice* (*Midvinterblot,* 1946), the landscape of Sweden, with its snow-wrapped mountains and crowded pines, was a pervasive element in the story. Werner has tended more than Sucksdorff to shun the conventional spoken commentary, relying instead on natural sounds and music to suggest a mood and to dictate the pace of a picture. He turned later to features, but his influence could be seen in a documentary like Gunnar Höglund's *Ferrum* (1953), while admiration—though never imitation—of Sucksdorff's films has run clearly through the work of Jan Troell (see Chapter Six). *pdc*

ANIMATION

Two events contributed to the startling developments which were to take place in animation after the Second World War. The first was the war itself which had a powerful effect in the Eastern European countries where the spread of Communist domination created a new cultural atmosphere. Animation was fostered by the state in many countries, although this bureaucratic control did not prevent artists from making barbed comments on Socialism in many of their films. The second event was the strike at Disney's studio in 1941, as a result of which several artists, including **Stephen Bosustow**, departed.

In 1945 Bosustow founded United Productions of America (UPA) whose distinctive films were distributed by Columbia. They soon established their own character, the short-sighted Mr. Magoo, who, supported by Jim Backus's admirable vocal characterisation, blundered his way through an amazing series of unlikely situations, collecting an Oscar en route for *Magoo's Puddle Jumper* (1956, *dir* Pete Burness). At their best, UPA's films were sharply satirical and the technique of limited animation was intelligently handled. They also eschewed the violence which predominated in other Hollywood films and frequently turned to literary sources for their material as with their versions of James Thurber's *The Unicorn in the Garden* (1953, *dir* William T. Hurtz) and Edgar Allan Poe's *The Tell-tale Heart* (1953, *dir* Ted Parmalee). In later years, however, the freshness of their approach hardened into monotony and most of the final Magoo films showed that myopia is restricted as a theme and there was a concomitant deterioration in quality.

The Foundation of UPA

The great strength of Hollywood animation has always been the creation of characters with whom audiences can to some extent identify since they display recognisable human characteristics. Whilst this anthropomorphism has obvious benefits in the popularity stakes it has meant that Hollywood cartoons have generally been identified by the characters who appear in them and their directors have been sadly neglected. Each major studio had its own team of directors and names with which the finest films have been associated include **Tex Avery, William Hanna** and **Joseph Barbera** at M-G-M, **Jack King, Jack Kinney** and **Jack Hannah** at Disney's and **Friz Freleng** and **Chuck Jones** at Warner Bros.

In Canada, there has been the pace-setting work of **Norman Mc-Laren** (*b* 1914) whose films, like those of UPA and Len Lye, have had a profound influence on postwar animation. McLaren had a varied career in Britain, including a spell with the GPO Film Unit, before joining the National Film Board of Canada in 1941 at the invitation of John Grierson. He has made a number of films using the direct technique pioneered by Len Lye including *Begone Dull Care* (1949). He has used the cut-out technique in *Alouette* (1944), made abstract films like *Lines Vertical* (1960), used processed live-action in *Neighbours* (1953) and *Pas de Deux* (1968) and introduced his "pastel method" by which gradual changes in a drawing are photographed, as in *A Little Phantasy on a Nineteenth Century Painting* (1946).

Norman McLaren

Initially the European studios produced vapid Hollywood imitations but as they gained confidence their styles became more individual. In England **John Halas** and **Joy Batchelor** established their famous company Halas and Batchelor in 1940. They have produced a tremendous number of films ranging from entertainment films for the cinema, including *Animal Farm* (1954), the first feature-length British cartoon, to a large quantity of public relations, promotional, scientific, instructional and educational films as well as film titles, television commercials and several series for television.

Halas & Batchelor

The Rank Organisation imported Disney director **David Hand** in 1945 to head their animation unit but the idea was not a success and British artists found difficulty in imitating the brash, florid style which was prevalent in America at that time. British animation received a powerful boost with the advent of Independent Television in 1955. The demand for animated commercials spawned a number of new companies, including Biographic and TV Cartoons. Biographic, personified by the ebullient **Bob Godfrey,** made a number of uneven but invigorating films including *The Do-it-yourself Cartoon Kit* (1961) and *The Rise and Fall of Emily Sprod* (1964). TV Cartoons, headed by Canadian **George Dunning,** concentrated on commercials and sponsored films but found time to make theatrical shorts including *The Apple* (1962) and *The Insects* (1964). Their best-known work is the feature *Yellow Submarine* (1968) inspired by the John Lennon and Paul McCartney song of the same name. Designed by leading German graphic artist **Heinz Edelmann,** *Yellow Submarine* has already generated several imitations and is notable for its excellent colour and novel character design. Edelmann has since set up Trickfilm Ltd., with accomplished artist and technician **Charlie Jenkins.** There have been other offshoots: **Richard Williams,** another Canadian who once worked with TV Cartoons and made the classic *The Little Island* (1958), has subsequently established a reputation as a designer of film credit titles including those for *What's New Pussycat?* and *Casino Royale.* He has also made a small number of entertainment cartoons, including *Love Me, Love Me, Love Me* (1962) and *The Sailor and the Devil* (1967). Two of Williams's former associates, **Ron Wyatt** and **Tony Cattaneo,** have formed their own company specialising in

One of the innumerable Zagreb cartoons that dominated European animation in the Fifties and Sixties. KREK, by Borivoj Dovniković-Bordo

Puppetry at its best: Jiri Trnka's ARCHANGEL GABRIEL AND MOTHER GOOSE

advertising and educational work although they have found time to make an entertainment film, the charming *Fairy Story* (1968).

One of the most important studios in the postwar development of European animation has been the Yugoslavian Zagreb Film Studio, founded in 1956. One of their finest directors is founder member **Dušan Vukotić** (*b* 1927) whose films include *Concerto for Submachine Gun* (*Koncert za Masinsku Pusku,* 1959), *Piccolo* (1960) and *Ersatz* (*Surogat,* 1961) for which he won an Oscar—the first occasion on which the award went to a non-American cartoon. Other members of the early Zagreb team included **Boris Kolar, Vatroslav Mimica, Zlatko Bourek** and **Vlado Kristl** and names that have emerged since the initial impact of Zagreb include **Zlatko Grgic** and **Nedeljko Dragić.**

Yugoslavia

In Czechoslovakia a major figure had already established himself by the time Zagreb commenced production. He is **Jiří Trnka** (1912–1969) who, after early experience with puppet theatres, turned to animation in 1945 with *Grandpa Planted a Beet.* His first puppet film appeared in 1947: *Bethlehem,* which was part of a cycle called *The Czech Year.* In 1959 he completed the film which is widely regarded as his masterpiece, *A Midsummer Night's Dream,* a feature-length puppet film based on Shakespeare's play. A notable contemporary of Trnka's is **Karel Zeman** whose career embraces ordinary cartoons, puppet films and films combining live-action and animation, particularly *Baron Münchhausen* (*Baron Prásil,* 1962).

Czechoslovakia

These new styles began to seep back to America and one or two artists produced work influenced by the European innovators and the stylists at UPA. **Ernest Pintoff** (*b* 1931) had been with UPA in 1955 and 1956 and in 1957 he made *Flebus,* which was followed by *The Violinist* (1959), *The Interview* (1960), *The Old Man and the Flower* (1962) and *The Critic* (1963), all quintessentially American. Another ex-UPA director who has established a sound reputation as an independent producer is **John Hubley** who, with his wife Faith, established his Storyboard studio in 1955. The following year he released his first short, *The Adventures of an* * which was succeeded by *The Tender Game* (1958), *Moonbird* (1960), *Children of the Sun* (1961), *Of Stars and Men* (1961), *The Hole* (1963), *The Hat* (1964), *Windy Day* (1968) and *Zuckerkandl* (1968). Hubley's style, whilst distinctive and pleasing, has remained virtually unchanged since *The Hole* and his hour-long version of Harlow Shapley's *Of Stars and Men,* although sincere, tends towards the dull and pompous. The new graphicism invaded the hitherto impregnable bastions of traditional animation when Disney animator **Ward Kimball** directed *Toot, Whistle, Plunk and Boom* (1953). Disney was not keen on the new style although other films were made in this fashion, including Jack Kinney's delightful *Pigs Is Pigs* (1964). At Warner Brothers Chuck Jones, creator of the highly successful Coyote and Road Runner series, succumbed and made *High Note* (1959) and *The Dot and the Line* (1966).

The medium was further enriched by the films of **Walerian Borowczyk** (*b* 1923) which first appeared in the late Fifties. His early work includes the extraordinarily menacing *Dom* (1958) in which he animated an orange, a glass and a wig. In 1959 he moved to Paris where he has produced a variety of influential films, including a feature entitled *Le Théâtre de M. et Mme. Kabal* (1967) and *Les Jeux des Anges* (1964) in which he gave a nightmare account of the after-life, uncompromising in its pessimism and relentlessly sombre in its visual tone.

Walerian Borowczyk

Some of Borowczyk's earlier work was done in collaboration with **Jan Lenica** (*b* 1928) who subsequently produced films with **Henri Gruel** and, later, on his own. His solo films include *Janko the Musician* (1961) and *Labyrinth* (1962). His highly personalised style is rather obscure, sometimes to the point of almost entirely excluding the viewer.

The bulk of Western Europe's animation output is tied up in commercial work but some pleasing theatrical films have been made in Italy. **Bruno Bozzetto** has made several cartoons, among them *Alpha Omega* (1962) and a feature, *West and Soda* (1965). **Emanuele Luzzati** and **Giulio Gianini** have produced two richly textured cutout films: the enchanting *Paladini di Francia* (1962) and *La Gazza Ladra* (1964).

Of the variety of talents at work in France one of the most durable is **Paul Grimault** (*b* 1905) who started work in 1936. His most significant film is the feature-length *The Shepherdess and the Chimney Sweep* (*La Bergère et le Ramoneur,* 1952). In 1962 **René Laloux** made *Les Dents du Singe,* a strangely disturbing film for which the story was written by patients in a psychiatric hospital.

Looking further afield, animation is very popular in Japan where some attractive features have been made, notably *The White Snake Enchantress* (*Hakuja Den,* 1958, *dir* Taiji Yabushita), but much of the footage is dull television grind-outs. The best-known Japanese director is **Yoji Kuri** (*b* 1928) whose violent, outrageous films began with *Clap Vocalism* (*Ningen Dōbutsen,* 1960) which set the tone for his subsequent output (broadly based on the battle of the sexes). His style, although limited to the point of containing no animation whatsoever, is appealing because of its very directness. In 1964 came *Aos,* a horrific, almost obscene, vision of life and in 1966 *Au Fou* (*Satsujinkyo Shidai*) which contains a series of savage jokes far more violent than anything created in Hollywood.

Animation techniques have changed and expanded over the years, from the early cartoons which were simply photographed drawings to the intricacies of a Disney feature. The invention of the cell system was a great improvement and the addition of sound in 1928 and colour in 1930 completed the animator's armoury. Puppet animation, perfected by **George Pal** in the Thirties and Jiří Trnka in the Forties, was heralded by fantasies such as *The Lost World* (1925) and *King Kong* (1933) in which model monsters were animated by **Willis O'Brien**. His successor in this field is **Ray Harryhausen** whose work in *The 7th Voyage of Sinbad* (1958), *Jason and the Argonauts* (1963) and similar pictures is extremely impressive. In *King Kong* O'Brien painted his scenery on glass sheets, mounted vertically on the animation table, and a few years later this idea re-appeared in a different form as Disney's Multiplane camera. In this device the scenery and action were contained on a series of horizontally mounted plates which permitted realistic tracking shots and imparted an improved sense of depth to the projected picture. Len Lye had by then made his first "direct" films, a technique later adopted by Norman McLaren. The adaptation to animation purposes of the Xerox copying system by Disney technicians dispensed with the laborious manual tracing of animator's drawings on to the cells and permitted a freer style, first seen in *101 Dalmatians* (1960). In England, George Dunning's *The Flying Man* (1962) demonstrated the possibilities of animated painting rather than drawing and brush work has become increasingly common since then. One of the finest exponents of this technique is Polish director **Witold Giersz** whose film *Kon* (1967) is primarily executed in glistening oils with overlaid white outline drawings on cells. *dr*

Bulgarian cartoons leapt into the world class largely through the

Developing Techniques

work of **Todor Dinov** (*b* 1919), who is not only a brilliant animator himself, but has also trained a whole new group of young and talented animators. Documentaries and popular science films range over a very wide field; a special source of material is Bulgaria's immense store of archeological treasures which are gradually being uncovered. *nh*

CINEMA VERITE

Cinéma-vérité (or "direct cinema") is a branch of documentary that emerged simultaneously in North America and in France in the early Sixties. Made possible by the development of lighter (16mm) cameras, faster film stock and, especially, portable professional tape recorders easily synchronised with the camera, the *vérité* method was a reaction against the orthodox documentary approach as much in philosophy as in technique. It rejected the old style: action that was carefully scripted and scrupulously staged, the tenuous linking of widely disparate materials, weighty or "witty" commentaries that bludgeoned the viewer with a mass of facts and information. Instead, deriving its inspiration from the work of Dziga Vertov and Flaherty, it relied upon bare filmed records of factual situations and events; it stressed fluidity, spontaneity, respect for and empathy with the subject, alertness to the unexpected and to the subtle details of human behaviour.

In the United States the movement was pioneered by a journalist-producer, **Robert Drew** (*b* 1921) and a cameraman-director, **Richard Leacock** (*b* 1921). In 1960 they combined forces to produce a television documentary on the battle between Jack Kennedy and Hubert Humphrey for the Democratic nomination, *Primary,* and in the years that followed made many more films in the "Living Camera" series financed by the Time-Life Organisation. In each case the film-makers, usually a two-man crew of cameraman and sound recordist, simply photographed their subjects going about their daily tasks, often following a single person for a period of weeks or months. The Drew-Leacock team was responsible for *The Children Were Watching* (about the attempt to integrate public schools in New Orleans in 1960); *Pete and Johnnie* (1961, a Negro social worker and the leader of a Puerto Rican gang in Harlem); *Eddie Sachs at Indianapolis* (1961, a racing driver preparing for a big event); *David* (1962, a group of ex-drug addicts); *Susan Starr* (1962, the efforts of a young pianist in competition); *Football* (1962, an interschool football competition); *The Chair* (1963, the struggle to reprieve from execution a Negro convicted of murder over ten years previously); and *Jane* (1963, Jane Fonda preparing for the opening night of a play which turns out to be a disaster); while broader, more political subjects included *Yankee No!* (1960, a study of poverty in Latin America), *Kenya* (1961), *Nehru* (1962) and *Crisis: Behind a Presidential Commitment* (the 1963 legal fight between the Kennedy administration and Governor George Wallace of Alabama). Since 1964 Leacock has worked for his own production company and has continued to direct films in the *vérité* style, notable among which are *Happy Mother's Day* (1964, a study of the American publicity machine bearing down on the mother of quintuplets in a small South Dakota town) and *A Stravinsky Portrait* (1966).

A longstanding collaborator of Leacock's is **Don Alan Pennebaker** whose most important films *Don't Look Back* (1967, about Bob Dylan's tour of Britain) and *Monterey Pop* (1968, an impression of the Pop Festival events) explore territory which had earlier been touched upon by **Wolf Koenig** (*b* 1927) and **Roman Kroitor** (*b* 1927) in *Lonely Boy* (1961), a film about Paul Anka shot in *vérité* style for the National Film Board of Canada. Another former associate of Leacock, **Albert Maysles** normally works with his brother **David** (*b* 1932) as sound recordist/editor. Their films include *Showman* (1962), for which they followed Joseph E. Levine to Europe in the hope of recording him sealing a big business deal that never eventuated, and *Salesman* (1969), a comic and compassionate study of Bible peddlers.

The major figures in the French *cinéma-vérité* movement have been discussed elsewhere (see Chapter Three). It is important here not to overlook the contribution of the Canadian **Michel Brault** (*b* 1928) who, after working for the National Film Board, went to France in 1960 to act as cameraman on *Chronique d'un Été*, and subsequently photographed Rouch's *La Punition* as well as Ruspoli's *Les Inconnus de la Terre* and *Regard sur la Folie*. In 1961, back in Canada, Brault directed *Seul ou avec d'autres*, shot at the University of Montreal with a story line about a newly-arrived girl student who finds that the other students seem preoccupied with love-making. Two years later Brault collaborated with the Canadian ethnologist **Pierre Perrault** (*b* 1927) to make *Pour la Suite du Monde*, a filmed record, shot over a one-year period, of a self-enclosed French Canadian community living on an island in the St. Lawrence. Another significant contributor to the Canadian *cinéma-vérité* movement has been **Allan King** (*b* 1930), whose major films include *Warrendale* (1967), a harrowing and controversial portrayal of life at a home for emotionally disturbed children, and *A Married Couple* (1969), a frank impression of a marital relationship.

"Direct cinema" methods of working have come to exercise a significant influence on fictional, in addition to documentary film-making. The *vérité* interview, distinguished by its informality and spontaneity, is used to good effect in such films as Rozier's *Adieu Philippine,* Godard's *Une Femme Mariée* and *Masculin-Féminin,* Shirley Clarke's *Portrait of Jason* and Vilgot Sjöman's *I Am Curious;* while the impact of *vérité* techniques may also be observed in the films of John Cassavetes (especially *Shadows* and *Faces*) and such recent works as Haskell Wexler's *Medium Cool* and Robin Spry's *Prologue. rc*

10. Economic Trends

IN EUROPE production was again disrupted by war. A few films were made in France during the occupation. In Italy there was a burst of activity when the Fascist era ended. *Rome—Open City* (1945, *dir* Roberto Rossellini) was even begun clandestinely while the Germans remained; it was completed with captured cameras and, like many other neo-realist films that followed, relied on slender co-operative finance and often un-paid actors. Guilt and national animosity tended to keep the German film industry in isolation even after the war, though West Germany was handicapped because many studios fell in the Eastern zone. There a nationalised company, DEFA, was established. The Agfa plant, the foremost European film stock manufacturer, was also in East Germany and early samples of the Agfacolor stock developed by the Germans were despatched to Russia where it was used by Eisenstein for the colour sequence of *Ivan the Terrible*. This process became the basis of Sovcolor. Meanwhile some of the Agfa scientists went to America where their knowledge was used in developing the Eastmancolor process.

The Soviet influence in Eastern Europe led to the nationalisation of film production in Poland, Yugoslavia, Bulgaria and Czechoslovakia. The Czechs had an established industry even before the war and the Nazis had used Prague as their film production centre for a while, leaving behind impressive studio facilities. Czech production was therefore able to resume quickly, but for Poland and the others it was a more painful process to reassert their national identity on the screen.

One benefit of nationalisation was the strength it gave to the short film which, in the American and British markets, was usually elbowed out by the harsher commercial realities of the double-feature programme. Czechoslovakia nurtured the delicate and tasteful animated films of Jiří Trnka and more recently several East European countries have developed impressive outputs of animated shorts.

In Britain after the war Rank set about capturing the overseas markets. He established branches and agents in many countries and bought an interest in cinema chains in Canada, Africa, Australia and New Zealand. Encouraged by the success of *Henry V* (1945) he opened his own American distribution company. Rank's goodwill visit to America in 1947 seemed likely to succeed in obtaining a wider showing for British films but hopes were dashed by an economic measure introduced by the British government. Faced with a serious dollar crisis it imposed a prohibitive duty on American films entering Britain. It was a futile and damaging measure, but Rank attempted to fill the void by stepping up production. Forty-seven films were to be made at a cost of £9¼m. Talent was spread thin, and the first picture reached the screens just as the American embargo was lifted. By October 1948 the Rank overdraft was more than £13½m. Ruthless economies followed, instituted by John Davis—an accountant who had become Rank's most powerful executive. It signalled the departure of most of Rank's best creative talent—Carol Reed, David Lean, Launder and Gilliat, Powell and Pressburger.

British production was in a critical condition. Out of the healthy box-office receipts of £109m in 1948—only slightly below the peak of 1946—about £7½m found its way back to British producers, though the Government were taking out some £39m in Entertainment Tax. In 1949 the Government responded and set up the National Film Finance Corporation to invest in production. £3m of its initial capital of £5m was channelled into British Lion with Alexander Korda in charge of production. Korda signed up the best of Rank's runaway directors and sustained production at Shepperton for some five years before the revolving credit ran out.

The N.F.F.C. also used its funds to set up an independent unit, Group 3, under John Grierson to encourage new talent but the results were disappointing and not widely shown. Other investments were made in individual films, with the N.F.F.C. usually contributing the final 30% to a budget already backed by a bank or distributor's guarantee.

A further aid to producers known as the Eady Plan, after Sir Wilfrid Eady of the Treasury, placed a levy of one penny on all cinema admissions. Like the N.F.F.C., the scheme still continues to help British production and to encourage American investment. The plan has however been criticised because it rewards the most successful films and gives little help to those producers who need it most. It has also, in the past, encouraged the two major groups to enhance their own share of the fund by producing and showing series of films like *Look at Life* and *Pathe Pictorial* which qualified for an attractively large contribution, while excluding the showing of short films by other producers.

Hollywood began to feel the first impact of television in 1948, though cinema attendances had already fallen away from their peak in 1946. It was not until the introduction of Cinerama, with its gigantic screen and triple projectors, in 1952 that an effective method of competition became apparent. Cinerama itself was too cumbersome and expensive to be generally adopted, but a more flexible system using a single 70mm film was developed jointly by the showman, Mike Todd, and the American Optical Company. Even Todd-AO, however, could only be used for presentations in key cities and it was CinemaScope, introduced by Twentieth Century-Fox in 1953, that found general acceptance throughout the industry.

CinemaScope was soon imitated or used under license by all the other major companies and there were other variations—VistaVision

Latest Phase
1948–1970

and Technirama—which aimed at enhancing the size and quality of the picture. Latterly, and as a result of an agreement with Fox, the Panavision system—achieving the same results as CinemaScope—has been generally adopted by the American industry for wide-screen production. The wide screens seemed to do their job: box-office receipts in the U.S.A. had declined steadily from the 1946 peak of $1,512m to $1,134m in 1952 but revived to $1,415m in 1955.

Television was however only part of a changing pattern of leisure activities in America, Britain and elsewhere. Car ownership and increasing prosperity brought a wider range of pastimes to the urban populations who previously had sought to escape their environment in weekly visits to the cinema. Suburban cinemas tended to fall below the social standards of their old audiences, and eventually many suffered the same fate as the Nickelodeons after 1912. In the U.S.A. the rising number of drive-in theatres reflected the other side of the situation.

By the mid-Fifties the market for second features had seriously declined, and Republic and Monogram both ceased production, though the trend was partially offset by the success of American-International who specialised in the more sensational horror films like *I Was a Teenage Werewolf*. The most traumatic event was the closure of the RKO studios in 1957; they were taken over for television production. By this time the prosperity of American television made it possible to produce many of the programmes on film and several major companies turned over some of their facilities for this purpose.

Fear of reprisals by cinema interests kept most feature films off television for some time. In Britain cinema owners even paid a small levy to the Film Industry Defence Organisation which used the money to secure covenants from owners of British films preventing their being screened on television. FIDO was fairly effective until two large groups of American films were sold to British television in 1964.

In America a number of companies sold their backlog of pre-1948 films to other distributors to avoid trading directly with the enemy. Many fortunes were made by the astute middlemen. Associated Artists Productions under Eliot Hyman bought the Warner Bros. backlog and traded profitably before selling the company to United Artists. Operating under the Seven Arts banner, Hyman then secured television rights in a substantial number of Fox films, benefiting from the financial crisis over delays in completing *Cleopatra* (1963). Seven Arts prospered to the point where Hyman was able to purchase Warner Bros., outright, in 1967. Similarly, the Music Corporation of America, originally a talent agency, acquired the Paramount backlog, profits from which helped to finance MCA's takeover of American Decca with its subsidiary—Universal. Older Hollywood's films thus assumed a new lease of life and the television market has preserved in circulation many films that might well have been lost for ever. At present the ultimate value of a feature film for sale to television can be an important factor in financing the initial production and all the three American television networks are now active in feature film production either directly or through financial participation.

In the late Fifties the lower labour costs of European studios began to attract production away from Hollywood. Alongside the American financed films the local industries also started to make films of more direct international appeal. In Italy there was a revival of spectaculars, one of which—*Hercules Unchained* (1959, *dir* Pietro Francisci), was extremely successful in the U.S.A. Joseph E. Levine, who had imported it, founded a new company, Embassy Pictures, to handle a range of similar pictures; they are now one of the major Hollywood producers. *Dr. No* (1962, *dir* Terence Young), adapted from the James Bond story by Ian Fleming and produced in Britain on a modest budget by American producer Harry Saltzman, was an even more overwhelming success. It created a mould in which dozens of other "special agent" films were cast. For several years Bond became that rarest of all phenomena in the film industry—a formula for success.

As spectacle and spies began to pall their place was taken by horror films from Italy and Westerns from Germany and Yugoslavia. Often an American star filled the leading role, effectively disguising the film's European origin. One of the Westerns, *A Fistful of Dollars* (*Per un pugno di dollari*, 1964, *dir* Sergio Leone) came close to rivalling Bond: it exploited a degree of ruthless violence in the same way that Bond exploited luxurious promiscuity.

Most European production of course remained geared to home markets. Governments came to realise that some financial support was necessary to sustain film production on a purely national basis, as Britain had when it set up the N.F.F.C. In Sweden the industry was reorganised in 1963, and the newly-founded Swedish Film Institute directly assisted production, and also promoted Swedish cinema abroad. In 1966 the Kuratorium "Junger Deutscher Film" (Young German Film Board) was established to help young short film-makers to graduate to feature production, with budget loans of up to £30,000. Initial results have been promising and the first group of about twenty pictures returned a substantial part of their investment. In Britain the British Film Institute helps young film-makers on a much more modest scale with its Production Fund, but most of its work is beyond the limits of the normal commercial industry. In 1969 the possibility of a recession of American production in Britain persuaded the government to revitalise the N.F.F.C. with additional funds, but .the decision to set up a National Film School has also highlighted the problems of young people who want to enter an already overcrowded industry.

During the period of intense American activity in Britain, the Rank

Organisation, under John Davis, has been content to rent its remaining studios at Pinewood to visiting producers. Its own production programme dwindled to two or three films a year and has now virtually ended. A.B.P.C. output suffered a similar decline until the Warner Bros. holdings were sold to EMI, the giant recording company, in 1968. In 1969 writer-director Bryan Forbes, newly appointed head of production at Elstree, announced an ambitious list of some fifteen features.

In America the more sophisticated European films imported during the Sixties openly challenged the censorship system, while putting Hollywood productions at a disadvantage because they remained bound by the old Production Code. In 1968 a system of classification was introduced, rather on the British pattern. G, M, and R categories, corresponding roughly to the British U, A, and X, reflect subjects increasingly unsuitable for young people, while an additional X category encompasses films which go beyond the limits of approval but which still fall within the limits of the law.

Ownership and control of the major companies are now going through a period of rapid change. Anti-trust legislation in the early Fifties forced the production companies to sell off their cinema chains in the U.S.A., ending the trend towards vertical integration that had been part of the pattern from the earliest days. Legal pressures have therefore directed subsequent mergers into a horizontal pattern, while the asset value of their stocks of old films traditionally written off as of little value, has made the established film company an attractive investment for the large industrial complex looking for a toehold in the expanding "leisure business." Universal was one of the first to go; they were bought by American Decca in 1952 before Decca passed to MCA. More recently, in 1966 Paramount was merged with Gulf and Western Industries, whose principal business is fuel oil, while soon afterwards United Artists was bought by Transamerica Corporation, an industrial conglomerate with interests in a vast range of products and services. And within two years of the Warner-Seven Arts merger the new group was sold to Kinney Services, yet another conglomerate, whose original primary business was mortuaries. Control of M-G-M has recently passed to a Las Vegas property millionaire, Kirk Kerkorian, creating a situation not unlike RKO-Radio when it was owned by Howard Hughes from 1948 until 1955. Hughes sold the assets of RKO to a subsidiary of The General Tire and Rubber Company—one of the first industrial groups to buy a Hollywood company. Columbia and Twentieth Century-Fox have so far avoided similar changes of control, though Fox is itself now contemplating a programme of diversification, perhaps taking its example from the Rank Organisation which has built up a wide range of other interests including the Xerox copying process.

A further breakdown in vertical integration now shows signs of developing with the sale of studios. Paramount have sold theirs while the sale of M-G-M's Culver City studios and Warner Brothers studios at Burbank seems virtually assured. Many companies may now follow the patterns adopted by United Artists, with individual producers making films under contract and renting studio facilities only when they are needed. Improving technology and heavy studio costs have already made it both possible and desirable to do as much filming as possible on location, and the possibility of one or two "super-studios" built to incorporate the most modern techniques and replace the individual company-owned studios has recently been suggested.

In exhibition both cinemas and broadcast television now face a threat from new systems of marketing films in cassettes which can be plugged into a unit connected to the home television set. Such cassettes are already technically feasible and though at present they are too expensive for home use they promise to become, eventually, the pictorial equivalent of the long-playing record. Just as radio and concert halls have survived the gramophone so—almost certainly—the cinemas and television will survive the cassette, but it will create in time a new area of commercial activity in the industry and further enhance the value of the libraries of films owned by the established companies. *ah*

11. Technical Developments

TECHNICOLOR was for a long time the most successful colour system, but it was gradually followed by others. The Technicolor system was dependent on a bulky "three-strip" camera, and has been superseded by systems such as Eastmancolor, which use a single negative film, and do not require any special camera equipment.

Other colour negative films similar in principle to Eastmancolor which have been used in various regions of the world include Ferrania-color, Agfacolor, Gevacolor, Fujicolor and Sovcolor; while terms such as Columbiacolor, DeLuxe Color, Metrocolor, Pathécolor and Warner-color refer to the laboratories at which the original negative is processed. The Technicolor company now concentrates on a unique method of release printing by means of dye transfer.

Modern colour systems are versatile, rich and sensitive. The director can exercise control over a colour film at three stages: First, in drafting a colour script for the film and co-ordinating the preliminary work of the art director, set designer, etc.; second, in using lights, filters and paint sprays during the actual shooting; third, in the laboratory where control during printing will determine the final result.

3-D   An interlude, now of minor importance, but still part of film history, is the brief use of three-dimensional photography. Stereoscopic vision is of more importance than stereophonic sound, and pairs of stereoscopic photographs viewed through a double eyepiece had a long and successful career in Victorian times. A system of two superimposed images, unscrambled by wearing special glasses, and giving the impression of a solid image, was introduced into the cinema in the early Fifties, when the competition of television was becoming acute in America and England. But the films were mediocre, the novelty palled, the system failed to spread, and was dropped after a few years.

The profusion of screen dimensions prevalent in the early years of film-making as a result of the widely differing film gauges and camera aperture sizes in use was curtailed shortly after 1900 when the Edison format was adopted as a standard. This utilised 35mm film, with a picture having a width to height ratio of 1.33:1. With the introduction of sound, and the consequent use of part of the film area for the soundtrack, the image area was reduced in size but the 1.33:1 ratio was maintained by the insertion of a frame line, the dimensions of the new standard picture area being termed the "Academy" aperture. Despite sporadic experiments, the 35mm 1.33:1 ratio remained standard in the cinemas for a further twenty years.

SCREEN DIMENSIONS   In the early Fifties, however, about the same time as 3-D came and went, larger screens and different screen ratios were introduced on a major commercial scale in order to make the cinema screen look different from the television screen. The systems which were introduced eventually came to include four distinct techniques of attaining a wide screen effect: (a) cropping the top and bottom of the standard picture area (b) using multiple interlocked cameras and projectors (c) using anamorphic lenses (d) using wide gauge film.

The easy answer to giving the screen a new look was Wide-Screen, and wide-screen ratios (usually between 1.66:1 and 1.85:1) have almost entirely replaced the Academy ratio in modern cinemas. The normal 35mm film is used for shooting, but when it is projected a metal plate masks off the top and bottom of every frame thus reducing the height, but keeping the same width. The cameraman has lines marked on his viewfinder so when filming he can keep the action away from the top and bottom of the picture.

Cinerama grew from an exhibit created by Fred Waller for the 1939 New York World's Fair and no doubt owed much to Abel Gance's use of the triple screen in *Napoléon* (1926). Launched in 1952, Cinerama uses a huge "wrap-around" screen which, because of the peripheral vision it makes possible, gives spectators the effect of being in the centre of the action. The film was taken in three separate strips by triple linked cameras and shown by triple projectors. The joins were concealed by moving masks, but were nevertheless frequently obtrusive. Triple-camera Cinerama was popular for a time, but it was very cumbersome and has now been discontinued in favour of a system employing 70mm film projected on the same deeply curved screen.

CinemaScope

CinemaScope, introduced by 20th Century-Fox in 1953, used a special anamorphic lens (originally patented by the Zeiss Company in 1898, and further developed by Henri Chrétien) to squeeze a wide picture on to 35mm film and a corresponding lens in the projector to spread it out again. It gave a very wide image, eventually fixed at an aspect ratio of 2.35:1, much the shape of an opening in a pillar box. CinemaScope was also used by other companies under license from 20th Century-Fox, and was employed for the majority of genuine expanded ratio productions in the Fifties. A number of other 35mm anamorphic systems were introduced both in America and in Europe, and during the Sixties Panavision, identical in concept to Cinema-Scope, came to occupy a pre-eminent position.

VistaVision used 35mm film which ran horizontally instead of vertically through the camera, resulting in an image approximately twice the normal size. In a few theatres the film was projected as it was photographed, horizontally, but for regular cinema release the Vista-Vision image was reduced in size and printed in the normal position on the film. Projected at a wide-screen ratio of up to 1.85:1, it produced an exceptionally clear, detailed picture. VistaVision was developed from a wide-screen system invented by George Hill and Professor Alberini in 1928; it was withdrawn after the release of *One Eyed Jacks* in 1961.

The use of 70mm film on a commercial scale was pioneered by Todd-AO with the release of *Oklahoma!* in 1955. A picture almost the size of Cinerama was produced, but without the expense or complexities of three separate films. Its success was assured after its use on the production of *Around the World in 80 Days*. Further systems employing wide-gauge film for the original photography have followed, prominent among which is Panavision 70. In some cases extra width again is attained by the use, in addition, of anamorphic lenses. With the improvement in quality of film emulsions it has been found possible to produce acceptable results by enlarging or "blowing up" a 35mm original to 70mm for release purposes, and this system also is now in general use for roadshow presentations.

Among the multitude of other systems that have been employed are Techniscope, Technirama, Super Vistarama, Glamorama, Warner-Scope, SearchlightScope, and Cinema 160. Circlorama and Walt Disney's Circarama aim to go further than Cinerama by presenting films on a completely circular screen, with the spectator standing in the middle. Such systems were first used by the French showman, Raoul Grimoin-Sanson, as early as 1896, and continue to provide spectacular entertainment at international expositions.

CONCLUSION   What of the future? The cinema seems to be moving towards a compact building, fairly plain and functional in its style, using light and shade rather than draperies for decoration, flexible enough without extravagant novelty to show different film shapes and gauges. It would cater for an audience of up to five hundred and use automation for handling the film and a combination of automation and self-service for dealing with the public. Another development likely to increase is the use of film as an incidental diversion, almost as a decoration—showing continuously in automatic projectors on walls and dance halls, galleries, public buildings, waiting places. Perhaps moving pictures, perhaps (for the still photograph is making a comeback) a series of slides.
rs, rc, as

Index to Film Titles

250

254

257